LEARNING DISABILITIES
A CHALLENGE TO TEACHING AND INSTRUCTION

STUDIA PAEDAGOGICA

New Series
40

Editorial Board
Prof. Dr. E. De Corte (Chairman)
Prof. Dr. A. De Munter
Prof. Dr. M. Depaepe
Prof. Dr. B. Maes
Prof. Dr. G. Vandemeulebroecke

Studia Paedagogica

LEARNING DISABILITIES
A Challenge to Teaching and Instruction

Edited by
P. GHESQUIÈRE
&
A.J.J.M. RUIJSSENAARS

University Press Leuven
2005

Uitgegeven met de steun van de
K.U.Leuven Commissie voor Publicaties

© 2005 Universitaire Pers Leuven/Leuven University Press/Presses Universitaires de Louvain, Blijde-Inkomststraat 5, B-3000 Leuven

All rights reserved. Except in those cases expressly determined by law, no parrt of this publication may be multiplied, saved in an automated datafile or made public in any way whatsoever without the express prior written consent of the publishers.

ISBN 90 5867 444 4

D / 2005 / 1869 / 2

NUR: 848

CONTRIBUTORS

Bart Boets, Centre for Disability, Special Needs Education and Child Care, Faculty of Psychology and Educational Sciences, University of Leuven, Belgium

Cecilia Bouwer, Faculty of Education, University of Pretoria, South Africa

Annemie Desoete, Department of Psychology, University of Ghent, Belgium

Els Gadeyne, Centre for Disability, Special Needs Education and Child Care, Faculty of Psychology and Educational Sciences, University of Leuven, Belgium

Pol Ghesquière, Centre for Disability, Special Needs Education and Child Care, Faculty of Psychology and Educational Sciences, University of Leuven, Belgium

Jane M. Hutchinson, Department of Psychology, University of Central Lancashire, Preston, United Kingdom

Mark Godwin, Department of Psychology, University of Central Lancashire, Preston, United Kingdom

Vasti Jordaan, Faculty of Education, University of Pretoria, South Africa

Evelyn H. Kroesbergen, Department of Special Education, Faculty of Social Sciences, University of Utrecht, the Netherlands

Bauke F. Milo, Inspectorate of Education, the Netherlands

Suzanne Oakley, Department of Psychology, University of Central Lancashire, Preston, United Kingdom

Patrick Onghena, Centre for Methodology of Educational Research, Faculty of Psychology and Educational Sciences, University of Leuven, Belgium

Judith Rivalland, Fogarty Learning Centre, Edith Cowan University, Perth, Western Australia, Australia

Herbert Roeyers, Department of Psychology, University of Ghent, Belgium

Mary Rohl, Fogarty Learning Centre, Edith Cowan University, Perth, Western Australia, Australia

Aloysius J.J.M. Ruijssenaars, Department of Special Education/ GION Institute for Educational Research, Faculty of Social Sciences, Groningen University, the Netherlands

Chris D. Smith, Department of Psychology, University of Central Lancashire, Preston, United Kingdom

Wim Van den Broeck, Department of Special Education, Faculty of Social Sciences, Leiden University, the Netherlands

Erik Vandenbussche, Laboratory for Neuropsychology, Faculty of Medicine, University of Leuven, Belgium

Mieke Van Ingelghem, Centre for Disability, Special Needs Education and Child Care, Faculty of Psychology of Educational Sciences, University of Leuven, Belgium

Christina E. van Kraayenoord, Schonell Special Education Research Centre, The University of Queensland, Brisbane, Queensland, Australia

Johannes E.H. van Luit, Department of Special Education, Faculty of Social Sciences, University of Utrecht, the Netherlands

Astrid Van Wieringen, Laboratory for Experimental ORL, Faculty of Medicine, University of Leuven, Belgium

Helen E. Whiteley, Department of Psychology, University of Central Lancashire, Preston, United Kingdom

Jan Wouters, Laboratory for Experimental ORL, Faculty of Medicine, University of Leuven, Belgium

PREFACE

Research on learning disabilities has known a tremendous growth the last 25 years. All kinds of scientific disciplines are involved. Yet, despite the progress that is made in diverse domains, learning disabilities still stay a serious challenge to teaching and instruction. Fortunately, in recent research we notice a growing interest for the educational consequences of research findings, even in more fundamental disciplines. We thought this was a good starting point for a collection of papers with this scope. In this book the authors try to link original research findings on learning disabilities with instructional methods and teaching practices. The papers were selected on the occasion of the 25th anniversary of the International Academy for Research in Learning Disabilities. Most of the authors are even a member of this prestigious scientific society.

We ordered the different contributions in two parts. In the first part we brought together contributions about the cognitive, metacognitive and socio-emotional correlates of learning disabilities. These factors generally form a core aspect of the challenge of learning disabilities to teaching and instruction. The first three chapters concern the phenomenon of dyslexia. *Van den Broeck* critically evaluates the disputable role of intelligence in the concept and definition of dyslexia. *Hutchinson, Whiteley and Smith* explore the role of cognitive linguistic skills (such as phonological awareness) in the early identification of reading problems in emergent bilingual children, an often neglected group in dyslexia research. *Van Ingelghem and colleagues* study auditory temporal processing in children with dyslexia. In chapter 4 *Desoete and Roeyers* summarize their research on metacognition in children with mathematics learning disabilities. Finally, *Gadeyne, Ghesquière and Onghena* explore the relationship between academic achievement and behaviour problems. Surely, the socio-emotional consequences of learning problems regularly charge teachers with a difficult task.

In the second part of this book we go deeper into research on intervention and instruction methods. We start again with three chapters focusing on reading problems. In chapter 6 *Whitely and her colleagues* try to analyze why some children do not benefit from early, phonologically based interventions, leading to implications for the development of early screening tools and intervention schemes for these non-beneficiaries. *Van Kraayenoord, Rohl and Rivalland* report findings of an Australian study examining the programs and strategies used to teach and intervene in Australian classrooms for students with learning problems. *Bouwer and Jordaan* argue for the use of imaging as a learning support technique for children with dyslexia. The last two chapters explore the differential effect of direct and guided instruction for children with arithmetic learning problems. *Kroesbergen and Van Luit* focus on the acquisition and use of multiplication strategies. *Milo and Ruijssenaars* do the same for addition and subtraction up to 100.

We are sure that after reading this book, not all challenges of learning disabilities to teaching and instruction will be tackled. But we are convinced that it can offer some contribution in getting away from some of them. We hope it gives a lot of inspiration to the diverse audience we had in mind, practitioners as well as researchers of different disciplines.

Pol Ghesquière
Wied Ruijssenaars

CONTENTS

Part I: Cognitive, metacognitive and socio-emotional correlates — 11

1. The role of intelligence in the definition of dyslexia
   Wim Van den Broeck — 13

2. The role of linguistic skills in the identification of reading problems in emergent bilingual children.
   Jane M. Hutchinson, Helen E. Whiteley and Chris D. Smith — 37

3. An Auditory Temporal Processing Deficit in Children with Dyslexia?
   Mieke Van Ingelghem, Bart Boets, Astrid van Wieringen, Patrick Onghena, Pol Ghesquière, Erik Vandenbussche, and Jan Wouters — 47

4. Cognition and metacognition in children with mathematics learning disabilities
   Annemie Desoete and Herbert Roeyers — 65

5. The relationship over time between academic performance and behaviour problems in young children
   Els Gadeyne, Pol Ghesquière and Patrick Onghena — 91

Part II: Intervention and instruction methods — 105

6. Early literacy intervention: who benefits and who does not?
   Helen Whiteley, Chris Smith, Mark Godwin and Suzanne Oakley — 107

7. Intervention approaches for learning difficulties in literacy: an Australian approach
   Christina E. van Kraayenoord, Mary Rohl and Judith Rivalland — 117

8. Development of reading comprehension of learners with dyslexia by means of a technique of imaging
   Cecilia Bouwer and Vasti Jordaan — 133

9. Effects of different forms of instruction on acquisition and use of multiplication strategies by children with math learning difficulties
   Evelyn H. Kroesbergen and Johannes E.H. van Luit   161

10. Strategy use and math instruction for students with special needs
    Bauke F. Milo and Aloysius J.J.M. Ruijssenaars   183

PART I

COGNITIVE, METACOGNITIVE AND SOCIO-EMOTIONAL CORRELATES

1
THE ROLE OF INTELLIGENCE IN THE DEFINITION OF DYSLEXIA

Wim Van den Broeck

Introduction

The disputable role of intelligence in the concept and definition of developmental dyslexia is critically evaluated. The implicit assumptions of the discrepancy concept connected with the underachievement conceptualization are explicated. Further it is shown that the regression-based operationalisation of a discrepancy is logically inconsistent with the underlying concept of underachievement. Finally, an attempt is made to explain the specificity paradox: the requirement that dyslexia be defined as a deficit that is reasonably specific to the reading task, while cognitive differences are ubiquitous between reading disabled and nondisabled children.

Since the very beginning of the research into dyslexia a hundred years ago, developmental dyslexia has been defined as a specific reading problem which is 'unexpected' considering the normal aptitudes of the affected individuals. This specificity requirement traditionally has been operationalized as a discrepancy between intellectual functioning and academic achievement (e.g., reading performance). Despite the recent critiques formulated against the discrepancy concept of learning disabilities (Aaron, 1997; Stanovich, 1991), most contemporary definitions of specific learning disabilities include aptitude-achievement discrepancy as an essential criterion. For instance, according to the ICD-10 Classification of Mental and Behavioural Disorders (World Health Organization, 1993), and to the Diagnostic and Statistical Manual of Mental Disorders-IV [DSM-IV] (American Psychiatric Association, 1994), the diagnosis of a specific reading disorder requires that reading achievement is substantially below the level expected on the basis of the person's chronological age and general intelligence score. Moreover, in practice, the identification of students with learning disabilities is usually based on one or the other operationalization of the discrepancy concept (Frankenberger & Fronzaglio, 1991; Mercer, Jordan, Allsopp, & Mercer, 1996). In this contribution I critically evaluate the role of intelligence and intelligence test scores in the concept and definition of developmental dyslexia.

Unexpectedness, underachievement and the discrepancy formula

The reading problems of children with dyslexia are "unexpected" because they cannot readily be ascribed to obvious causal factors. This is the reason why poor reading after a period of school absence (e.g. due to an illness) or as the result of serious sensorial, mental or emotional disorders is not diagnosed as dyslexia. Therefore, most definitions include some exclusionary criteria. Whereas the traditional definitions (e.g. World Federation of Neurology, 1968, cited in Critchley, 1970) stipulate that children should not have sensory impairments, detrimental instructional circumstances or very low IQ's (e.g. under 70), contemporary definitions allow for these conditions but require that the reading problems are not their consequences (e.g. DSM IV, 1994). For example, the reading ability of children with hearing problems can be compared meaningfully with the reading level of a relevant norm-referenced group, that is other children with hearing difficulties. Consequently, when the reading difficulties are in excess of those usually associated with a sensory or mental deficit, the diagnosis of dyslexia is still conceivable. Although the unexpectedness of the reading problems forms the "raison d'être" of the concept of dyslexia, it would be a fundamental mistake (e.g. in Dumont, 1976) to include "unexpectedness" per se as a necessary condition in the definition of dyslexia. Because human knowledge is not static, such a definition would destroy the very concept of dyslexia once the causes of dyslexia are revealed. In that case, nothing happens against expectations, turning dyslexia into an empty concept.

The discrepancy concept

For a clear understanding of the discrepancy concept of dyslexia, we need a small historical detour. According to Hammill (1993; see also Wiederholt, 1974) the roots of the present conceptual core of dyslexia are situated at the beginning of the nineteenth century. At that time observations were made that adults who had sustained head injuries, had lost the capacity to express themselves through speech, while preserving their intellectual abilities (a condition known as aphasia). In 1892 Dejerine reported a case of acquired dyslexia in an adult with an affection of the left gyrus angularis, while retaining his language abilities. When reading problems can be the result of brain injuries, then developmental reading difficulties without intellectual impairment, could be the outcome of minor congenital brain defects: this was the hypothesis expressed by Hinshelwood (1917). This line of reasoning gave birth to the idea of a discrepancy between intact intellectual functioning and specific academic disabilities. It is important to note that according to this historical tradition, exclusionary IQ criteria were imposed primarily as a means of ruling out confounding variables in order to enable researchers to discover more specific causal antecedents (Taylor, 1984; Taylor & Schatschneider, 1992).

The role of intelligence in the assessment of specific reading disabilities (and learning disabilities in general) increased tremendously by the introduction of the concept of underachievement (Burt, 1950). Advocates of this concept argued that purely interindividual norm-referenced comparisons should be supplemented or even replaced by an ipsative measurement model which defines the disorder largely by the individuality of the student (Reynolds, 1992; Rutter & Yule, 1973; Thorndike, 1963). In this model the child's score on the achievement measure is compared with the score of the same child on an aptitude measure reflecting the child's potential for learning. In practice, the concept of underachievement has been translated into a discrepancy score between measured reading ability and general intelligence measured by an IQ-test (Frankenberger & Harper, 1987; Reynolds, 1992). An important implication of this new conceptualization is that poor readers with below average IQ's are often excluded from the dyslexic population (when not discrepant), whereas average readers with high IQ's can be labeled as dyslexic when satisfying the discrepancy criterion. Despite the critiques leveled against the operationalization of the discrepancy concept, most recent definitions are still based on some form of this concept. For that reason, it is useful to explicate the implicit assumptions underlying the discrepancy notion.

The crucial premise of the underachievement conceptualization is the idea that intellectual capacity normally determines reading achievement. Only in a minority of children some specific disturbing factors are responsible for a reading level far below the level one would have expected considering the normal intellectual disposition (cf. Aaron, 1997; Stanovich, 1996). Notably, the assumption of a causal relationship between intelligence and reading performance surpasses largely the assumption that only very low IQ's impede reading development (cf. the exclusionary criteria).

The regression-based discrepancy formula

In a little but influential book Thorndike (1963) criticized the simple standard score discrepancy formula, that is IQ – AS (Achievement Score), for its failure to recognize the regression effect (see also Cone & Wilson, 1981; McLeod, 1979; Reynolds, 1985, 1992). Generally, regression toward the mean occurs whenever two standardized variables are not perfectly correlated. In the case of a positive but imperfect correlation, subjects who are high on one of the variables will also tend to be high on the other variable, but relatively less so, thus "they regress toward the mean". Similarly, subjects who are low on one of the variables will also tend to be low on the other variable, but relatively less so (e.g. Pedhazur-Schmelkin, 1991; Rogosa & Willet, 1985). Because of the imperfect correlation between IQ and reading scores, children with above average IQ's tend to have reading scores that are lower than their IQ-scores, resulting in statistically expected discrepancies which "should" be considered normal. Conversely, children with below average IQ-scores tend to have reading scores that are higher than their IQ-scores, resulting in an underestimation of discrepancies (Shaywitz, Fletcher, Holahan & Shaywitz, 1992). In order to avoid the overidentification of dyslexic children with high IQ's, and the underidentification of dyslexic children with low IQ's, Thorndike proposed a regression-based discrepancy formula that accounts for the imperfect relationship between IQ and achievement. According to this formula, which is generally considered as the proper one since Thorndike, a difference score is calculated between the predicted reading score (based on the correlation with IQ) and the actual reading achievement score. When a child's regression-based discrepancy score exceeds a predetermined number of standard deviations of the discrepancy distribution (mostly 1.5 or 2 standard deviations), then the child could be characterized as "reading disabled" or "dyslexic".

It has gone unnoticed, however, that the adapted discrepancy formula is inconsistent with the basic premise of the under-achievement concept (Van den Broeck, 2002$_a$). Recall that according to the concept of underachievement, intellectual potential normally determines reading achievement. A discrepancy score is then an indication that the normal course of things has been perturbed by some disrupting factors. Now, taking into account the imperfect relationship between IQ and achievement, which itself is the consequence of the empirical fact that other factors than IQ determine reading achievement, neutralizes the goal of the discrepancy method. Clearly, a measure of the extent that specific causal factors depress the achievement score normally determined by the intellectual potential, should not be corrected for the influence of the same causal factors. The description of a difference (discrepancy) should not be influenced by the explanation of the difference. In short, what is wrong with the simple uncorrected discrepancy formula is not its mathematical form, but its underlying theory about the role of intelligence, which is empirically falsified by the far from perfect correlation between IQ and reading scores. In a review of the literature on the relationship between IQ and reading, Stanovich (1988) calculated that for beginning readers the median correlation between reading ability and intelligence measures was .34 (11.5% explained variance).

To elaborate this critique on the regression-based discrepancy formula two important consequences of the regression method should be emphasized. First, because the regression-based discrepancy scores actually reflect reading achievement scores partialled out for the influence of IQ, these discrepancy scores tend to be more determined by the actual reading scores the lower the correlation between IQ and reading is. In other words, the similarity between the regression-based discrepancy model and the interindividual norm-referenced approach of reading disability increases with a decreasing correlation between IQ and reading. Second, since the correlation between regression-based discrepancy scores and IQ-scores is exactly zero (a consequence of partialling out the influence of IQ), discrepant readers and non-discrepant readers have the same mean IQ-score. This last point illustrates the logical inconsistency of the regression-based approach connected with the concept of under-achievement of which it pretends to be the operationalization. Logically, there should be more "under-achievers" with high IQ's than with low IQ's, a requirement that is fulfilled with the simple standard score discrepancy formula.

The gradual decline of the discrepancy concept

Since more than two decades the discrepancy concept has been the subject of some critical inquiries. Although the field of learning disabilities seemed to have survived the first critical attacks which were primarily theoretical and methodological (Algozzine & Ysseldyke, 1983; Schlee, 1976), more recent critiques on the role of the IQ-score, and empirical comparisons between discrepant and non-discrepant poor readers accelerated the fall of the discrepancy concept.

Intelligence as "unlocked potential"

One of the many conceptualizations of intelligence is the view that intelligence reflects the general capacity for learning, included academic learning (Dearborn, as cited in Sternberg, 1985a, p. 324). The concept of underachievement has often implied the assumption that children are not performing up to their innate potential (Burt, 1950). According to this view the intelligence test score is a measure of the child's intellectual capacity, setting the maximum level of performance of which the child is capable. These assumptions, however, fared poorly under scrutiny. First, although genetic factors are unanimously accepted as important determinants of intellectual functioning, most recent theories incorporate environmental and contextual elements in their conceptualizations of intelligence (Ceci, 1990; Sternberg, 1985a; but see Vernon, 1987). Moreover, as Stanovich (1991) pointed out, IQ-scores are at their best gross measures of current cognitive functioning (see also Detterman, 1982), and Siegel (1989) has made it clear that typical IQ-tests, as the Wechsler Intelligence Scale for Children-Revised (Wechsler, 1974), do not measure "potential" or basic reasoning skills but depend more on expressive language skills, memory, fine motor abilities, and specific factual knowledge. Second, it has been shown that many children do achieve at a level well above their intellectual capacity, an anomalous outcome under the hypothesis of intelligence as potential for learning (Yule, Rutter, Berger & Thompson, 1974).

In an attempt to do justice to children with dyslexia, some scholars have argued against the use of verbal intelligence tests, favoring instead performance IQ measures which are deemed to be "fairer" measures of the children's potential (Birnbaum, 1990; Thomson, 1982; see also Miles, 1996). When the IQ-score is affected by the underlying dyslexic deficit, so the argument goes, the "real potential" of the child with dyslexia is underestimated. Stanovich (1991) countered this argument persuasively. He questioned the tacit assumption of the fairness argument that performance tests would provide the best measure of the subject's potential to comprehend *verbal* material. On the contrary, verbally loaded measures are arguably better estimates of future reading achievement (Hessler, 1987).

From an a-theoretical position, intelligence test scores are achievement scores just as much as reading scores, because an intelligence test assesses the child's *performance* on a variety of tasks (Rutter & Yule, 1975). By implication, it would be just as valid to consider reading ability as a cause of intelligence as vice versa. As a matter of fact, there is sufficient empirical evidence that reading ability is a moderate determinant of vocabulary growth, verbal intelligence, and general comprehension ability (Hayes, 1988; Hayes & Ahrens, 1988; Juel, 1988; Share, McGee & Silva, 1989; Share & Silva, 1987; Stanovich, 1986a; Stanovich & West, 1989; van den Bos, 1989). Stanovich (1986) places these causal effects of reading on verbal cognition in the broader developmental framework of "rich-get-richer and poor-get-poorer effects" and organism-environment interactions[1].

---

[1]. The "rich-get-richer and poor-get-poorer" effects are dubbed by Stanovich (1986) "Matthew effects" following Walberg (Walberg & Tsai, 1983) after the Gospel according to Matthew: "For unto every one that hath shall be given, and he shall have abundance: but from him that hath not shall be taken away even that which he hath" (XXV:29).

According to Stanovich, initial differences in reading skill grow larger as a consequence of the reciprocal or "bootstrapping" relationships with print exposure, vocabulary growth and motivational influences. Typically, a poor-reading child is not inclined to engage in reading activities, by which the delay in vocabulary and decoding ability grows larger. This framework offers an elegant explanation of the observed increasing correlation with age between reading ability and verbal competence (Bisshop & Butterworth, 1980; Brainerd, Kingma & Howe, 1986; Cohen, 1982; Stanovich, Cunningham & Feeman, 1984). Apparently, the vindication of the practice to exclude poor reading children with low IQ's from the definition of dyslexia becomes exceedingly dubious when their low IQ's are at least partly the consequence of their reading disability.

To conclude, there is reasonable doubt that an intelligence test is an appropriate measure of the concept of learning potential, understood as an invariable disposition.

Discrepancy as a means to ensure specificity

The aforementioned arguments were directed primarily against the concept and measurement of intelligence in the definition of dyslexia. However, the discrepancy concept itself was not really questioned (e.g. Lyon, 1995; Stanovich, 1993). On the contrary, it was felt that abandoning the discrepancy concept would undermine the very foundation of dyslexia, namely the assumption of specificity. In the words of Stanovich (1988):

> *"this assumption ... is the idea that a dyslexic child has a brain/cognitive deficit that is reasonably specific to the reading task. That is, the concept of a specific reading disability requires that the deficit displayed by the disabled reader not extend too far into other domains of cognitive functioning. Were this the case, there would already exist educational de-signations for such children (e.g., underachiever, slow learner, low intelligence), and the concept of reading disability or dyslexia would be superfluous. That is, if the deficits displayed by such children extended too far into other domains of cognitive functioning, this would depress the constellation of abilities we call intelligence, reduce the reading/intelligence discrepancy, and the child would no longer be dyslexic! His reading problem would become predictable from his problems in a range of other cognitive domains and no other explanation would be necessary."* (p. 155)

Stanovich' formulation of a brain/cognitive deficit hypothesizes specificity at the causal, explanatory level: this is "causal specificity". Although causal specificity is a viable hypothesis when a disorder is characterized by phenotypic specificity, the common idea that causal specificity is essential for the concept of dyslexia leads to a number of problems in the diagnosis and research of dyslexia.

Pertaining to diagnostic issues, the requirement of a specific underlying deficit divides the group of poor readers theoretically into two subgroups: those whose poor reading is explained by the deficit (the dyslexics), and those whose poor reading is the consequence of other non-specific factors (e.g. low intelligence), often called the "garden-variety" poor readers (Gough & Tunmer, 1986). In order to substantiate this theoretical subdivision in the assessment of an individual's reading disability, the causal specificity requirement is often translated into the discrepancy criterion. To be sure that a child has a specific deficit, its reading level should be below a measure of reading potential. To avoid the disadvantages of the intelligence test, an alternative test procedure was proposed: the discrepancy between reading ability and listening comprehension (Aaron, 1989; Spring & French, 1990; Stanovich, 1991, 1993). As Stanovich explains: *"Presumably, their listening comprehension [of discrepant readers] exceeds their reading comprehension because their word recognition processes are inefficient, causing a 'bottleneck' that impedes comprehension."* (Stanovich, 1991, p. 20; see also Perfetti, 1985). Completely in line with the underachievement premise of different causation of dyslexic versus other readers, children who are simultaneously low in reading and listening comprehension are said to have no "unexplained" or "unexpected" reading problem (Hoover & Gough, 1990; Stanovich, 1991). Importantly, a measure of listening comprehension is considered as superior to verbal IQ for its capacity to isolate a specific, "modular" deficit. Since listening comprehension correlates higher with reading than verbal IQ does, the deficit displayed by discrepant readers will be more likely a very specific one.

The fundamental problem with any discrepancy measurement procedure is that it contradicts the basic observation that reading problems are largely independent from any readily identifiable cognitive ability. It was exactly this independence that gave rise to the concept of dyslexia. In other words, the relative domain-specificity of word recognition (dis)ability is an observable fact, not a theoretical assumption or principle that should be substantiated in every particular case. The demand to observe a discrepancy in every child with dyslexia actually implies a dependence relationship between reading and general cognition: whether poor reading will be characterized as dyslexia depends on the height of the IQ or listening comprehension score. But to the extent that reading ability is really domain-specific and modular, an IQ or listening comprehension score is irrelevant for the nature or explanation of the reading problem. The idea that the reading problems of children with low IQ or listening comprehension scores are explained by their weak general cognitive ability, contradicts the domain-specificity of reading. For instance, a child that is poor in reading, arithmetic and has a low IQ still has an unexplained specific reading problem by virtue of the domain-specificity of reading ability. Comparably, to get the diagnosis of the flu, it is not necessary to be otherwise completely healthy (Van den Bos, 1998; see also Stanovich, 1996 for a comparable example). It seems that the deeply entrenched experimental logic of ruling out confounding variables was unperceived but erroneously translated into a diagnostic procedure. In explanatory research designed to discover the causal factors of dyslexia, to rule out confounding variables (e.g. IQ) in trying to exemplify the causal status of a hypothesized factor is utterly justified (Torgesen, 1989).

The requirement of causal specificity leads also to a conceptual paradox in the research on individual differences in the cognitive processes related to reading disability. This paradox was clearly pointed out by Stanovich (1986b, 1988). He reported that cognitive differences between reading-disabled and nondisabled children were found virtually everywhere. It has been demonstrated that children with reading problems obtain lower achievement levels compared to normal children on syntactic awareness tasks (Bentin, Deutsch, & Liberman, 1990; Byrne, 1981; Siegel & Ryan, 1984; Vogel, 1974), on measures of general linguistic awareness (Johnson, 1993; Kotsonis & Patterson, 1980; Menyuk & Flood, 1981; Siegel & Ryan, 1984), on general rule learning tasks (Fletcher & Prior, 1990; Manis et al., 1987; Morrison, 1984, 1987), on short term memory and processing strategy tasks (Bauer, 1977, 1979; Brady, 1991; Newman & Hagen, 1981; Share, 1994; Siegel, 1994; Torgesen, 1978-1979), and on measures of metacognitive strategies (Baker, 1982; Foster & Gavelek, 1983; Wong, 1991). These observations are also in agreement with the one-half standard-deviation-IQ deficit displayed by children with learning disabilities (Stanovich, 1986b). Although some of these cognitive processing liabilities can partly be attributed to reading or reading-related deficits (cf. reciprocal and Matthew effects), the generalized nature of the depressed cognitive abilities of children with dyslexia threatens to undermine the assumption of causal specificity. To avoid the impending deadlock, Stanovich suggests that research into the underlying causal deficits of dyslexia should not aim at these general cognitive processes, but should be directed at more modular cognitive mechanisms, particularly phonological processing.

Explaining the specificity paradox

To reconcile the idea of a specific cognitive deficit with the finding of more general cognitive problems in poor readers, Stanovich formulated his "phonological-core variable-difference model" (Stanovich, 1988, 1991, 1993). In this model a deficit in phonological processing is thought to be common to all poor readers, discrepant or non-discrepant, although the phonological deficit is hypothesized to be more severe in dyslexic (discrepant) readers. Indeed, a vast volume of evidence has established that poor readers exhibit deficits in various aspects of phonological processing. They have difficulty to detect, compare or manipulate phonemic segments in words, they are slower at naming objects and symbols, they show problems with short-term memory tasks (presumably due to inefficient phonological rehearsal), and they reveal subtle difficulties with speech perception and speech production tasks (Ackerman, Dykman & Gardner, 1990; Blachman, 1984; Bowers & Wolf, 1993; Brady, 1991; Brady, Mann & Schmidt, 1987; Catts, 1986; de Weirdt, 1988; Kahmi & Catts, 1989; Katz, Shankweiler & Liberman, 1981; Pallay, 1986; Rapala & Brady, 1990; Snowling, Goulandris, Bowlby, & Howell, 1986; Wagner & Torgesen, 1987; Werker & Tees, 1987; Wimmer, Landerl, Linortner, & Hummer, 1991; Wolf, 1986, 1991). The term "variable difference" refers to the differences in cognitive skills between discrepant (dyslexic) and non-discrepant poor readers. These differences between dyslexic and non-discrepant poor readers magnify when one moves on the continuum from children with a discrepancy toward children without a discrepancy. Because the cognitive deficits of the garden-variety poor readers *do* extend into a variety of cognitive domains, the phonological difficulties of these children are considered in this model as epiphenomenal to their general cognitive deficits. Thus, a developmental lag model is thought to be an appropriate description of the cognitive status of the garden-variety poor reader. In other words, albeit the common phonological problem of discrepant and non-discrepant poor readers, the differing etiology of non-discrepant poor readers offers an explanation of the reported relationship between poor reading and general cognitive functioning. Again, the subdivision in two distinct etiological categories, reflecting the discrepancy concept, comes to the rescue to warrant specificity. In a recent study, Stanovich and Siegel (1994) could reject the prediction that the phonological core deficit would be more severe for discrepant poor readers than for non-discrepant poor readers. The authors explain this finding by referring to the "acquired modularity" of word recognition ability. However, by disconnecting the phonological problems of the garden-variety poor readers from their general cognitive deficits, the phonological-core variable-difference model no longer explains the moderate association between poor reading and general cognitive disability.

Before discussing an alternative proposal to explain the specificity paradox without relying on the discrepancy concept, a caveat about the specificity of explanations is in place. The idea that specific phenomena require specific causes, as an application of the "representativeness heuristic" (Nisbett & Ross, 1980), is consistent with the dominant habit in cognitive science to induce a cognitive structure from the observation of a behavioral effect: the effect = structure assumption (Lakoff, 1987; see also Van Orden, Jansen op de Haar & Bosman, 1997). Although the effect = structure heuristic is often an indispensable tool for deriving a first-order description of behavior (Bechtel & Richardson, 1993), it fails to reduce the complexity of the behavioral phenomena (Van Orden & Goldinger, 1994). Most scientific explanations reduce empirical phenomena as special cases of more comprehensive regularities. Clearly, explaining specific reading disability by a specific reading deficit doesn't explain much. This is of course the reason for the qualification in Stanovich' formulation that the deficit may extend into other domains of cognitive functioning, although not too far! Moreover, an entirely reading-specific brain/cognitive deficit as the cause of dyslexia, is theoretically implausible, if not impossible. Such a deficit would require an extremely fast Darwinian evolution, since "homo sapiens sapiens has been illiterate for more than 40,000 years, and universal education is only about 100 years old, much too short a time span for such a complex behavior to evolve" (McGuiness, 1997, p. 124). What might be heritable is one or the other "natural" underlying aptitude involved in learning to read, instead of the "unnatural" ability of reading that depends on instruction and requires a cultural evolution (Gough, 1996; Gough & Hillinger, 1980; Liberman & Liberman, 1990). Also, a phonological deficit, although rather specific and therefore an excellent candidate cause, is clearly not entirely specific to reading. The hypothesis of a phonological deficit predicts phonological processing difficulties outside the reading domain (e.g. in dyslexic children's preliterate language development).

Stanovich' recommendation not to search for causes in the domain of *general* cognitive processes, lest the concept of dyslexia would become superfluous, is justified as concerning the *central* cognitive processes. Central processes like metacognitive and strategic functioning are surely too allied to intelligence to be good places to look for the cognitive locus of reading disability. They are bad candidates, not because they violate a theoretical principle of causal specificity, but because they are incompatible with the empirical fact showing a low correlation between intelligence and word recognition ability. Not all general cognitive processes are necessarily central processes. To name a few examples of general non-central cognitive processes that were proposed as candidate causes for dyslexia: a general language disorder (Catts & Kamhi, 1999; Metsala & Walley, 1998), a skill automatization deficit (Nicolson & Fawcett, 1990, 1994, 1995), and a deficit in temporal processing speed (Tallal, 1980; Tallal, Miller & Fitch, 1993). Naturally, these hypotheses should explain why the proposed deficits manifest themselves primarily in the process of reading development, and less so in other cognitive tasks. In short, they should explain phenotypic specificity. As a common scheme in hypotheses assuming a general cognitive deficit, phenotypic specificity is explained by referral to an interaction of the underlying deficit with task specific characteristics. For example, to explain why dyslexic children do not exhibit serious problems in the automatization of all cognitive skills, the "dyslexic automatization deficit" hypothesis assumes that the reading task is extremely vulnerable because of its specific resource-intensity (Nicolson & Fawcett, 1990). Notably, the demand to explain phenotypic specificity is not confined to these general cognitive hypotheses. As already argued, every viable causal hypothesis is to a certain extent non-specific, included the more specific ones. In a similar vein, the phonological deficit hypothesis has to explain why the phonological processing deficit doesn't manifest itself, or at least much less strikingly, outside the reading process. One would indeed expect that the extremely complex phonological processes in speech perception and production are even more vulnerable than the phonological processes involved in reading relatively simple words at the start of reading development. How is it possible that children who prove to be experts in speech phonology (by producing and understanding the most complex utterances) still have a subtle phonological deficit explaining their poor reading? (for attempts to answer these questions, see Fowler, 1991; Liberman, 1971; Liberman, Shankweiler, Liberman, Fowler, & Fisher, 1977; Metsala & Walley, 1998).

The fundamental point is that phenotypic specificity is a necessary and sufficient condition for the meaningfulness of the dyslexia concept. Causal specificity, on the other hand, is not a requirement for the tenability of the dyslexia concept, but is a possibility or hypothesis that has to be established empirically (Stanovich, personal communication, March 24, 2000). A priori imposing causal specificity on a theoretical basis endangers the concept of dyslexia (instead of saving it), when no single specific cause can be discovered. To strengthen the case for phenotypic specificity, it may be pointed out that this proposal is entirely compatible with medical practice. Many medical diagnoses are based exclusively on phenotypic specificity (symptom patterns). Furthermore, many diseases are known for which definite causes are not yet been found. In medical science causal factors are only included in the diagnosis if the cause of the disease is empirically established as a fact by the scientific community.

Let us return now to the specificity paradox. Although the correlation between IQ and reading ability is very modest, it is reliably larger than zero. For one thing, this means that the major determinants of reading (dis)ability are not to be found in the central processes: the explained variance of reading being only 10 à 15 %. At the other hand, the relationship has to be explained. Besides the already mentioned reciprocal relationship between reading and IQ, there appears to be some additional sources to explain the correlation. First, because an IQ-test is no pure measure of central processes, it is plausible that an IQ-score is partly determined by lower-order processes like for example, phonological processing in digit span, associative learning in digit symbol (WISC-R). If this assumption is reasonable, then the observed correlation between IQ and reading is even an overestimation of the real relationship between reading ability and comprehension or thought processes. Second, it is conceivable that central processes have no direct effect on the reading process itself, but exercise an indirect influence on reading ability in two ways. (a) Less intelligent children, who have weak attentional capabilities, are probably less inclined to engage in sustained reading sessions. (b) Engendered by organism-environment interactions, these children get probably less stimulation from their environment to read, resulting in a lag of print exposure (cf. Stanovich, 1986a). The detrimental entailments of low print exposure on reading ability are well-documented (Allington, 1984; Biemiller, 1977-1978; Cunningham & Stanovich, 1991; McBride-Chang, Manis, Seidenberg, Custodio & Doi, 1993; Nagy & Anderson, 1984; Stanovich & West, 1989). Finally, in all existing models of word recognition it is assumed that vocabulary knowledge facilitates the process of word recognition directly. In sum, there may be a multitude of factors determining reading (dis)ability, some of which are direct and others indirect, and some of which are intra-individual and others external (e.g. the influence of instruction methods). After all, learning to read is a learning process and any learning process can go awry for a multitude of reasons. Therefore, it will usually prove very difficult to pin down which determinant or which complex of determinants caused the reading problem of a reading disabled individual. Whether the child's reading problem is the result of a specific cognitive weakness, say a phonological deficit, exacerbated by low motivation and stimulation and a mediocre instruction method, or any other combination, is very difficult to tell. Therefore, although most reading problems are probably determined partly by intrinsic specific factors, a realistic definition of dyslexia should leave open the possibility for multidimensional causality.

Are intelligent poor readers different from unintelligent poor readers?

The demonstration of the independence of word recognition from higher order central processes is reason enough to discard the discrepancy notion. However, it was not until direct comparisons between discrepant and non-discrepant poor readers revealed no qualitative differences in their reading-related processes, that most scholars were prepared to abandon the discrepancy concept.

Remember that the basic premise of the underachievement-discrepancy concept is the thesis of different etiology of the reading problems of unexpected (smart) poor readers and expected (dull) poor readers. By implication, it was predicted that the cognitive makeup, the nature of reading processes, the educational prognosis and the sensitivity for remedial interventions would be different for both groups (for an extensive review of these issues, see Aaron, 1997). Empirical studies have failed to show significant differences in psychometric profiles (e.g. WISC profiles) of discrepant and non-discrepant poor readers, despite the overall lower cognitive level of the last group (e.g. Fletcher, Francis, Rourke, Shaywitz & Shaywitz, 1992; Kavale & Forness, 1994; Ysseldyke, Algozzine, Shinn & McGue, 1982). A series of studies, using diverse measurements of phonological processing abilities in reading, couldn't reveal any substantial differences between discrepant and non-discrepant poor readers. Both groups performed equally on pseudoword (nonexistent pronounceable words) reading (Badian, 1994; Ellis & Large, 1987; Ellis, McDougall & Monk, 1996_a; Felton & Wood, 1992; Fredman & Stevenson, 1988; Jorm, Share, Maclean & Matthews, 1986; Share, 1996; Siegel, 1988, 1989; Stanovich & Siegel, 1994) and on other phonological skills (Ellis et al., 1996_a; Johnston, Rugg, & Scott, 1987; Siegel, 1992; Stanovich & Siegel, 1994). Nor have differences been found between both groups in the reading of regular words and exception words, indicating a failure to find a differing regularity effect (Fredman & Stevenson, 1988; Share, Jorm & Maclean, 1988; Siegel, 1992; Stanovich & Siegel, 1994; see Metsala, Stanovich & Brown, 1998 for a meta-analysis).

Concerning the issue of differential etiology, in a twin study Olson, Rack, Connors, DeFries and Fulker (1991) couldn't find a statistical significant difference in the heritability of both groups' reading deficit. In the Colorado Reading Project, Pennington, Gilger, Olson and DeFries (1992) compared an IQ-regression based discrepant group with a group of backward readers and concluded that *"The heritability analyses are primarily consistent with the hypothesis that the same genes influence each diagnostic phenotype"* (p. 570). In another study, Olson, Forsberg, Gayan, and DeFries (1999) did find a higher heritability-score for high IQ poor readers versus low IQ poor readers. The authors suggest that a poor home and educational environment could be determinants for both the poor reading and low IQ, an interpretation that is consistent with the idea, expressed in the previous section, of a moderate indirect influence of IQ on reading disability. In their classic study Rutter and Yule (1975) reported that the educational prognosis for the discrepant poor readers was better than that for the non-discrepant poor readers. However, this finding could not be replicated in subsequent studies using longitudinal growth curve analyses of reading development (Francis, Shaywitz, Stuebing, Shaywitz & Fletcher, 1994; Share, McGee, McKenzie, Williams & Silva, 1987). Finally, concerning the differential sensitivity for remedial interventions, Aaron concludes from his review that *"no overall, compelling evidence of educational gains has been obtained to warrant the continuation of the policy of classifying poor readers into learning-disabled and non-learning-disabled categories"* [discrepant vs. non-discrepant] (Aaron, 1997, p. 475).

Respecting the methodology to compare discrepant and non-discrepant poor readers, an important remark about these studies should be made. As was already explained, when using regression-based discrepancy scores the mean IQ-score of discrepant and non-discrepant readers is the same. So, the natural meaning of discrepant as "smart but poor reader" vanishes because these readers are not smarter than non-discrepant readers are. Moreover, taking the median correlation between IQ and reading (.34) as a reference, the correlation between the reading scores and the regression based discrepancy scores is -.94. This means that most (regression-based) discrepant readers are also poor readers, and vice versa. Therefore, it is not easy to find a group of (regression-based) non-discrepant readers that are also poor readers. This is probably the reason why in the reported studies all kind of groups were compared with each other: groups with regression based discrepancies, groups with simple standard score discrepancies and groups of low reading achievement with or without discrepancies. Nevertheless, despite the methodological and conceptual ambiguity of these studies, the overall conclusion that intelligence is quite irrelevant for the characterization of reading disability remains uncontested and is consistent with the empirical documentation of the modularity of reading. There is however some irony in the fact that the field has been persuaded most about the irrelevance of the discrepancy concept by studies which were only partly capable of disconfirming the discrepancy concept. To the extent that these studies made use of the generally commended but invalid regression based method, a priori implying the irrelevance of intelligence by statistically controlling for IQ, the discrepancy concept was not really challenged. Fortunately, the simple observation of a low correlation between IQ and reading is a sufficient reason for the definitive falsification of the discrepancy notion. With respect to the history of reading disabilities research, one can only endorse Stanovich' admonition that:

One might have thought that researchers would have begun with the broadest and most theoretically neutral definition of reading disability – reading performance below some specified level on some well-known and psychometrically sound test – and then proceeded to investigate whether there were poor readers with differing cognitive profiles within this broader group. Unfortunately, the history of reading disabilities research does not resemble this logical sequence. Instead, early definitions of reading disability assumed knowledge of differential cognitive profile (and causation) within the larger sample of poor readers and defined the condition of reading disability in a way that actually served to preclude empirical investigation of the unproven theoretical assumptions that guided the formulation of these definitions! (Stanovich, 1994, p.16).

Are intelligence tests obsolete in the research and clinical diagnosis of dyslexia?

Although we have come to the conclusion that intelligence is essentially irrelevant for the concept of dyslexia and is therefore not needed in the diagnosis of dyslexia, a more modest role of intelligence testing can be defended. First, in research it remains a perfectly legitimate question to ask what the exact role of intelligence is in specific learning disabilities; after all, the aptitude-achievement correlation is always larger than zero. This kind of research requires a design in which groups of individuals with learning disabilities with high IQ scores (i.e., discrepant) and low IQ scores (i.e., nondiscrepant) who are matched on all possible confounding variables are compared. Secondly, in a clinical diagnosis it may be informative to segregate the role of intelligence-related and intelligence-unrelated determinants of an individual reading achievement score. This can be achieved by comparing the simple discrepancy score (IQ minus achievement score) with the regression-based discrepancy score (IQ-expected achievement score minus achievement score) (see Van den Broeck, 2002b).

References

Aaron, P.G. (1989). *Dyslexia and hyperlexia.* Dordrecht, The Netherlands: Kluwer Academic.

Aaron, P.G. (1997). The impending demise of the discrepancy formula. *Review of Educational Research, 67,* 461-502.

Ackerman, P.T., Dykman, R.A., & Gardner, M.Y. (1990). ADD students with and without dyslexia differ in sensitivity to rhyme and alliteration. *Journal of Learning Disabilities, 23,* 279-283.

Algozzine, B., & Ysseldyke, J.E. (1983). Learning disabilities as a subset of school failure: The over-sophistication of a concept. *Exceptional Children, 50,* 242-246.

Allington, R.L. (1984). Content coverage and contextual reading in reading groups. *Journal of Reading Behavior, 16,* 85-96.

American Psychiatric Association. (1994). *Diagnostic and statistical manual of mental disorders* (4th ed. rev.). Washington, DC: American Psychiatric Press.

Badian, N.A. (1994). Do dyslexic and other poor readers differ in reading-related cognitive skills? *Reading and Writing: An Interdisciplinary Journal, 6,* 45-63.

Baker, L. (1982). An evaluation of the role of metacognitive deficits in learning disabilities. *Topics in Learning and Learning Disabilities, 2,* 27-35.

Bauer, R. (1977). Memory processes in children with learning disabilities: Evidence for deficient rehearsal. *Journal of Experimental Child Psychology, 24,* 415-430.

Bauer, R. (1979). Memory, acquisition, and category clustering in learning-disabled children. *Journal of Experimental Child Psychology, 27,* 365-383.

Bechtel, W., & Richardson, R.C. (1993). *Discovering complexity: Decomposition and localization as strategies in scientific research.* Princeton, NJ: Princeton University Press.

Bentin, S., Deutsch, A., & Liberman, I.Y. (1990). Syntactic competence and reading ability in children. *Journal of Experimental Child Psychology, 49,* 147-172.

Biemiller, A. (1977-1978). Relationships between oral reading rates for letters, words, and simple text in the development of reading achievement. *Reading Research Quarterly, 13,* 223-253.

Birnbaum, R. (1990). IQ and the definition of LD. *Journal of Learning Disabilities, 23,* 330.

Bishop, D., & Butterworth, G. (1980). Verbal-performance discrepancies: Relationship to both risk and specific reading retardation. *Cortex, 16,* 375-389.

Blachman, B. (1984). Relationship of naming ability and language analysis skills to kindergarten and first-grade reading achievement. *Journal of Educational Psychology, 76,* 610-622.

Bowers, P.G., & Wolf, M. (1993). Theoretical links between naming speed, precise timing mechanisms and orthographic skill in dyslexia. *Reading and Writing: An Interdisciplinary Journal, 5,* 69-85.

Brady, S.A. (1991). The role of working memory in reading disability. In S.A. Brady & D.P. Shankweiler (Eds.), *Phonological processes in literacy: A tribute to Isabelle Y. Liberman* (pp. 129-151). Hillsdale, NJ: Erlbaum.

Brady, S., Mann, V., & Schmidt, R. (1987). Errors in short-term memory for good and poor readers. *Memory and Cognition, 15,* 444-453.

Brainerd, C., Kingma, J., & Howe, M. (1986). Long-term memory development and learning disability: Storage and retrieval loci of disabled/nondisabled differences. In S. Ceci (Ed.), *Handbook of cognitive, social, and neuropsychological aspects of learning disabilities* (Vol. 1, pp. 161-184). Hillsdale, NJ: Erlbaum.

Burt, C. (1950). *The backward child.* (3rd ed.). London: University of London Press.
Byrne, B. (1981). Deficient syntactic control in poor readers: Is a weak phonetic memory code responsible? *Applied Psycholinguistics, 2,* 201-212.
Catts, H. (1986). Speech production/phonological deficits in reading-disordered children. *Journal of Learning Disabilities, 19,* 504-508.
Catts, H., & Kamhi, A. (1999). *Language and reading disabilities.* Needham Heights, MA: Allyn and Bacon.
Ceci, S.J. (1990). *On intelligence... more or less: A bio-ecological treatise on intellectual development.* Englewood Cliffs, NJ: Prentice-Hall.
Cohen, R.L. (1982). Individual differences in short-term memory. In L. Ellis (Ed.), *International review of research in mental retardation* (Vol. 2, pp. 43-77). New York: Academic Press.
Cone, T.E., & Wilson, L.R. (1981). Quantifying a severe discrepancy: A critical analysis. *Learning Disability Quarterly, 4,* 359-371.
Critchley, M. (1970). *The dyslexic child.* London: Heinemann.
Cunningham, A.E., & Stanovich, K.E. (1991). Tracking the unique effects of print exposure in children: Associations with vocabulary, general knowledge, and spelling. *Journal of Educational Psychology, 83,* 264-274.
de Weirdt, W. (1988). Speech perception and frequency discrimination in good and poor readers. *Applied Psycholinguistics, 9,* 163-183.
Dejerine, J. (1892). Contribution à l'étude anatomoclinique et clinique des differences varietés de cécité verbale. *Mémoires de la Société de Biologie, 4,* 61-90.
Detterman, D. (1982). Does "G" exist? *Intelligence, 6,* 99-108.
Dumont, J.J. (1976). *Leerstoornissen deel 1: theorie en model* [Learning disabilities Part 1: theory and model]. Rotterdam: Lemniscaat.
Ellis, A.W., McDougall, S., & Monk, A.F. (1996a). Are dyslexics different? I. A comparison between dyslexics, reading age controls, poor readers, and precocious readers. *Dyslexia, 2,* 31-58.
Ellis, N., & Large, B. (1987). The development of reading: as you seek so shall you find. *British Journal of Psychology, 78,* 1-28.
Felton, R.H., & Wood, F.B. (1992). A reading level match study of nonword reading skills in poor readers with varying IQ. *Journal of Learning Disabilities, 25,* 318-326.
Fletcher, C.M., & Prior, M.R. (1990). The rule learning behavior of reading disabled and normal children as a function of task characteristics and instruction. *Journal of Experimental Child Psychology, 50,* 39-58.
Fletcher, J.M. (Ed.) (1992). The validity of distinguishing children with language and learning disabilities according to discrepancies with IQ: introduction to the Special Series. [Special issue] *Journal of Learning Disabilities, 25* (9).
Fletcher, J.M., Francis, D., Rourke, B.P., Shaywitz, S.E., & Shaywitz, B.A. (1992). The validity of discrepancy-based definitions of reading disabilities. *Journal of Learning Disabilities, 25,* 555-561.
Foster, R., & Gavelek, J. (1983). Development of intentional forgetting in normal and reading-delayed children. *Journal of educational Psychology, 75,* 431-440.
Fowler, A. (1991). How early phonological development might set the stage for phoneme awareness. In S.A. Brady, & D.P. Shankweiler (Eds.), *Phonological processes in literacy* (pp. 97-117). Hillsdale, N.J.: Erlbaum.
Francis, D.J., Shaywitz, S., Stuebing, K., Shaywitz, B., & Fletcher, J.M. (1994). Measurement of change: Assessing behavior over time and within a developmental context. In G.R. Lyon (Ed.), *Frames of reference for the assessment of*

learning disabilities: New views on measurement issues (pp. 29-58). Baltimore, MD: Paul Brookes.

Frankenberger, W., & Fronzaglio, K. (1991). A review of states' criteria and procedures for identifying children with learning disabilities. *Journal of Learning Disabilities, 24,* 495-500.

Frankenberger, W., & Harper, J. (1987). States' criteria and procedures for identifying learning disabled children: A comparison of 1981/82 and 1985/86 guidelines. *Journal of Learning Disabilities, 20,* 118-121.

Fredman, G., & Stevenson, J. (1988). Reading processes in specific reading retarded and reading backward 13-year-olds. *British Journal of Developmental Psychology, 6,* 141-161.

Gough, P.B. (1996). How children learn to read and why they fail? *Annals of Dyslexia, 46,* 3-20.

Gough, P.B., & Hillinger, M.L. (1980). Learning to read: an unnatural act. *Annals of Dyslexia, 30,* 179-196.

Gough, P.B., & Tunmer, W.E. (1986). Decoding, reading, and reading disability. *Remedial and Special Education, 7,* 6-10.

Hammill, D.D. (1993). A brief look at the learning disabilities movement in the United States. *Journal of Learning Disabilities, 26,* 295-310.

Hayes, D.P. (1988). Speaking and writing: Distinct patterns of word choice. *Journal of Memory and Language, 27,* 572-585.

Hayes, D.P., & Ahrens, M. (1988). Vocabulary simplification for children: A special case of "motherese"? *Journal of Child Language, 15,* 395-410.

Hessler, G.L. (1987). Educational issues surrounding severe discrepancy. *Learning Disabilities Research, 3,* 43-49.

Hinshelwood, J. (1917). *Congenital word blindness.* London: H.K. Lewis.

Hoover, W.A., & Gough, P.B. (1990). The simple view of reading. *Reading and Writing: An Interdisciplinary Journal, 2,* 127-160.

Johnson, D.J. (1993). Relationship between oral and written language. *School Psychology Review, 22,* 595-609.

Johnston, R.S., Rugg, M.D. & Scott, T. (1987). The influence of phonology on good and poor readers when reading for meaning. *Journal of Memory and Language, 26,* 57-68.

Jorm, A.F., Share, D.L., Maclean, R., & Matthews, R. (1986). Cognitive factors predictive of specific reading retardation and general reading backwardness: A research note. *Journal of Child Psychology and Psychiatry, 27(1),* 45-54.

Juel, C. (1988). Learning to read and write: A longitudinal study of 54 children from first through fourth grades. *Journal of Educational Psychology, 80,* 437-447.

Kahmi, A., & Catts, H. (1989). *Reading disabilities: A developmental language perspective.* Boston: College-Hill.

Katz, R., Shankweiler, D., & Liberman, I. (1981). Memory for item order and phonetic recoding in the beginning reader. *Journal of Experimental Child Psychology, 32,* 474-484.

Kavale, K.A., & Forness, S.R. (1994). Learning disabilities and intelligence: An uneasy alliance. In T.E. Scruggs & M.M. Mastropieri (Eds.), *Advances in learning and behavioral disabilities* (pp. 1-63). Greenwich, CT: Jai Press.

Kotsonis, M., & Patterson, C. (1980). Comprehension-monitoring skills in learning-disabled children. *Developmental Psychology, 16,* 541-542.

Lakoff, G. (1987). *Women, fire, and dangerous things: What categories reveal about the mind.* Chicago, IL: University of Chicago Press.

Lerner, J.W. (1989). Educational interventions in learning disabilities. *Journal of the*

American Academy of Child and Adolescent Psychiatry, 28, 326-331.

Liberman, I.Y. (1971). Basic research in speech and lateralization of language: Some implications for reading disability. *Bulletin of the Orton Society, 21,* 71-87.

Liberman, I.Y., & Liberman, A.M. (1990). Whole language vs. code emphasis: Underlying assumptions and their implications for reading instruction. *Annals of Dyslexia, 40,* 51-76.

Liberman, I.Y., Shankweiler, D., Liberman, A.M., Fowler, C., & Fisher, W.F. (1977). Phonetic segmentation and recoding in the beginning reader. In A.S. Reber & D.L. Scarborough (Eds.), *Toward a psychology of reading: the proceedings of the CUNY conference* (pp. 207-225). Hillsdale, N.J.: Erlbaum.

Lyon, G.R. (1995). Toward a definition of dyslexia. *Annals of Dyslexia, 45,* 3-27.

Manis, F.R., Savage, P.L., Morrison, F.J., Horn, C.C., Howell, M.J., Szeszulski, P.A., & Holt, L.J. (1987). Paired associate learning in reading-disabled children: Evidence for a rule-learning deficiency. *Journal of Experimental Child Psychology, 43,* 25-43.

McBride-Chang, C., Manis, F.R., Seidenberg, M.S., Custodio, R.G., & Doi, L.M. (1993). Print exposure as a predictor of word reading and reading comprehension in disabled and nondisabled readers. *Journal of Educational Psychology, 85,* 230-238.

McGuinness, D. (1997). *Why our children can't read and what we can do about it.* New York: The Free Press.

McLeod, J. (1979). Educational underachievement: Toward a defensible psychometric definition. *Journal of Learning Disabilities, 12,* 42-50.

Menyuk, P., & Flood, J. (1981). Linguistic competence, reading, writing problems, and remediation. *Bulletin of the Orton Society, 31,* 13-28.

Mercer, C.D., Jordan, L., Allsopp, D.H., & Mercer, A.H. (1996). Learning disabilities definitions and criteria used by state education departments. *Learning Disability Quarterly, 19,* 217-232.

Metsala, J.L., Stanovich, K.E., & Brown, G.D.A. (1998). Regularity effects and the phonological deficit model of reading disabilities: A meta-analytic review. *Journal of Educational Psychology, 90,* 279-293.

Metsala, J.L., & Walley, A.C. (1998). Spoken vocabulary growth and the segmental restructuring of lexical representations: Precursors to phonemic awareness and early reading ability. In J.L. Metsala & L.C. Ehri (Eds.), *Word recognition in beginning literacy* (pp. 89-120). NJ: Lawrence Erlbaum.

Miles, T.R. (1996). Do dyslexic children have IQs? *Dyslexia, 2,* 175-178.

Morrison, F.J. (1984). Word decoding and rule-learning in normal and disabled readers. *Remedial and Special Education, 5,* 20-27.

Morrison, F.J. (1987). The nature of reading disability: Toward an integrative framework. In S. Ceci (Ed.), *Handbook of cognitive, social, and neuropsychological aspects of learning disabilities* (pp. 33-62). Hillsdale, NJ: Erlbaum.

Nagy, W.E., & Anderson, R.C. (1984). How many words are there in printed school English? *Reading Research Quarterly, 19,* 304-330.

Newman, D.S., & Hagen, J.W. (1981). Memory strategies in children with learning disabilities. *Journal of Applied Developmental Psychology, 1,* 297-312.

Nicolson, R.I., & Fawcett, A.J. (1990). Automaticity: a new framework for dyslexia research? *Cognition, 35,* 159-182.

Nicolson, R.I., & Fawcett, A.J. (1994). Comparison of deficits in cognitive and motor skills among children with dyslexia. *Annals of Dyslexia, 44,* 147-164.

Nicolson, R.I., & Fawcett, A.J. (1995). Dyslexia is more than a phonological disability. *Dyslexia, 1,* 19-37.

Nicolson, R.I, & Siegel, L.S. (Eds.) (1996). Special issue on dyslexia and intelligence: Editors' foreword. [Special issue] *Dyslexia, 2.*

Nisbett, R.E., & Ross, L. (1980). *Human inference: Strategies and shortcomings of social judgment.* Englewood Cliffs, NJ: Prentice-Hall.

Olson, R.K., Forsberg, H., Gayan, J., & DeFries, J.C. (1999). A behavioral-genetic analysis of reading disabilities and component processes. In R.M. Klein & P.A. Mullen (Eds.), *Converging methods for understanding reading and dyslexia.* (pp. 133-153). Cambridge Mass.: MIT Press.

Olson, R.K., Rack, J.P., Connors, F., DeFries, J.C., & Fulker, D. (1991). Genetic etiology of individual differences in reading disability. In L. Feagans, E. Short, & L. Meltzer (Eds.), *Subtypes of learning disabilities* (pp. 113-135). Hillsdale, NJ: Erlbaum.

Pallay, S. (1986). *Speech perception in dyslexic children.* Dissertation: The City University of New York.

Pedhazur, E.J., & Pedhazur Schmelkin, L. (1991). *Measurement, design, and analysis: An integrated approach.* Hillsdale, NJ: Lawrence Erlbaum.

Pennington, B.F., Gilger, J., Olson, R.K., & DeFries, J.C. (1992). The external validity of age- versus IQ-discrepancy definitions of reading disability: Lessons from a twin-study. *Journal of Learning Disabilities, 25,* 562-573.

Perfetti, C.A. (1985). *Reading ability.* New York: Oxford University Press.

Rapala, M.R., & Brady, S. (1990). Reading ability and short term-memory: The role of phonological processing. *Reading and Writing: An Interdisciplinary Journal, 2,* 1-25.

Reynolds, C.R. (1985). Measuring the aptitude-achievement discrepancy in learning disability diagnosis. *Remedial and Special Education, 6 (5),* 37-48.

Reynolds, C.R. (1992). Two key concepts in the diagnosis of learning disabilities and the habilitation of learning. *Learning Disability Quarterly, 15,* 2-12.

Rogosa, D.R., & Willett, J.B. (1985). Understanding correlates of change by modeling individual differences in growth. *Psychometrika, 2,* 203-228.

Rutter, M., & Yule, W. (1973). Specific reading retardation. In L. Mann & D.A. Sabatino (Eds.), *The first review of special education* (pp. 49-62). Philadelphia: Buttonwood Farms.

Rutter, M., & Yule, W. (1975). The concept of specific reading retardation. *Journal of Child Psychology and Psychiatry, 16,* 181-197.

Schlee, J. (1976). *Legasthenieforschung am Ende?* München.

Share, D.L. (1994). Deficient phonological processing in disabled readers implicates processing deficits beyond the phonological module. In K.P. Van den Bos, L.S. Siegel, D.J. Bakker, & D.L. Share (Eds.), *Current directions in dyslexia research* (pp. 149-167). Lisse, The Netherlands: Swets & Zeitlinger.

Share, D.L. (1996). Word recognition and spelling processes in specific reading disabled and garden-variety poor readers. *Dyslexia, 2,* 167-174.

Share, D.L., Jorm, A.F., & Maclean, R. (1988). Lexical decision and naming times of young disabled readers with function and content words. *Australian Journal of Psychology, 40,* 11-18.

Share, D.L., McGee, R., McKenzie, D., Williams, S., & Silva, P.A. (1987). Further evidence relating to the distinction between specific reading retardation and general reading backwardness. *British Journal of Developmental Psychology, 5,* 35-44.

Share, D.L., McGee, R., & Silva, P.A. (1989). IQ and reading progress: A test of the capacity notion of IQ. *Journal of the American Academy of Child and Adolescent Psychiatry, 28,* 97-100.

Share, D.L., & Silva, P.A. (1987). Language deficits and specific reading retardation: Cause or effect? *British Journal of Disorders of Communication, 22*, 219-226.

Shaywitz, B.A., Fletcher, J.M., Holahan, J.M., & Shaywitz, S.E. (1992). Discrepancy compared to low achievement definitions of reading disability: Results from the Connecticut longitudinal study. *Journal of Learning Disabilities, 25*, 639-648.

Siegel, L.S. (1988). Evidence that IQ scores are irrelevant to the definition and analysis of reading disability. *Canadian Journal of Psychology, 42*, 210-215.

Siegel, L.S. (1989). IQ is irrelevant to the definition of learning disabilities. *Journal of Learning Disabilities, 22*, 469-478.

Siegel, L.S. (1992). An evaluation of the discrepancy definition of dyslexia. *Journal of Learning Disabilities, 25*, 618-629.

Siegel, L.S. (1994). Working memory and reading: A life-span perspective. *International Journal of Behavioral Development, 17*, 109-124.

Siegel, L.S., & Ryan, E. (1984). Reading disability as a language disorder. *Remedial and Special Education, 5*, 28-33.

Snowling, M., Goulandris, N., Bowlby, M., & Howell, P. (1986). Segmentation and speech perception in relation to reading skill: A developmental analysis. *Journal of Experimental Child Psychology, 41*, 489-507.

Spring, C., & French, L. (1990). Identifying children with specific reading disabilities from listening and reading discrepancy scores. *Journal of Learning Disabilities, 23*, 53-58.

Stanovich, K.E. (1986a). Matthew effects in reading: Some consequences of individual differences in the acquisition of literacy. *Reading Research Quarterly, 21*, 360-407.

Stanovich, K.E. (1986b). Cognitive processes and the reading problems of learning disabled children: Evaluating the assumption of specificity. In J. Torgesen & B. Wong (Eds.), *Psychological and educational perspectives on learning disabilities* (pp. 87-131). New York: Academic Press.

Stanovich, K.E. (1988). The right and wrong places to look for the cognitive locus of reading disability. *Annals of Dyslexia, 38*, 154-177.

Stanovich, K.E. (1991). Discrepancy definitions of reading disability: has intelligence led us astray? *Reading Research Quarterly, 26*, 7-29.

Stanovich, K.E. (1993). A model for studies of reading disability. *Developmental Review, 13*, 225-245.

Stanovich, K.E. (1994). Are discrepancy-based definitions of dyslexia empirically defensible? In K.P. Van den Bos, L.S. Siegel, D.J. Bakker, & D.L. Share (Eds.), *Current directions in dyslexia research* (pp. 15-30). Lisse, The Netherlands: Swets & Zeitlinger.

Stanovich, K.E. (1996). Toward a more inclusive definition of dyslexia. *Dyslexia, 2*, 154-166.

Stanovich, K.E., Cunningham, A.E., & Feeman, D.J. (1984). Intelligence, cognitive skills, and early reading progress. *Reading Research Quarterly, 19*, 278-303.

Stanovich, K.E., & Siegel, L.S. (1994). Phenotypic performance profile of children with reading disabilities: A regression-based test of the phonological-core variable-difference model. *Journal of Educational Psychology, 86*, 24-53.

Stanovich, K.E., & West, R.F. (1989). Exposure to print and orthographic processing. *Reading Research Quarterly, 24*, 402-433.

Sternberg, R.J. (1985a). *Beyond IQ: A triarchic theory of human intelligence.* Cambridge, England: Cambridge University Press.

Tallal, P. (1980). Auditory temporal perception, phonics and reading disabilities in children. *Brain and Language, 9*, 182-198.

Tallal, P., Miller, S., & Fitch, R.H. (1993). Neurological basis of speech: A case of the preeminence of temporal processing. *Annals of the New York Academy of Sciences, 682,* 27-47.

Taylor, H.G. (1984). Minimal brain dysfunction in perspective. In R.E. Tarter & G. Goldstein (Eds.), *Advances in clinical neuropsychology* (Vol. 2, pp.207-229). New York: Plenum Press.

Taylor, H.G., & Schatschneider, C. (1992). Academic achievement following childhood brain disease: implications for the concept of learning disabilities. *Journal of Learning Disabilities, 25,* 630-638.

Thomson, M. (1982). Assessing the intelligence of dyslexic children. *Bulletin of the British Psychological Society, 35,* 94-96.

Thorndike, R.L. (1963). *The concepts of over- and under-achievement.* New York: Bureau of Publications, Teachers College, Columbia University.

Torgesen, J. (1978-1979). Performance of reading disabled children on serial memory tasks. *Reading Research Quarterly, 14,* 57-87.

Torgesen, J.K. (1989). Why IQ is relevant to the definition of learning disabilities. *Journal of Learning Disabilities, 22,* 484-486.

Van den Bos, K.P. (1989). Relationship between cognitive development, decoding skill, and reading comprehension in learning disabled Dutch children. In P. Aaron & M. Joshi (Eds.), *Reading and writing disorders in different orthographic systems* (pp. 75-86). Dordrecht, The Netherlands: Kluwer Academic.

Van den Bos, K.P. (1998). Orthopedagogische dyslexiebehandeling gaat altijd uit van 'dyslexie-plus'. [Orthopedagogical treatment of dyslexia always starts from dyslexia-plus.] *Tijdschrift voor Orthopedagogiek, 37,* 300-304.

Van den Broeck, W. (2002a). The misconception of the regression-based discrepancy operationalization in the definition and research of learning disabilities. *Journal of Learning Disabilities, 35,* 194-204.

Van den Broeck, W. (2002b). Will the real discrepant learning disability please stand up? *Journal of Learning Disabilities, 35,* 209-213.

Van Orden, G.C., & Goldinger, S.D. (1994). Interdependence of form and function in cognitive systems explains perception of printed words. *Journal of Experimental Psychology: Human Perception and Performance, 20,* 1269-1291.

Van Orden, G.C., Jansen op de Haar, M.A., & Bosman, A.M.T. (1997). Complex dynamic systems also predict dissociations, but they do not reduce to autonomous components. *Cognitive Neuropsychology, 14,* 131-165.

Vernon, P.A. (Ed.). (1987). *Speed of information-processing and intelligence.* Norwood, NJ: Ablex.

Vogel, S. (1974). Syntactic abilities in normal and dyslexic children. *Journal of Learning Disabilities, 7,* 103-109.

Wagner, R.K., & Torgesen, J.K. (1987). The nature of phonological processing and its causal role in the acquisition of reading skills. *Psychological Bulletin, 101,* 192-212.

Wechsler, D. (1974). *Manual for the Wechsler Intelligence Scale for Children-Revised.* San Antonio, TX: Psychological Corp.

Werker, J., & Tees, R. (1987). Speech perception in severely disabled and average reading children. *Canadian Journal of Psychology, 41,* 48-61.

Wiederholt, J.L. (1974). Historical perspectives on the education of the learning disabled. In L. Mann & D.A. Sabatino (Eds.), *The second review of special education* (pp. 103-152). Austin, TX: PRO-ED.

Wimmer, H., Landerl, K., Linortner, R., & Hummer, P. (1991). The relationship of phonemic awareness to reading acquisition: More consequence than precondition but still important. *Cognition, 40,* 219-249.

Wolf, M. (1986). Rapid alternating stimulus naming in the developmental dyslexias. *Brain and Language, 27,* 360-379.

Wolf, M. (1991). Naming speed and reading: The contribution of the cognitive neurosciences. *Reading Research Quarterly, 26,* 123-141.

Wong, B.Y.L. (Ed.) (1989). Is IQ necessary in the definition of learning disabilities? Introduction to the special series. [Special issue] *Journal of Learning Disabilities, 22*(8).

Wong, B.Y.L. (1991). The relevance of metacognition to learning disabilities. In B.Y.L. Wong (Ed.), *Learning about learning disabilities* (pp. 231-258). San Diego, CA: Academic Press.

World Health Organization (1993). *ICD-10 classification of mental and behavioural disorders: Diagnostic criteria for research.* Geneva, Switzerland.

Ysseldyke, J.E., Algozzine, B., Shinn, M.R., & McGue, M (1982). Similarities and differences between low achievers and students classified learning disabled. *Journal of Special Education, 16,* 73-85.

Yule, W., Rutter, M., Berger, M., & Thompson, J. (1974). Over- and underachievement in reading: distribution in the general population. *British Journal of Educational Psychology, 44,* 1-12.

2
THE ROLE OF COGNITIVE LINGUISTIC SKILLS IN THE IDENTIFICATION OF READING PROBLEMS IN EMERGENT BILINGUAL CHILDREN

Jane M. Hutchinson, Helen E. Whiteley and Chris D. Smith

Introduction

Early identification of dyslexia is needed to minimise subsequent educational and behavioural difficulties. Whilst progress has been made in the early identification of dyslexia in monolingual English-speaking children, diagnosis is more complex when children have English as an Additional Language (EAL). Reading problems are often attributed to problems with English language acquisition, with the consequence that dyslexia in EAL children may remain undetected resulting in long-term difficulties. In addition, EAL children will be less able to use comprehension to compensate for poor word recognition skills. This too is likely to contribute to more persistent problems.

A vast amount of research into reading problems has focused on the role of word level decoding and related phonological skills, especially phonological awareness. The link between phonological skills and reading success is well documented for monolingual English speaking children (Muter, Hulme, Snowling & Taylor, 1997), and conversely, the link between reading accuracy difficulties and phonological processing deficits. This research has led to the development of a number of screening and diagnostic tests (e.g. The Dyslexia Early Screening Test; Nicolson & Fawcett, 1996; The Phonological Assessment Battery; Frederickson, Frith & Reason, 1997) and intervention programmes (e.g. Phonological Linkage; Hatcher, Hulme & Ellis, 1994).

Within the UK about 4% of the population are dyslexic (Crisfield, 1994) with the prevalence of dyslexia at a similar or higher level in many countries (Belgium 5%; Japan 6%; U.S.A. 8.5%; Salter & Smythe, 1997), suggesting that dyslexia is an international concern. Early identification of children at risk of being dyslexic is important as it generally leads to more effective remediation and facilitates the development of individual education plans.

Within the English education system approximately 7.5% of the school population learn English as an Additional Language (Cline & Shamsi, 2000). In a multicultural society, such as the UK, the finding that EAL children are under-represented among pupils who are assessed as having specific learning disabilities (SLD) must raise concerns (Deponio, Landon, Mullin, & Reid, 2000; Cline & Shamsi, 2000). The under-identification of dyslexia in this group of children has been attributed to several factors: language related problems, a lack of first language assessment tools, a low awareness of the issues relating to bilingualism and dyslexia within both the literacy research and educational practice (Deponio et al., 2000), and the way in which dyslexia is defined (Cline, 2000). Although the assessment of the bilingual child may be complicated by English language learning problems (Cline & Reason, 1993) the possible negative effects of failure to identify dyslexia are no less damaging. Early research indicates that measures developed for use with monolingual English speaking children can also be used when assessing the phonological skills of the bilingual child (Frederickson & Frith, 1998; Everatt, Adams & Smythe, 2001).

Research suggests that decoding skill is not a specific area of difficulty for the bilingual learner, in fact it is suggested that many of these children have enhanced phonological awareness that often results in good phonic decoding skill (Deponio, Landon, & Reid, 2001). Whilst poor language skills may complicate the identification of dyslexia, Landon (1999) suggests that bilingual children's development of good phonic skills when first starting to read may result in their reading accuracy progress masking the difficulties that these children are experiencing with their comprehension of the text.

When looking at reading development it is important to remember that reading (understanding the meaning of text) is the product of two skills, decoding ability and linguistic comprehension (Gough & Tunmer, 1986). Many EAL children start school with little or no experience of the English language, with monolingual children having a four/five year advantage in oral language experience. EAL children are faced with the enormous task of closing the vocabulary knowledge gap. According to Tunmer and Hoover (1993) text comprehension will not exceed general language ability, even with very high levels of decoding skill. Therefore vocabulary knowledge is especially important when considering the reading problems of EAL children. Furthermore, for EAL children with dyslexia, lower levels of linguistic comprehension may cause further difficulties, monolingual children with dyslexia have been found to use their understanding of the text to facilitate the reading of partially decoded words (Nation & Snowling, 1998), and thus the EAL child with dyslexia is likely to experience a double disadvantage.

The small amount of research following the literacy development of EAL children makes it difficult to identify the precise nature of their literacy difficulties within the context of a 'normal' pattern of development when learning English within the classroom setting. All children are individuals, each bringing their own previous experiences to the learning situation. In order to interpret assessment information and provide support that meets the individual needs of EAL children there needs to be a greater understanding of the developmental progression of literacy skills for this group of children.

The key aims of this research project are to examine the developmental progression of cognitive linguistic skills and related literacy achievement for both monolingual and EAL children. The study examines the similarities and differences between the two groups of children at each point in time and their progress over time. The data is used to evaluate the usefulness of diagnostic tools in the identification of dyslexia in EAL children.

Method

Design

Forty-three monolingual and forty-three bilingual children were tested on a range of measures in the first stage of a longitudinal design with follow-up testing twelve months later.

Participants

The participating children attend one of ten primary schools in the North West of England. For the monolingual children, English is the only language spoken at home. The bilingual children speak mother tongue, to some extent, in the home (21 Gujerati; 12 Urdu; 7 Punjabi; 2 Bengali; 1 Pushto). The sample includes the same number of male and female monolingual and bilingual children with the same number of monolingual and bilingual children from each school. Each bilingual child was matched for gender, age (monolingual = 81.7 months; bilingual children = 81.8) and general ability (Raven's Coloured Matrices – mean scores monolingual children = 21.91; bilingual children = 21.72; range = 15 – 29) with a monolingual child.

Measures

Raven's Coloured Progressive Matrices (Raven, Court & Raven, 1990) was used to match the monolingual and EAL children on general non-linguistic ability. Form 1 of The Neale Analysis of Reading – Revised (Neale, 1977) was used to measure the accuracy and comprehension of oral reading, whilst Form 2 was used to measure Listening Comprehension (the first four passages were recorded onto tape and children answered orally delivered questions after listening to each passage). Spelling and single word reading were measured using The Wide Range Achievement Test 3 (WRAT3) (Wilkinson, 1993) in which coding skills are measured whilst minimising the influence of comprehension.

Phonological skills were measured using The Phonological Assessment Battery (PhAB) (Frederickson, Frith & Reason, 1997), results of eight out of the nine subtests of the PhAB are reported, these include alliteration, rhyme, non-word reading, spoonerisms, rapid naming of numbers and pictures, and alliteration and rhyme fluency.

The Test of Reception of Grammar (TROG) (Bishop, 1989) was used to assess the understanding of grammatical contrasts in English, and The Test of Word Knowledge (TOWK) (Wigg & Secord, 1992) to measure aspects of both receptive and expressive language ability.

Procedure

All tests were conducted in a quiet area within the children's schools during seven half-hour sessions between March and July 1999 and repeated between March and July 2000. All tests were completed on an individual basis as per manual instructions.

Results

The mean raw scores obtained by the monolingual and bilingual children on each of the accuracy related measures at Time 1 and Time 2 are presented in Table 1 and the comprehension related measures are presented in Table 2.

A series of 2-tailed independent t-tests were conducted to examine the differences between the monolingual and bilingual children on each measure at Time 1 and Time 2.

Accuracy measures: There was a significant difference between the monolingual and bilingual children on measures of rhyme and rapid naming of numbers at both Time 1 and Time 2. On the measure of rhyme the monolingual children achieved higher scores than their bilingual peers ($p<.01$ and $p<.05$ respectively) whilst on the measure of rapid naming of numbers bilingual children named the numbers faster than the monolingual children ($p<.01$ and $p<.001$ respectively). There was no significant difference between the two groups of children on each of the remaining accuracy related measures.

Comprehension measures: On each of the comprehension related measures there was a highly significant difference between the monolingual and bilingual children with the monolingual children achieving higher scores on each of the comprehension related measures (p<.001 on all measures).

Further analysis was undertaken to compare the developmental progress (Time 1 and Time 2 scores) separately for the monolingual and bilingual children. A series of 1-tailed related t-tests revealed that both groups of children made significant progress on each of the measures (accuracy and comprehension related) between Time 1 and Time 2. All comparisons were highly significant (p<.005) except for the monolingual Time 1 and Time 2 comparisons on the measures of alliteration and rhyme fluency, which were significant at the .05 level.

Table 1 Overall mean score (and standard deviation) for the accuracy related measures at both Time one and Time two for both groups of children

Measures	Time 1		Time 2	
	Bilingual	Monolingual	Bilingual	Monolingual
1. Reading Accuracy	34.63 (15.41)	33.74 (16.67)	47.93 (17.03)	45.16 (18.28)
2. Spelling	22.65 (3.63)	21.86 (3.77)	27.93 (4.86)	26.77 (4.72)
3. Single word reading	39.56 (9.70)	37.35 (10.64)	46.53 (9.64)	47.58 (10.48)
4. Alliteration	8.21 (2.19)	8.74 (1.97)	9.58 (0.91)	9.63 (1.09)
5. Rhyme	12.21 (5.10)	15.07 (4.85)	16.28 (4.25)	18.02 (3.27)
6. Non-word reading	13.14 (6.11)	13.05 (5.96)	16.56 (4.24)	16.42 (4.51)
7. Spoonerisms	10.30 (5.76)	11.28 (5.88)	15.88 (6.15)	16.77 (5.83)
8. Rapid naming of numbers (secs to name 100 digits)	61.16 (16.96)	72.42 (20.43)	48.35 (11.24)	64.84 (16.25)
9. Rapid naming of pictures (secs to name 100 pictures)	111.67 (20.92)	113.47 (23.69)	97.12 (16.71)	99.39 (22.55)
10. Alliteration fluency	8.91 (3.64)	10.16 (3.73)	10.84 (3.45)	11.14 (3.91)
11. Rhyme fluency	7.14 (2.88)	8.00 (3.09)	8.44 (2.75)	9.02 (3.24)

Table 2 Overall mean score (and standard deviation) for the comprehension related measures at Time one and Time two for both groups of children

Measures	Time 1		Time 2	
	Bilingual	Monolingual	Bilingual	Monolingual
12. Reading comprehension	9.40 (4.43)	13.98 (6.95)	14.63 (5.14)	21.26 (8.43)
13. Listening comprehension	5.44 (2.72)	9.70 (3.86)	7.09 (3.59)	13.65 (4.99)
14. Reception of grammar	63.33 (5.58)	69.88 (4.31)	65.44 (5.97)	73.42 (3.54)
15. Expressive vocabulary	21.14 (6.18)	32.33 (6.12)	28.56 (7.47)	40.16 (7.87)
16. Receptive vocabulary	24.74 (6.80)	37.63 (8.25)	31.14 (7.44)	47.07 (7.27)

Although all differences between Time 1 and Time 2 were significant, the level of developmental progress made by the two groups of children varied. In order to illustrate the differences in developmental progress made by the monolingual and bilingual children from Time 1 to Time 2, the difference between the two scores was calculated separately for each group of children. The differences between Time 1 and Time 2 are presented in graphical format; the measures are numbered as the measures presented in Tables 1 and 2. Differences in accuracy related scores are presented in Figure 1 illustrating the similarity in the level of progress that both groups of children have made between the two points in time. The comprehension related differences presented in Figure 2 illustrate the higher level of progress that the monolingual children have made with aspects of comprehension compared to their bilingual peers.

Figure 1
Differences between the mean Time one and Time two scores on the accuracy-related measures calculated separately for the monolingual and bilingual children

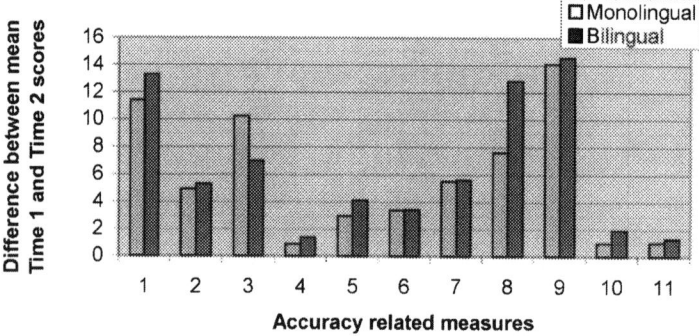

Figure 2
Differences between the mean Time one and Time two scores on the comprehension-related measures calculated separately for the monolingual and bilingual children

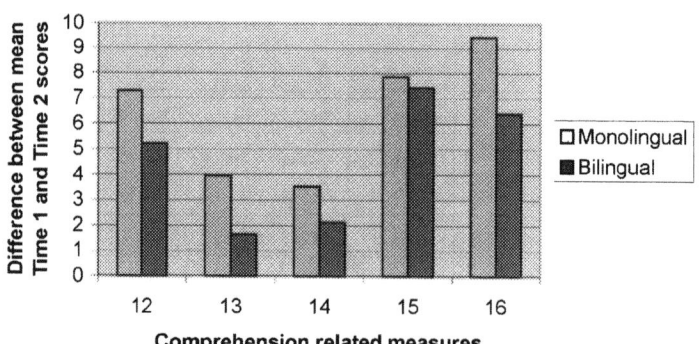

Discussion

Results highlight the similarities and differences between the two groups of children at both Time 1 and Time 2. While there are similar levels of achievement on most of the accuracy related measures monolingual children achieve significantly higher scores on the measures related to comprehension. Only two accuracy related measures revealed differences between the groups with higher rhyme scores for the monolingual children and faster number naming speed for the bilingual children at both points in time.

When comparing developmental progression, both groups of children made significant progress between Time 1 and Time 2 on all measures, however for some of the measures, the amount of progress varied. There is a similar level of progress on measures of spelling, non word reading, spoonerisms, alliteration, rhyme, rapid naming of pictures and rhyme fluency. The slightly higher level of bilingual progress on the measures of alliteration and rhyme, and the smaller difference between the rhyme scores of the two groups of children at Time 2 may be due to a number of monolingual children performing at ceiling on both measures. Bilingual children make more progress with reading accuracy and rapid naming of number, and monolingual children make more progress with single word reading. On the comprehension related measures the monolingual children increased their Time 1 advantage when tested at Time 2.

The finding of similar levels of achievement on the accuracy related measures supports the finding that reading accuracy is not a specific area of difficulty for EAL children (Deponio et al., 2001). A number of monolingual and bilingual children experience decoding problems. The distribution of phonological skills are similar for both groups of children, supporting the use of the phonological diagnostic measures (e.g. The PhAB, Frederickson, Frith & Reason, 1997) developed to identify the reading problems of monolingual children with their EAL peers (Everatt et al., 2001, Frederickson & Frith, 1998).

Whilst it is important to identify difficulties with aspects of phonological awareness and reading accuracy in all children, for EAL children problems with vocabulary and comprehension also need to be considered. On each of the measures, at both Time 1 and Time 2 the difficulties that many EAL children experienced were highlighted. The difference between the two groups of children on measures of expressive and receptive vocabulary suggests that it takes longer than the three years that these EAL children have been speaking English within the school environment to close the vocabulary knowledge gap. In fact, the vocabulary knowledge gap is still getting wider. Difficulties with both reading and listening comprehension suggest that lower levels of linguistic comprehension are having a negative impact on the understanding of English, whether written or spoken. EAL children's general difficulties with the understanding of both the written and spoken word suggest that this group of children will experience some difficulties in their curriculum learning.

In many instances EAL children with good decoding skills experience difficulties with comprehension related measures. If EAL readers can present themselves as being 'good readers' (Landon, 1999), assessment of reading ability needs to separately measure both accuracy and comprehension skill. Tests that focus on decoding skill (e.g. single word reading) will not identify the difficulties that these children are experiencing.

The difficulties that EAL children experience with their understanding of text suggests that EAL dyslexic children cannot rely on their understanding of text to facilitate the reading of partially decoding words (Nation & Snowling, 1998). This suggests that for EAL children experiencing problems with decoding, early identification is important as these children may need support to facilitate the development of both accuracy and comprehension related skills.

References

Bishop, D. (1989) *Test of Reception of Grammar.* University of Manchester, Department of Psychology.

Cline, T. & Reason, R. (1993) Specific learning difficulties (Dyslexia): Equal opportunities issues. *British Journal of Special Education, 21,* 30-34.

Cline, T. & Shamsi, T. (2000) *Language Needs or Special Needs? The Assessment of Learning Difficulties in Literacy among Children Learning English as an Additional Language: A Literature Review.* Department for Education and Employment.

Crisfield, J. (1994) *The Dyslexia Handbook, 1995.* Reading: The British Dyslexia Association.

Deponio, P., Landon, J. & Reid, G. (2001) Dyslexia and Bilingualism – Implications for Assessment, Teaching and Learning. In L. Peer & G. Reid (Eds.) *Multilingualism, Literacy and Dyslexia: A Challenge for Educators.* London: David Fulton Publishers.

Deponio, P., Landon, J., Mullin, K. & Reid, G. (2000) An audit of the processes involved in identifying and assessing bilingual learners suspected of being dyslexic: A Scottish study. *Dyslexia,* 6 (1), 29-41.

Everatt, J., Adams, E. & Smythe, I. (2001) Bilingual Children's Profiles on Dyslexia Screening Measures. In L. Peer & G. Reid (Eds.) *Multilingualism, Literacy and Dyslexia: A Challenge for Educators.* London: David Fulton Publishers.

Frederickson, N., Frith, U. & Reason, R. (1997) *Phonological Assessment Battery.* Windsor: NFER-Nelson.

Frederickson, N. & Frith, U. (1998) Identifying dyslexia in bilingual children: A phonological approach with inner London Sylheti speakers. *Dyslexia, 4,* 119-131.

Gough, P.B. & W. E. Tunmer, W.E. (1986) Decoding, reading, and reading disability. *Remedial and Special Education, 7* (1), 6-10.

Hatcher, P.J., Hulme, C. & Ellis, A.W. (1994) Ameliorating early reading failure by integrating the teaching of reading and phonics: The phonological linkage hypothesis. *Child Development,* 65, 41-57.

Landon, J. (1999) Early intervention with bilingual learners: Towards a research agenda. In H. South (Eds.) *Literacies in Community and School, 84-86.* Watford: National Association for Language Development in the Curriculum (NALDIC).

Muter, V., Hulme, C., Snowling, M. & Taylor, S. (1997) Segmentation, not rhyming, predicts early progress in learning to read. *Journal of Experimental Child Psychology,* 65, 370-396.

Nation, K. & Snowling, M. (1998b) Individual differences in contextual facilitation: Evidence from dyslexia and poor reading comprehension. *Child Development, 69 (4),* 996-1011.

Neale, M.D. (1997) Neale Analysis of Reading Ability (Second Revised British Edition). Windsor: NFER-Nelson.

Nicolson, R.I. & Fawcett, A.J. (1996) *The Dyslexia Early Screening Test.* London: The Psychological Corporation.

Raven, J.C.; Court, J.H. & Raven, J. (1990) *Coloured Progressive Matrices.* Windsor: NFER-Nelson.

Salter, R. & Smythe, I. (Eds) (1997) *The International Book of Dyslexia.* London: World Dyslexia Network Foundation.

Tunmer, W.E. & Hoover, WA. (1993) Language-related factors as sources of individual differences in the differences of word recognition skills. In G. B. Thompson, W. E. Tunmer, & T. Nicholson (eds) *Reading Acquisition Processes.* Clevedon: Multilingual Matters Ltd.

Wiig, E.H. & Secord, W. (1992) *Test of Word Knowledge.* London: The Psychological Corporation Limited.

Wilkinson, G.S. (1993) *Wide Range Achievement Test 3.* London: Psychological Corporation Limited.

3
AN AUDITORY TEMPORAL PROCESSING DEFICIT IN CHILDREN WITH DYSLEXIA?

Mieke Van Ingelghem, Bart Boets,
Astrid van Wieringen, Patrick Onghena, Pol Ghesquière,
Erik Vandenbussche[†] and Jan Wouters

Introduction

Developmental dyslexia is characterised by serious reading and spelling problems that are persistent and resistant to the usual didactic measures and remedial efforts (Gersons-Wolfensberger & Ruijssenaars, 1997). However, a lot of research has shown that problems of individuals with dyslexia extend beyond the domain of written language and affect their performance on tasks that require phonological processing (see Snowling, 2000 for a review). It is therefore widely acknowledged that in cognitive terms, individuals with dyslexia have a phonological deficit, which is causal to their reading and spelling difficulties.

Investigation into the underlying neurological dysfunction of dyslexia suggests these phonological problems result from a more fundamental deficit in the basic perceptual mechanisms responsible for auditory temporal processing. This hypothesis was put forward by Tallal (1980), who found that children with dyslexia, in comparison to normal readers, were impaired in discriminating and sequencing acoustic stimuli that are brief and occur in rapid succession. This impairment was supposed to apply to both non-linguistic and linguistic auditory stimuli and have particular impact on the perception of syllables containing stop consonants, such as /ba/ and /da/ (Tallal, Miller & Fitch, 1993). Perception of these syllables critically depends on accurate detection of the rapid frequency changes in the first milliseconds of voicing (formant transitions). Inaccurate detection of these formant transitions inevitably interferes with the identification of the phonological cues that are typical for spoken language. To summarise, the theory of Tallal and colleagues states that individuals with dyslexia have a deficit in perceiving brief duration and rapidly occurring temporal cues, i.e. within a time frame of milliseconds. This basic perceptual deficit causes a problem for the accurate detection of the rapid acoustical changes in speech. Consequently, the speech-perception problem causes a cascade of effects, starting with the disruption of normal development of the phonological system and resulting in problems learning to read and to spell (see also studies of Nagarajan et al., 1999; Wright et al., 1997).

Studdert-Kennedy and Mody (1995) challenge this theory because of its implicit assumption that rapid sequences of brief stimuli are acoustically equivalent to the integral spectral sweeps of formant transitions. According to these authors, stimulus processing is temporal only when the defining features of the stimuli are changing in time (later called "dynamic stimuli", see Talcott et al., 2000; Talcott & Witton, 2002; Witton, Stein, Stoodley, Rosner & Talcott, 2002). Besides their criticism on Tallal's "rapid and brief" operationalization of temporal processing, Studdert-Kennedy and Mody also argue that the observed phonological impairments in dyslexics are in origin speech-specific and cannot be attributed to a more general lower-level auditory deficit. Therefore, dyslexics' difficulties to distinguish stop-vowel syllables do not unquestionably reflect an auditory temporal processing deficit, meaning a deficit in the perception of rapid spectral changes (Mody, Studdert-Kennedy & Brady, 1997; see also Nittrouer, 1999).

Moreover, McAnally and Stein (1996) found that adults with dyslexia were not significantly different from normal readers for detection of a temporal gap in broadband noise and detection of a tone in a diotic noise masker when the tone was in phase at two ears. On the contrary, significant group differences were found for a frequency discrimination task and the tone-in-noise detection task when the tone was presented with opposite phase at two ears. This may indicate that the dyslexics' neural coding of stimulus onsets and offsets was normal, but that they were impaired in their ability to generate or exploit neural discharges phase-locked to the fine structure of acoustic stimuli. Data consistent with these findings were reported by Baldeweg, Richardson, Watkins, Foale & Gruzilier (1999), Dougherty, Cynader, Bjornson, Edgell & Giaschi (1998) and Schulte-Körne, Deimel, Bartling, & Remschmidt (1998). Also Talcott et al., (2002) reported similar observations from a large-scale primary school study in which auditory frequency resolution differed between groups of children with different literacy skills.

The latter evidence and Studdert-Kennedy and Mody's criticism on Tallal's theory have lead to studies that investigate auditory temporal processing in dyslexia using stimuli that specifically change in time. In these studies, in which adult samples were used, dyslexics were found to be less sensitive than controls to amplitude modulation (AM) (McAnally & Stein, 1997; Menell, McAnally & Stein, 1999) and frequency modulation (FM) (e.g. Stein & McAnally, 1995). A remarkable study in this context is from Witton, Talcott, Hansen, Richardson, Griffiths et al. (1998) who have shown that adults with dyslexia were less sensitive than controls to 2Hz and 40Hz FM, but not to 240 Hz FM. In the first two cases detection is achieved by tracking the actual frequency change of the carrier over time (= a temporal process), whereas in the third case, detection is achieved by detecting a pair of extra spectral components separated from the carrier frequency by the modulating frequency (= a spectral process). In addition, Witton et al., (1998) found that sensitivity to 2 and 40 Hz FM, for both dyslexics and controls, highly correlated with their measure of phonological decoding skill. This relationship between FM sensitivity and phonological ability was also demonstrated by Talcott et al. (1999, 2000) in a random group of children.

These studies again point to an auditory temporal processing deficit as a possible cause of dyslexics' phonological problems. Accurate tracking of amplitude and frequency changes is exactly what is needed for the perception of speech, which is characterised by spectral and temporal variations (Shannon, Zeng, Kamath, Wygonski & Ekelid, 1995). Since speech perception is the basis to develop phonological skills, it is likely that impairments in AM and FM detection affect phonological skill development via speech perception (McBride-Chang, 1996).

However, there are still studies that question the hypothesis of an auditory temporal processing deficit in dyslexia. For example Hill, Bailey, Griffiths and Snowling (1999) and Adlard and Hazan (1998) have not found significant group differences between dyslexics and controls for several tasks of auditory temporal processing. Other investigators, such as Heath, Hogben and Clark (1999) and McArthur and Hogben (2001), have found the deficit only in particular subgroups of dyslexics. Also the evidence for a relationship between auditory temporal processing and phonological skills has not been unequivocal (Marshall, Snowling & Bailey, 2001; Nittrouer, 1999).

To conclude, there are two major lines of studies that have shown an auditory temporal processing deficit in individuals with dyslexia: studies of Tallal and colleagues that have demonstrated a deficit in processing brief stimuli or stimuli that occur in rapid succession, and studies that have demonstrated a deficit in processing changes in acoustic stimuli such as AM and FM. Most of these studies have been carried out with adults. Nevertheless, there is yet no consensus whether the auditory temporal processing deficit exists in children with dyslexia and how this deficit can be specified. Moreover, it is not clear in what way this deficit can be related to the reading process.

In this study we want to deal with these issues. We tested the hypothesis of an auditory temporal processing deficit in a group of 10- to 12-year old children with dyslexia as compared with a normal reading group of the same age. Auditory temporal processing was assessed by means of two psychophysical threshold tests, one for gap-detection in broadband noise (GAP) and one for 2Hz FM-detection (FM). With the GAP-detection test, Tallal's hypothesis was tested by measuring temporal resolution, i.e. the ability to perceive as separate two events closely occurring in time. With the FM-detection test, we measured the ability to perceive 2 Hz changes in an acoustic stimulus. Assessing both GAP and FM detection ability in the same children with dyslexia and calculating the relations with literacy skills makes it possible to answer three questions. First, whether *children with dyslexia*, in comparison to normal readers, perform significantly worse on psychophysical tasks for auditory temporal processing. Second, whether they perform worse in *both* the GAP and FM detection tasks or just in one of them. Third, whether these temporal processing abilities are *related* to reading and phonological skills. As a consequence, it is possible to determine whether children with dyslexia have an auditory temporal processing deficit and how this deficit can be specified.

Method

Participants

Participants of the experimental group were 6 boys and 4 girls with developmental dyslexia (dyslexic readers; DR). Mean age of the DR-group was 11;4 years (SD = 0;9 yr). The participants had been diagnosed as reading disabled by an authorised educational psychology service and were in a special education school for children with specific learning disabilities. Selection criteria were a) native Dutch speaking, b) average or above average intelligence (Wechsler IQ Δ 85), c) no gross deficiencies in ophthalmology (Snellen acuity > .8) or audiology (audiometric pure-tone thresholds < 20 dB HL at octave frequencies in the range of 250-4000 Hz) and d) scoring below percentile 10 on both of two standardised Dutch word-reading tests: the One-minute Real-Word reading Test (Brus & Voeten, 1973) and the Pseudo-Word reading Test (Van den Bos et al., 1994; see below for a detailed description). Criterion b was used to exclude the so-called "garden variety" poor readers whose literacy is poor because their intelligence quotient is low (see Snowling, 2000, p. 30).

Participants of the control group were 10 normal reading children (normal readers; NR) matched to the experimental group for sex (6 boys) and chronological age (t (18) = -0.35, p = 0.73). Mean age of the NR-group was 11;5 yr (SD = 0;7 yr). Normal readers were selected in the senior classes of a primary school. They met the same criteria as the dyslexic readers for language, intelligence and sensory acuity (see criteria a-c). Since in Flanders children with low IQ are in special education schools instead of regular primary schools, intelligence was not tested, but assumed to be average or above average. NR's performance on both standardised word-reading tests (criterion d) was at least higher than percentile 50.

Informed consent was obtained from all children and from at least one of their parents. During the experiments the children were motivated with small rewards. Detailed characteristics of both participant groups are given in Appendix.

Apparatus

Reading tests

Reading ability was assessed using two standardised Dutch word recognition tests: the One-Minute Real-Word reading Test, RWT (Brus & Voeten, 1973) and the Pseudo-Word reading Test, PWT (Van den Bos et al., 1994). Both tests consist of 116 single words of increasing difficulty. In the PWT, the words (i.e. pseudo-words) have the same syllabic structure than those of the RWT. Participants were instructed to read aloud the words correctly and as quickly as possible. The raw score on the tests is the number of words read correctly in one minute for the RWT, in two minutes for the PWT. Raw scores on RWT and PWT were converted into standard scores with $M = 10$ and $SD = 3$ (Van den Bos et al., 1994).

GAP-detection test

In the GAP-detection test, white noise stimuli were used. The target stimulus was a white noise stimulus containing a silent gap. The reference stimulus was an uninterrupted white noise. In the target stimulus, the length of the markers (i.e. the parts of the stimulus surrounding the gap) varied between 200 and 700 ms. The length of the reference stimulus was 500 or 1000 ms. These different lengths were used to prevent participants from using overall duration as a cue for detection (van Wieringen & Wouters, 1999). Stimuli were cosine gated on and off with 50 ms rise and fall times. Gap rise and fall times were 0.5 ms. Stimuli were generated in MATLAB 5.1 and saved as 16-bit wav-files (sample frequency 44100 Hz) on the hard disc of a Toshiba 486DX4 portable computer. They were presented using a PCMCIA audio PC-card and rooted to an audiometer (Madsen OB622) in order to have control over the level of presentation. The stimuli were presented monaurally (through the right ear) at 65 dB SPL over a calibrated TDH-39 headphone. Testing took place in a quiet room and responses were recorded using a standard computer mouse.

FM-detection test

In the FM-detection test, stimuli can be defined as $A\sin[2\pi f_c t + \beta \sin(2\pi f_m t)]$ in which β is the modulation index ($\beta = \Delta f / f_m$), f_c the carrier frequency, f_m the modulation frequency and Δf the frequency deviation. The target stimulus was a 2 Hz frequency modulation (f_m) of a 1 kHz carrier tone (f_c). The reference stimulus was a pure tone of 1 kHz ($\beta=0$). The length of each stimulus was 1000 ms including 20 ms cosine-gated onsets and offsets. Frequency modulation in the target was sinusoidal and the modulation envelope was always in sine phase. Stimuli were generated and presented in a similar way and with the same equipment and software as in the GAP-detection test (Geurts & Wouters, 2000).

Psychophysical procedure

In both the GAP and FM-test, detection thresholds were estimated using a two interval, two-alternative forced-choice procedure with the target stimulus randomly presented in either the first or the second interval. Intervals were separated by a 500 ms silent inter-stimulus interval. On the computer screen, the intervals were represented by two panels respectively indicated with number 1 and 2. Participants, wearing the headphone, were sitting in front of the computer screen and were required to report verbally which interval, first or second, contained the target. They were given an unlimited time to respond. The experimenter, seated beside the participant, recorded the responses by clicking on the corresponding panel. Immediately after responding, participants were presented with visual feedback on the screen for 2000 ms. After termination of feedback the next trial began.

The length of the gap or the frequency deviation (Δf), according to the test, was adjusted adaptively using a two-down, one-up rule, which targeted the threshold corresponding to 70.7% correct responses (Levitt, 1971). In the GAP-test, each threshold run began with a gap length of 100 ms. The gap length was decreased by a factor of 1.2 from 100 to 10 ms and with a step size of 1 ms between 10 ms and 0 ms. An additional stimulus with a gap length of 0.5 ms was added for those listeners who may even detect a gap smaller than 1 ms. In total 25 different target stimuli were generated. In the FM-test, each run began with a frequency deviation (Δf) set to 2% of the carrier frequency. The frequency deviation (Δf) was decreased by a factor of 1.25. In total 14 different target stimuli were generated. In both tests, a threshold run was terminated after 10 reversals. Thresholds for an individual run were calculated by averaging the values of the last 6 reversals. For each participant, 4 threshold estimates were determined (4 runs on 4 different days for both GAP and FM). These repeated measures were taken to check for potential differences in learning rate. Prior to data collection, participants were given a short period of practice -comprising supra-threshold trials- to familiarise them with the stimuli and the task.

Statistical Analysis

Psychophysical thresholds were analysed using Mixed Model Analysis for repeated measures designs (Littell et al., 1996). Normal quantile plots for thresholds of the different threshold runs did not show extreme skewness or outliers. Mixed Model Analysis was chosen to avoid violating the sphericity assumption of repeated measures designs with three or more treatment levels (Max & Onghena, 1999). In the model the within-subjects factor was threshold run (1 to 4), the between-subjects factor participant group (DR vs NR) and the covariates sex and age. Appropriate covariance structures were modelled as outlined in Littell et al. (1996, p. 101). Relationships between variables were analysed using Spearman correlation coefficients.

Psychophysical control task

To check whether any deficit on the auditory temporal tasks in the DR-group does not result from failing performance on auditory psychophysical tasks in general, the audiometric pure-tone detection task (used in the participant selection procedure) was included in the analysis as a non-temporal control task. In the audiometric detection task, pure-tone thresholds at octave frequencies in the range of 250–4000 Hz were obtained using the Hughson-Westlake procedure, which is also an adaptive staircase method. Stimuli were presented in a similar way as in the GAP and FM-detection tests and the same equipment was used. Thresholds of the different frequencies were summarised in one index, the so-called Fletcher-index or Pure Tone Average (PTA), which represents the mean hearing loss in dB HL at 500, 1000 and 2000 Hz. The data of the control task were analysed with a t-test for differences in group means.

Results

GAP-detection experiment

Participants' individual threshold estimates for GAP-detection are given in Appendix. The mean GAP threshold over all threshold runs was 3.3 ms (SD = 0.5 ms) for the DR-group and 2.7 ms (SD = 0.3 ms) for the NR-group. For some participants, thresholds of the different runs varied a lot. Mixed Model Analysis showed that there was a significant effect of participant group, $F(1,16) = 12.06$, $p = .003$. There was no significant effect of threshold run, $F(3,16) = 0.39$, $p = .76$ and no significant run by group interaction effect, $F(3,16) = 0.25$, $p = .86$. This means that the thresholds of the dyslexic readers were significantly higher (0.6 ms) than those of the normal readers over the 4 successive threshold runs. Thresholds did not change during the runs, what indicates that there was no training effect, either for dyslexic or for normal readers (Figure 1).

To analyze the relationship between participants' GAP-detection ability and their reading skills, Spearman correlation coefficients were calculated between the participants' average GAP-thresholds of the 4 threshold runs (see AVGAP in Appendix) and their RWT and PWT raw scores. The use of the average threshold was justified, as there was no within-subject effect in the Mixed Model Analysis. Spearman r_s was -0.60 ($p = .005$) for the relationship between AVGAP and RWT and -0.58 ($p = .007$) for the relationship between AVGAP and PWT.

Figure 1
Mean GAP-detection threshold per threshold run for dyslexic (DR) and normal readers (NR).

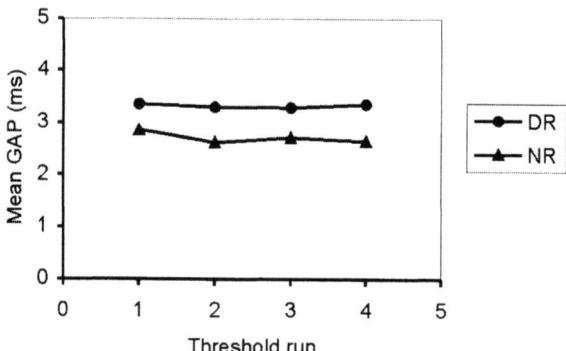

FM-detection experiment

Participants' individual threshold estimates for FM-detection are given in Appendix. The mean FM threshold over all threshold runs was 6.0 Hz (SD = 3.3 Hz) for the DR-group and 3.7 Hz (SD = 1.2 Hz) for the NR-group. Again, for some participants, thresholds of the different runs varied a lot. Mixed Model Analysis showed that there was a significant effect of participant group, F (1,16) = 5.06, p = .04, no significant effect of threshold run, F (3,16) = 0.05, p = .98 and no significant run by group interaction effect, F (3,16) = 0.41, p = .75. This means that, as for the GAP experiment, the thresholds of the dyslexic readers were significantly higher (2.3 Hz) than those of the normal readers over the 4 successive threshold runs. Thresholds did not change during the runs, indicating that there was no training effect, either for dyslexic or for normal readers (Figure 2).

Spearman r_s was -0.19 (p = .41) for the relationship between the participant's average FM-thresholds of the 4 runs (AVFM in Appendix) and RWT, and –0.42 (p = .07) for the relationship between AVFM and PWT.

Figure 2
Mean FM-detection threshold per threshold run for dyslexic (DR) and normal readers (NR).

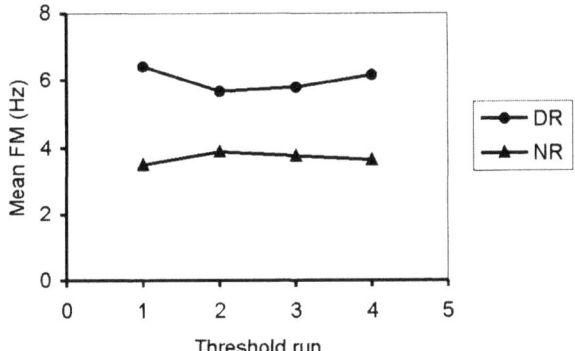

GAP and/or FM-detection deficit?

In Figure 3 (a and b) dyslexic readers' average thresholds of the 4 runs for GAP and FM detection (see AVGAP and AVFM in Appendix) are plotted against the 95% upper confidential level of the respective average thresholds of the normal readers. The figure shows that 6 of 10 dyslexic readers had significantly higher thresholds than the averaged normal readers for both the GAP and FM detection task. For three of the dyslexic readers (n° 1, 8, 9), thresholds were only higher for the GAP, but not for the FM-detection task. For one dyslexic reader (n° 2), the average threshold was higher for the FM, but not for the GAP-detection task. Spearman r_s between AVGAP and AVFM (r_s = 0.31, p = .19) showed that the relationship between GAP and FM detection ability was not significant.

Figure 3
a. Dyslexic readers' average GAP thresholds (AVGAP) in comparison with the GAP 95% upper confidential level for normal readers (horizontal line).
b. Dyslexic readers' average FM thresholds (AVFM) in comparison with the FM 95% upper confidential level for normal readers (horizontal line).

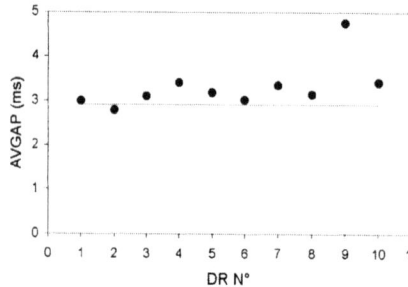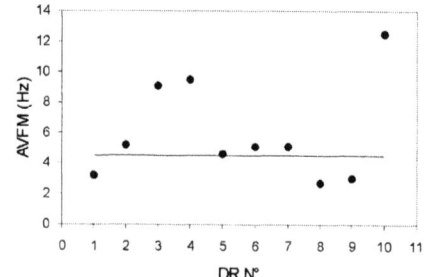

Control task

The results of the non-temporal control task show that the audiometric pure-tone thresholds are not significantly different for the DR and the NR-group. The mean PTA-threshold was 4.2 dB HL (SD = 4.9) for the DR-group and 3.2 dB HL (SD = 5.1) for the NR-group (t (18) = 0.45, p = .66).

Discussion

In this study, psychophysical thresholds were estimated for auditory GAP and FM-detection in a group of 10 children with dyslexia (10- to 12-year-old) and 10 age-matched normal reading controls. We tested children because we wanted to determine whether the hypothesis of an auditory temporal processing deficit also applies to children with dyslexia. We administered both GAP and FM-detection ability to determine whether children with dyslexia have problems with both the GAP and FM-detection tasks or just with one of them. Finally, we correlated the temporal detection thresholds with obtained reading and phonological measures to explore the meaning of a possible deficit.

Significant group differences were found for both the GAP and FM-detection test. GAP and FM-detection thresholds of the dyslexic readers were significantly higher than those of the normal readers over the 4 successive threshold runs. Moreover, 6 of 10 dyslexic readers had significantly higher thresholds than the controls for both the GAP and FM-detection test. This means that the dyslexic readers perform worse than the normal readers on both auditory temporal tasks. Thresholds did not change over the successive runs, indicating that there was no training effect, either for dyslexic or for normal readers. This suggests that the dyslexics' temporal deficit not simply results from the fact that they need more time to learn a difficult psychophysical task. Equal performance on the non-temporal control task also confirms that the significant higher thresholds of the dyslexic readers on both the GAP and FM-detection task is likely to result from a specific temporal processing deficit, rather than a failing performance on auditory psychophysical tasks in general.

Concerning the relationship between auditory temporal psychophysical thresholds and literacy skills, we found significant negative correlations between GAP-detection thresholds and reading and phonological scores. This confirms that the observed group difference for GAP-detection between the DR and NR-group can be related to a difference in literacy. On the contrary, the FM-detection thresholds are not correlated with reading or phonological measures. This indicates that the observed group difference for FM-detection is not related to the specific difference in literacy between the DR and NR-group. Instead, it suggests that the observed FM group difference results from another underlying third factor that is not specific to dyslexia but unequally represented in both groups (for example intelligence). Moreover, the finding that GAP and FM-detection thresholds are not mutually related also indicates that both auditory tasks measure different processing skills that might rely on a different underlying processing mechanism.

The group differences on the GAP-detection experiment are not consistent with findings of other studies that used a gap detection paradigm (Adlard & Hazan, 1998; McAnally & Stein; 1996, Schülte-Korne et al., 1998). However, it is difficult to compare our study with these studies. McAnally and Stein tested adult subjects and Schülte-Korne et al. and Adlard and Hazan reported mean gap thresholds that were significantly higher than our average thresholds. In the latter study, this can easily be understood because the smallest gap that could be technically administered in the test was 4 ms, which is larger than the thresholds that we found. Moreover, different psychophysical procedures were used. Nevertheless, our GAP-detection results do confirm those of McCroskey and Kidder (1980). They are thus in line with Tallal's original findings (1980) and Nagarajan et al.'s replication of these findings (1999) that children with dyslexia require a longer inter-stimulus interval to perceive brief acoustic stimuli that occur in rapid succession. Our observed correlations between GAP-detection thresholds and phonological measures are also in line with Tallal's original data. However, they are conflicting with the findings of Marshall, Snowling and Bailey (2001) who could not find any evidence for a relationship between phonological skills and rapid auditory processing.

A possible neurophysiological explanation for this observed deficit in auditory temporal resolution is that dyslexic readers have a prolonged refractive period in their neurological firing pattern. This may be the result of a slower transmission time of neural information (Stein & Walsh, 1997). A similar temporal resolution deficit has been found in the visual modality where it has been related to a subtle impairment in a specific visual subsystem, namely the magnocellular system (Lovegrove, 1996; Van Ingelghem et al, 2001). This system, characterised by large and heavily myelinated axons, is particularly responsible for processing fast and transient information. Although the auditory system does not have an anatomically distinct magnocellular pathway, there is supposed to be an auditory subsystem that is responsible for analysing acoustic transients (see Stein & Talcott, 1999). This auditory subsystem should be similarly characterised by large neurones and located in the medial geniculate nucleus (MGN). Galaburda and colleagues have demonstrated that, like visual magnocells, auditory 'magnocells' in the MGN show abnormalities in the brains of dyslexic readers (Galaburda, Menard & Rosen, 1994; Livingstone, Rosen, Drislane & Galaburda, 1991). Even though the existence of a similar magnocellular fast-transmitting auditory subsystem is still controversial, the results on the GAP-detection experiment do at least suggest impairment in this system for dyslexics.

The group differences on the FM-detection experiment are conflicting with the findings of Adlard and Hazan (1998) and Hill et al., (1999). However, it is again difficult to compare with these studies. In the first study, FM rates were higher (between 60 and 300 Hz) than in our study. Similarly, Witton et al., (1998) failed to find impaired FM sensitivity in dyslexic readers with 240 Hz FM (probably because at higher modulation rates FM detection depends mainly on spectral instead of temporal cues). The lack of significant differences in the study of Hill et al. (1999) might be attributed to the small difference between the dyslexic and control group's phonological skills (see Talcott & Witton, 2002). It is also difficult to compare with Hill's study because adult samples were used. Converging evidence for the observed group differences on the FM detection task is found in both Witton's studies on adult samples (Witton et al., 1998, 2002).

In the present study we didn't find any significant correlation between FM-detection thresholds and scores on a real word reading and pseudoword reading task. However, Talcott, Witton and colleagues consistently found significant correlations between reading and phonological measures and FM-detection skills with a slow modulation rate as the 2 Hz FM. These correlations were found in studies with dyslexic and normal reading adults (Witton et al., 1998, 2002), as well as in studies with unselected children covering the normal range of reading abilities (Talcott et al., 1999, 2000, 2002). However, they never conducted a comparable child study with contrasting DR and NR-groups. Moreover, their use of a psychophysical paradigm with constant stimuli differs from our adaptive staircase procedure, which offers a more optimal learning situation due to a gradual increase in stimulus difficulty. On the other hand, our observed correlation with phonology is not negligible (r_s = -0.42, p = .07) and almost reaches significance. It is very probable that significance would have been reached when more subjects were included in the study.

An alternative explanation for the conflicting FM results can be found in the impact of intelligence on any measured variable. As Hirsh and Watson (1996) have shown, the variance in psychophysical task performance is associated with individual differences in cognitive skills. This means that our correlations can be blurred by a non-perfect matching of intelligence. From the three psychophysical tasks we administered, the FM-detection task is conceptually the most difficult one and, consequently, the most sensitive to differences in general intelligence. Future studies will include a larger sample of IQ-matched subjects to avoid this possible interference.

To conclude, we found evidence that dyslexic reading children perform worse than normal reading controls on both auditory temporal processing tasks. However, both temporal impairments are unrelated to each other, suggesting that they might depend on different underlying mechanisms. Moreover, GAP-detection seems to be a reading and phonology related (and as such a dyslexic-specific) deficit. On the contrary, FM-detection seems to be unrelated to reading and phonological skills.

References

Adlard, A., & Hazan, V. (1998). Speech perception in children with specific reading disabilities (dyslexia). *Quarterly Journal of Experimental Psychology, 51A*, 153-177.

Baldeweg, T., Richardson, A., Watkins, S., Foale, C., & Gruzilier, J. (1999). Impaired auditory frequency discrimination in dyslexia detected with mismatch evoked potentials. *Annals of Neurology, 45*, 495-503.

Brus, B. Th., & Voeten, M. J. M. (1973). *Eén-minuut-test vorm A en B. Verantwoording en handleiding.* [One minute test form A and B. Manual] Nijmegen: Berkhout.

Dougherty, R. F., Cynader, M. S., Bjornson, B. H., Edgell, D., & Giaschi, D. E. (1998). Dichotic pitch: A new stimulus distinguishes normal and dyslexic auditory function. *Neuroreport, 9*, 3001-3005.

Galaburda, A. M, Menard, M. T, & Rosen, G. D. (1994). Evidence for aberrant auditory anatomy in developmental dyslexia. *Proceedings of the National Academy of Sciences USA, 91*, 8010-8013.

Gersons-Wolfensberger, D. C. M., & Ruijssenaars, A. J. J. M. (1997). Definition and treatment of dyslexia: A report by the Committee on Dyslexia of the Health Council of the Netherlands. *Journal of Learning Disabilities, 30*, 209-213.

Geurts, L., & Wouters, J. (2000). A concept for a research tool for experiments with cochlear implant users. *Journal of the Acoustical Society of America, 108*, 2949-2956.

Heath, S. M., Hogben, J. H., & Clark, C. D. (1999). Auditory temporal processing in disabled readers with and without oral language delay. *Journal of Child Psychology and Psychiatry, 40*, 637-647.

Hill, N. I., Bailey, P. J., Griffiths, Y. M., & Snowling, M. J. (1999). Frequency acuity and binaural masking release in dyslexic listeners. *Journal of the Acoustical Society of America, 106*, 53-58.

Levitt, H. (1971). Transformed up-down methods in psychoacoustics. *Journal of the Acoustical Society of America, 49*, 467-477.

Littell, R. C., Milliken, G. A., Stroup, W. W., & Wolfinger, R. D. (1996). *SAS system for mixed models.* Cary, NC: Sas Institute Inc.

Livingstone, M. S, Rosen, G. D, Drislane, F. W, & Galaburda, A. M. (1991). Physiological and anatomical evidence for a magnocellular defect in developmental dyslexia. *Proceedings of the National Academy of Sciences USA, 88*, 7943-7947.

Lovegrove B. (1996). Dyslexia and a transient/magnocellular pathway deficit: The current situation and future directions. *Australian-Journal-of-Psychology, 48*, 167-171.

Marshall, C. M., Snowling, M. J., & Bailey, P. J. (2001). Rapid auditory processing and phonological ability in dyslexic and normal readers. *Journal of Speech, Language and Hearing Research, 44*, 925-940.

Max, L., & Onghena, P. (1999). Some issues in the statistical analysis of completely randomized and repeated measures designs for speech, language, and hearing research. *Journal of Speech, Language and Hearing Research, 42*, 261-270.

McAnally, K. I., & Stein, J. F. (1996). Auditory temporal coding in dyslexia. *Proceedings of the Royal Society London B., 263*, 961-965.

McAnally, K. I., & Stein, J. F. (1997). Scalp potentials evoked by amplitude-modulated tones in dyslexia. *Journal of Speech, Language, and Hearing Research, 40,* 939-945.

McArthur, G. M., & Hogben, J. H. (2001). Rate of auditory perceptual processing in children with a specific language impairment and children with a specific reading disability. *Journal of the Acoustical Society of America, 109,* 1092-1100.

McBride-Chang, C. (1996). Models of speech and phonological processing in reading. *Child Development, 67,* 1856-1876.

McCroskey, R. L., & Kidder, H. C. (1980). Auditory fusion among learning disabled, reading disabled and normal children. *Journal of Learning Disabilities, 13,* 18-25.

Menell, P., McAnally, K. I., & Stein, J. F. (1999). Psychophysical sensitivity and physiological response to amplitude modulation in adult dyslexic listeners. *Journal of Speech, Language, and Hearing Research, 42,* 797-803.

Mody, M., Studdert-Kennedy, M., & Brady, S. (1997). Speech perception deficits in poor readers: Auditory processing or phonological coding? *Journal of Experimental Child Psychology, 64,* 199-231.

Nagarajan, S., Mahncke, H., Saltz, T., Tallal, P., Roberts, T., & Merzenich, M. M. (1999). Cortical auditory signal processing in poor readers. *Proceedings of the National Academy of Sciences (USA), 96,* 6483-6488.

Nittrouer, S. (1999). Do temporal processing deficits cause phonological processing problems? *Journal of Speech, Language and Hearing Research, 42,* 925-942.

Schulte-Körne, G., Deimel, W., Bartling, J., & Remschmidt, H. (1998). Role of auditory temporal processing for reading and spelling disability. *Perceptual and Motor Skills, 86,* 1043-1047.

Shannon, R. V., Zeng F.G., Kamath, V., Wygonski, J., & Ekelid, M. (1995). Speech recognition with primarily temporal cues. *Science, 270,* 303-304.

Snowling, M. J. (2000). *Dyslexia* (2nd ed.). Oxford, UK: Blackwell Publishers Ltd.

Stein, J. F., & McAnally, K. (1995). Auditory temporal processing in developmental dyslexics. *The Irish Journal of Psychology, 16,* 220-228.

Stein, J., & Talcott, J. (1999). Impaired neuronal timing in developmental dyslexia. The magnocellular hypothesis. *Dyslexia, 5,* 59-77.

Stein, J., & Walsh, V. (1997). To see but not to read; the magnocellular theory of dyslexia. *Trends in Neuroscience, 20,* 147-152.

Studdert-Kennedy, M., & Mody, M. (1995). Auditory temporal perception deficits in the reading-impaired: A critical review of the evidence. *Psychonomic Bulletin & Review, 2,* 508-514.

Talcott, J. B., & Witton, C. (2002). A sensory-linguistic approach to normal and dysfunctional reading development. In E. Witruk, A. Friederici & T. Lachmann (Eds.), *Neuropsychology and Cognition (volume XX). Basic functions of language and language disorders.* Dordrecht: Kluwer Academic Publishers.

Talcott, J. B, Witton, C., Hebb, G. S, Stoodley, C. J, Westwood, E. A, France, S. J, Hansen, P. C, & Stein, J. F. (2002). On the relationship between dynamic visual and auditory processing and literacy skills; results from a large primary-school study. *Dyslexia, 8,* 204-225.

Talcott, J. B., Witton, C., McClean, M., Hansen, P. C., Rees, A., Green, G. G. R., & Stein, J. F. (1999). Can sensitivity to auditory frequency modulation predict children's phonological and reading skills? *Neuroreport, 10,* 2045-2050.

Talcott, J., Witton, C., McClean, M., Hansen, P., Rees, A., Green, G., & Stein, J. (2000). Dynamic sensory sensitivity and children's word decoding skills. *Proceedings of the National Academy of Sciences USA, 97,* 2952-2957.

Tallal, P. (1980). Auditory temporal perception, phonics, and reading disabilities in children. *Brain and Language, 9,* 182-198.

Tallal, P., Miller, S., & Fitch, R. H. (1993). Neurobiological basis of speech: A case for the preeminence of temporal processing. In P. Tallal, R. R. Galaburda, R. R. Llinás & C. von Euler (Eds.), *Temporal information processing in the nervous system: Special reference to dyslexia and dysphasia* (pp. 27-47). New York: The New York Academy of Sciences, DI. 682.

van den Bos, K. P., Spelberg, H. C. L., Scheepstra, A. J. M., & De Vries, J. R. (1994). *De Klepel. Vorm A en B. Een test voor de leesvaardigheid van pseudowoorden. Verantwoording, handleiding, diagnostiek en behandeling.* [De Klepel Form A and B. Pseudoword reading test. Manual] Nijmegen: Berkhout.

Van Ingelghem, M., van Wieringen, A., Wouters, J., Vandenbussche, E., Onghena, P., & Ghesquiere, P. (2001). Psychophysical evidence for a general temporal processing deficit in children with dyslexia. *Neuroreport, 12,* 3603-3607.

van Wieringen, A., & Wouters, J. (1999). Gap detection in single- and multiple-channel stimuli by LAURA cochlear implantees. *Journal of the Acoustical Society of America, 106,* 1925-1939.

Witton, C., Stein, J. F, Stoodley, C. J, Rosner, B. S, & Talcott, J. B. (2002). Separate influences of acoustic AM and FM sensitivity on the phonological decoding skills of impaired and normal readers. *Journal of Cognitive Neuroscience, 14,* 866-874.

Witton, C., Talcott, J. B., Hansen, P. C., Richardson, A. J., Griffiths, T. D., Rees, A., Stein, J. F., & Green, G. G. R. (1998). Sensitivity to dynamic auditory and visual stimuli predicts nonword reading ability in both dyslexic and normal readers. *Current Biology, 8,* 791-797.

Wright, B. A., Lombardino, L. J., King, W. M., Puranik, C. S., Leonard, C. M., & Merzenich, M. M. (1997). Deficits in auditory temporal and spectral resolution in language-impaired children. *Nature, 387,* 176-178.

Acknowledgements: *This study was supported by the Fund for Scientific Research-Flanders (Belgium) and the Queen Fabiola Fund. The authors thank Geert Verbeke for advice on Mixed Model Analysis and the staff, pupils and parents of Parkschool and Arkschool (Leuven, Belgium) for participation.*

Appendix:
Participants' Characteristics, Reading Scores and Psychophysical Threshold Estimates

Group	N°	Sex	Age	RWT	PWT	GAP1	GAP2	GAP3	GAP4	AV GAP	(SD)	FM1	FM2	FM3	FM4	AV FM	(SD)
DR	1	f	148	1	1	2,3	3,4	3,3	2,9	3,0	(0,5)	5,9	1,8	2,7	2,3	3,2	(1,8)
DR	2	m	141	1	1	2,3	3,2	2,4	3,3	2,8	(0,5)	6,4	2,9	6,7	5,0	5,2	(1,7)
DR	3	f	126	1	1	3,8	3,6	2,0	3,1	3,1	(0,8)	14,9	8,2	3,1	10,2	9,1	(4,9)
DR	4	m	125	1	1	3,4	3,5	3,3	3,4	3,4	(0,1)	9,3	12,2	6,9	9,6	9,5	(2,2)
DR	5	m	147	1	2	3,4	3,3	2,5	3,5	3,2	(0,5)	5,6	4,2	4,8	3,9	4,6	(0,8)
DR	6	F	142	1	2	3,9	1,8	2,7	3,7	3,0	(1,0)	2,8	4,4	8,5	4,9	5,1	(2,4)
DR	7	m	140	1	3	3,3	3,3	3,3	3,6	3,4	(0,2)	4,1	6,3	6,5	3,3	5,1	(1,6)
DR	8	m	135	1	3	3,3	3,7	2,7	3,0	3,1	(0,4)	3,5	1,4	2,2	3,8	2,7	(1,1)
DR	9	m	125	1	5	4,3	3,7	7,5	3,5	4,8	(1,9)	4,4	1,9	3,0	2,9	3,0	(1,0)
DR	10	f	130	3	5	3,6	3,5	3,1	3,5	3,4	(0,2)	7,3	13,4	13,6	15,9	12,5	(3,7)
M			136	1,2	2,4	3,4	3,3	3,3	3,4	3,3		6,4	5,7	5,8	6,2	6,0	
SD			9,1	0,6	1,6	0,6	0,5	1,5	0,3	0,5		3,5	4,3	3,5	4,3	3,3	
NR	1	m	132	10	10	3,3	3,4	3,0	2,8	3,1	(0,3)	4,4	4,4	2,8	4,8	4,1	(0,9)
NR	2	m	147	11	11	2,3	2,4	2,0	2,1	2,2	(0,2)	1,7	1,8	1,6	1,8	1,7	(0,1)
NR	3	m	146	12	16	3,3	2,8	2,5	1,8	2,6	(0,7)	3,9	4,7	2,1	2,4	3,3	(1,2)
NR	4	m	128	12	16	2,5	1,9	3,3	2,8	2,6	(0,6)	3,5	2,6	4,6	4,8	3,9	(1,0)
NR	5	f	127	12	19	2,6	2,8	2,6	2,8	2,7	(0,1)	3,6	2,0	4,8	2,8	3,3	(1,2)
NR	6	m	137	13	12	3,3	2,6	1,9	3,3	2,8	(0,7)	4,1	4,0	4,3	4,7	4,3	(0,3)
NR	7	m	134	13	15	2,7	2,9	3,0	2,7	2,8	(0,2)	3,0	3,3	2,7	2,8	2,9	(0,3)
NR	8	f	135	14	15	3,0	2,6	3,5	3,5	3,1	(0,4)	3,1	5,5	2,3	3,2	3,5	(1,3)
NR	9	f	144	16	12	3,0	2,2	2,2	2,3	2,4	(0,4)	4,2	6,9	8,8	5,6	6,4	(2,0)
NR	10	f	145	19	16	2,7	2,6	3,1	2,6	2,7	(0,2)	3,6	3,8	3,6	3,6	3,6	(0,1)
M			137	13,2	14,2	2,9	2,6	2,7	2,6	2,7		3,5	3,9	3,8	3,7	3,7	
SD			7,4	2,6	2,8	0,4	0,4	0,6	0,5	0,3		0,8	1,6	2,1	1,3	1,2	

Note: Group: DR: dyslexic readers, NR: normal readers / N°: participant number / Sex: f: female, m: male / Age: age given in months / RWT: standard scores on Real Word reading Test ($M = 10$, $SD = 3$) / PWT: standard scores on Pseudo-Word reading Test ($M = 10$, $SD = 3$) / GAP1-4: GAP thresholds in ms from run 1-4 / AVGAP (SD): average GAP thresholds in ms from the 4 runs (standard deviation) / FM1-4: FM thresholds Df in Hz from run 1-4 / AVFM (SD): average FM thresholds Df in Hz from the 4 runs (standard deviation).

4
COGNITION AND METACOGNITION IN CHILDREN WITH MATHEMATICS LEARNING DISABILITIES

Annemie Desoete and Herbert Roeyers

Introduction

Mathematics can be seen as a human made representational system of one or more numerical relationships presented in number-fact or word problem fact format. We use numbers (1, 2, 21), measures (meter, litter, kg, hour, degree, euro) and symbols (+, -, =) to communicate and share images with colleagues on abstract elements such as time, speed, distance, temperature and power. The dialectical constructivist approach of mathematical problem-solving stresses that understanding mathematics develops through active knowledge construction, transformation and discovery and not merely results from passive information acquisition (e.g., Verschaffel, 1999). Constructivists assume that metacognition plays a role in strategy selection after the child can represent numbers mentally (Carr & Biddlecomb, 1998). In addition different cognitive skills seem involved in mathematical problem-solving (Donlan, 1998; Geary, 2003).

Despite all the emphasis on cognition and metacognition, concepts mean different things to different people, making studies difficult to compare (Boekaerts, 1999). The purpose of this chapter is to clarify some of the issues on the conceptualisation of cognition and metacognition in lower-elementary-school children with mathematics learning disabilities. To provide background, we begin with a definition of mathematics learning disabilities and a description of a conceptual framework on cognition. Afterwards we present a review of the metacognitive concepts mediating mathematical problem-solving. We then document on our own work on cognitive and metacognitive skills in lower-elementary school children with mathematics learning disabilities in Flanders. We conclude with a discussion of research areas in which data from cognition and metacognition may further enhance our assessment of the problems of children with mathematical learning disabilities in general.

Conceptual framework

Mathematics learning disabilities

In Flanders between 3 and 8 percent of the children have mathematical learning disabilities (Desoete, Roeyers, & De Clercq, 2004). Similar prevalence rates have been found in other countries (e.g., Shalev, Manor, Kerem, Ayali, Dadichi, Friedlander, & Gross-Tsur, 2001). The number of students classified as having learning disabilities has furthermore increased substantially over the last 20 years (Swanson, 2000).

Although various authors agree that an operational definition of learning disabilities is meaningful (e.g., Kavale & Forness, 2000; Swanson, 2000), most studies are rather vague when it comes to characterizing the children who fit in their category of 'children with learning disabilities'. In addition, several authors use different concepts for 'disablement' in mathematical problem-solving ('mathematics learning difficulty', 'mathematics learning problem', 'mathematics learning disorder', 'mathematics learning disability', 'mathematics learning retardation', 'mathematics learning deficiency', 'dyscalculia') (Desoete, Roeyers, & De Clercq, 2004; Geary, 2004).

We further use three criteria to include participants within the group of children with 'mathematics learning disabilities' (MLD). At first, as suggested by the *'discrepancy criterion'* children have to perform significantly poorer on mathematics than we would expect based on their general school results and/or intelligence. Moreover, the *'severeness criterion'* is used, based on the DSM IV. So we only talk about a mathematics learning disability if children have difficulties with mathematics, measured with a validated test, where they perform minus two or more standard deviations (*SD*) below the norm. In addition a third criterion is used, namely the *'resistance criterion'* referring to the teacher's judgments or the fact that the difficulties remain severe, even with the usual remediation during 6 months at school (remedial teaching or school therapist). Teachers' judgments are used since, although some researchers question the trustworthiness of these data, reviews indicate that those judgments can serve as worthy assessments of students' achievement-related behaviours triangulated with data gathered by other protocols (Winne & Perry, 2000). Furthermore teacher's perception of student's use of strategies was found to be an important predictor of academic performances in children with learning disabilities (Meltzer, Roditi, Houser, & Perlman, 1998). Difficulties of children with mathematics learning disabilities often persist into the college years and many of these children continue to function below the mathematical level of a

13-year-old child, even as adults (Cawley & Miller, 1989). Nevertheless, mathematics is less researched than reading in young children (Noel, 2000; Wong, 1996). Furthermore, research on the relationship between metacognition and mathematics is usually conducted in older students (e.g., Montague, 1997) or in students with acquired deficits associated with brain injury (e.g., Mora & Saldana, 1995) and inconsistent results were found in younger children (e.g., Siegler, 1989).

Cognition and mathematical problem-solving

Several cognitive skills were found important for young children to solve mathematical problems adequately (Campbell, 1998; Collet, 2003; Dehaene, 1997; Fuson, Wearne, Hiebert, Murray, Human, Olivier, Carpenter, & Fennema, 1997; Geary, 2004; McCloskey & Macaruso, 1995; Montague, 1998; Noel, 2000; Rittle-Johnson, Siegler, & Alibali, 2001; Rourke & Conway, 1997; Sowder, 1992; Sweller, 1994).

Mathematical problem-solving depends on adequate *number naming or reading (NR)* skills where numbers are translated from one kind of presentation (e.g., the Arabic presentation '5') to another kind of representation (e.g., the verbal oral representation of the number word 'five'). In order to answer tasks such as '17+5=_' children need to know that '17' is not '71' or '710' and that '5' is not '2'. Problems with this cognitive skill give mistakes as 17+5 = 19 (confusion between 5 and 2).

The second problem-solving skill has to do with the translation within the mathematics lexicon. *Operation symbol comprehension and production skills (S)* enable the reading, writing and comprehension of operation symbols (such as +, -, x, =, <, >). Checking if operation symbols are known can be done with symbol or S-tasks. Problems with this cognitive skill give mistakes as 17x5 = 22.

Furthermore, mathematical problem-solving depends on the insight in the number structure or on the *knowledge (K)* of the position of decades and units and the ability to establish base-ten structure relationships. *Number system comprehension skills* (R) are required to be able to know that 17 is '1 more than 16' and '1 less then 18'. Children making K-mistakes have problems with the place of a number on a number line and do not know how many decades and units are for example in 17.

In addition, mathematics depends on *procedural (P) knowledge and skills* to calculate and to solve mathematical tasks in a number problem format (e.g., 17+5=_ or 71-5=_). Children have to know how to subtract to solve 71-5 as 66 (and not as 74 or 24). Problems with these cognitive skills give mistakes as 17+5 = 67 or 72.

Linguistic skills (L) are cognitive conceptual skills enabling children to understand and to solve one-sentence mathematical problems in a word-problem format (e.g., 5 more than 17 is_). Language has a central task according to several authors. If children do not know what 'more' means, word problems as '5 more than 17 are?' cannot be solved correctly.

Visualization skills (V) are cognitive skills enabling an adequate mental representation or visualization (V processes) of the problem or task. A mental representation is required in most word problems, since a simple 'translation' of keywords in a problem (e.g., 'more') into calculation procedures (e.g., 'addition'), without representation, leads to 'blind calculation' or 'number crunching'. This superficial approach leads to errors as answering '22 to tasks as '17 is 5 more than _', '27 is 5 less than _' and '44 is half of _'.

Contextual skills (C) are cognitive skills that enable the solving of tasks in word problems consisting of more than one sentence (e.g., Bert has 17 chaps. Judith has 5 chaps more than Bert. How many chaps does Judith have? __). Problems involving these tasks can be related to problems with working memory (and 'cognitive overload').

Relevance skills (R) are cognitive skills enabling the solving of word problems with irrelevant information included in the assignment (e.g., Bert has 17 Yu-Gi-Oh chaps and 3 Yu-Gi-Oh cards. Judith has 5 Yu-Chi-Oh chaps more than Bert. How many Yu-Gi-Oh chaps does Judith have? __). Children can have difficulty ignoring and not using information (e.g., 3 cards) in an assignment. They think all numbers have to be 'used' in order to solve a mathematical problem, and answer '25'. Indirect tasks with irrelevant information included are further referred on as relevance- or R-tasks.

Number sense skills (N) are the ninth cognitive skills enabling the solving of tasks as 'the answer on 5 more than 17 is nearest ? Choose between 5, 10, 50 and 70'. These skills to estimate without giving the exact answer are labelled 'number sense' and tasks depending on it are referred to as N-tasks. For more information, we refer to Desoete and Roeyers (in press).

Metacognition and mathematical problem-solving

In addition, it is nowadays widely accepted that metacognition influences mathematical problem-solving (Borkowski, 1992; Carr & Jessup, 1995; Hacker, Dunlosky, & Graesser, 1998; Montague, 1998; Veenman, Wilhelm & Beishuizen, 2004; Winne & Perry, 2000).

'Metacognitive knowledge' has been described as knowledge and deeper understanding of one's own cognitive processes and products. Within metacognitive knowledge, Cross and Paris (1988) and

Jacobs and Paris (1987) distinguished declarative knowledge, procedural knowledge and conditional knowledge or what, how, when and why knowledge.

Metacognitive skills are the voluntary control people have of their own cognitive processes. Substantial data have been accumulated on four metacognitive skills: orientation, planning, monitoring and evaluation (Brown, 1987).

Simons (1996) described a third metacognitive component ('metacognitive beliefs') as the broader general ideas and theories (e.g., self-concept, self-efficacy, motivation, attribution, conceptions of intelligence and learning), people have about their own (and other people's) cognition.

Numerical and geometrical problem-solving abilities in particular were found to be strongly related to metacognitive skills, whereas this relation was only present for some children in arithmetic performance tasks (Lucangeli & Cornoldi, 1997). Studies have also shown that metacognition is especially instrumental during the initial stage of mathematical problem-solving ('prediction') as well as in the final stage ('evaluation') of interpretation and checking the outcome of the calculations (Verschaffel, 1999).

To summarise, several (meta)cognitive parameters were found important in mathematical problem-solving. Although a certain consensus has been reached that those skills have an important effect on students' mathematics achievement, research has yielded inconsistent results in younger children and on children with mathematical learning disabilities. The first study was set up to investigate in a normal population whether children with mathematical learning disabilities show subnormal performance on cognitive skills and whether age-matched children with below-average achievement in mathematics and average performing peers exhibit general strengths on cognitive skills. Moreover, recent research has led to the discovery of a procedural and semantic memory subtype of mathematical learning disabilities (e.g., Geary, 2004; McCloskey & Macaruso, 1995). Therefore the second and third study was set up to investigate whether the differentiation between children with procedural problems, children with a semantic memory problems and children with a combination of those problems might have an additional value in the explanation of learning. In addition, although authors do agree that an operational definition of learning disabilities is meaningful, most studies do not differentiate between children with specific mathematics learning disabilities, specific reading disabilities and children with combined reading and mathematics learning disabilities. Therefore the fourth study was set up to investigate whether this differentiation might have an additional value in the explanation of learning. A relevant research issue, then, is whether or not (meta)cognition has some 'value added' in the assessment of those young children with learning disabilities.

Method

Participants

This chapter is based on four studies. The participants in these studies consisted of third-grade and second-grade children referred by teachers of regular schools, psychologists of multidisciplinary rehabilitation centres, teachers at schools for special education or paraprofessionals treating children with learning disabilities because of significantly a specific mathematics and/or reading achievement.

Children in study 1 had to have a score below percentile (pc) 3 (or −2SD) on tests for procedural calculation and number knowledge (KRT Cracco et al., 1995) or number facts retrieval (TTR De Vos, 1992), and at least one year below grade level according to the school psychologist to be accepted in our sample as children with mathematics learning disabilities (MLD). To be accepted in the low-performing group (BAP) children had to have a score below pc 25 on both mathematics tests. The label of 'low performing on mathematics' had to be acknowledged by the teacher (rating scale) and the school psychologist. Children in the age-matched group (NoD3) had to have a score above pc 25 on both tests, acknowledged by teacher and school psychologist.

In study 2 and 3 children with a mathematics learning disability due to insufficient procedural skills (PRD), children with a semantic memory disability (SMD) and children with a combined disability in both aspects of mathematical problem-solving (CoD) were screened, with the permission of the parents, based on the following criteria: (a) The average intelligence had to be $90 < TIQ < 120$. Furthermore, the participants had to demonstrate an ability-achievement discrepancy based on their total IQ and total standardized achievement test scores. (b) Scores had to be below −2SD on number facts retrieval tests for the SMD and CoD children, and below −2SD on tests for procedural calculation for the PRD and CoD group of children. The performance level of all children with mathematics learning disabilities was at least one year below grade level according to the school psychologist. (c) To be accepted in our sample as children with learning disabilities of that specific subtype (PRD, SMD, and CoD) the diagnosis had to be acknowledged and inefficient learning strategies had to be detected by the teacher, a school psychologist and a team of therapists. (d) In addition, only white native Dutch-speaking children without histories of extreme hyperactivity, sensory impairment, brain damage, a chronic medical condition, insufficient instruction or serious emotional or behavioural disturbance were included.

In study 4, children with and without learning disabilities in grade 2 and 3 were screened, with the permission of the parents, based on the following criteria: (a) The average intelligence had to be $90 < \text{TIQ} < 120$. Furthermore, the participants had to demonstrate an ability-achievement discrepancy based on their total IQ and total standardized achievement test scores. Scores had to be below –2SD on frequently used tests on mathematics for the children with a mathematics learning disability (MLD) and the children with a combined mathematics and reading disability (MRD) children, and below –2SD on reading tests for the children with a reading learning disability (RLD) and for the MRD group of children. The performance level of all children with mathematics learning disabilities was at least one year below grade level according to the school psychologist. (b) To be accepted in our sample as children with learning disabilities (MLD, MRD and RLD) the diagnosis had to be acknowledged and inefficient learning strategies had to be detected by a school psychologist or a team of therapists. (c) In addition, only white native Dutch-speaking children without histories of extreme hyperactivity, sensory impairment, brain damage, a chronic medical condition, insufficient instruction or serious emotional or behavioural disturbance were included. Two control groups (NoD2, NoD3) were included in the contrastive analysis. The first control group (NoD3) consisted of average-intelligent third-graders (ages 8-9) without a diagnosis of learning disability or other problems. These children were matched with the children with mathematics learning disabilities based upon not more than 1 week difference in date of birth. The second control group (NoD2) consisted of average-intelligent second-grade students (ages 7-8) without a diagnosis of learning disability or other problems. The sample was drawn at random, with the permission of the children's parents, from regular elementary classes. The matching was based on their mathematical problem-solving skills. Participants in both control groups (NoD2, NoD3) were native Dutch-speaking Belgian children, with average intelligence ($90<\text{TIQ}<120$) and an overall school result of at least level B (60%).

Measures

The metacognitive tests were specifically designed for the present studies and consisted of the *Evaluation and Prediction Assessment* paper and pencil test (EPA) and the computerized test (EPA2000) (De Clercq, Desoete & Roeyers, 2000) (see Figure 1). These instruments were tested in a pilot study in order to determine their usefulness for this age group and for their sensitivity in measuring individual differences.

Figure 1
Cognitive and metacognitive skills measured with EPA 2000

Before the task	During the task	After he task
Prediction (Pr)	Number reading (NR) Operation Symbol comprehension (S) Number system Knowledge (K) Procedural calculation (P) Language comprehension (L) Dealing with Context information (C) Mental representation or visualization (V) Selecting relevant information (R) Number sense (N)	Evaluation (Ev)

In the EPA and EPA2000 (De Clercq et al., 2000) cognition and metacognition is assessed (see Figure 1). Before solving the different mathematical tasks, children first have to 'predict' their performance (see Figure 2). After doing the exercise, children 'evaluate' on the same 4-point rating scale.

Metacognitive predictions (Pr) or evaluations (Ev) are awarded two points whenever they correspond with the child's actual performance on the task. Predicting and evaluating the rating 'sure to be correct' or 'sure not to be correct' receive one point whenever they correspond. Other answers receive no points, as they are considered to represent a lack of prediction / evaluation. For the cognitive mathematical problem-solving (NR, S, K, P, V, C, R and N), children obtain I point for every correct answer. Results on the three subscales of EPA and EPA2000 (prediction, cognition and evaluation) were the basis for developing cognitive and metacognitive profiles for individual students. These profiles could provide a graphic display of a student's cognitive and metacognitive mathematical problem-solving strengths and weaknesses and can be used as a guide to tailor instruction by teachers for individual students (Desoete, Roeyers, Buysse, & De Clercq, 2002). The psychometric value of EPA and EPA2000 has been demonstrated on a sample of 550 Dutch-speaking children. For more information, we refer to Desoete, Roeyers, and De Clercq (2002b) and Desoete, Roeyers, Buysse and De Clercq (2002).

Figure 2
EPA2000 measurement of prediction

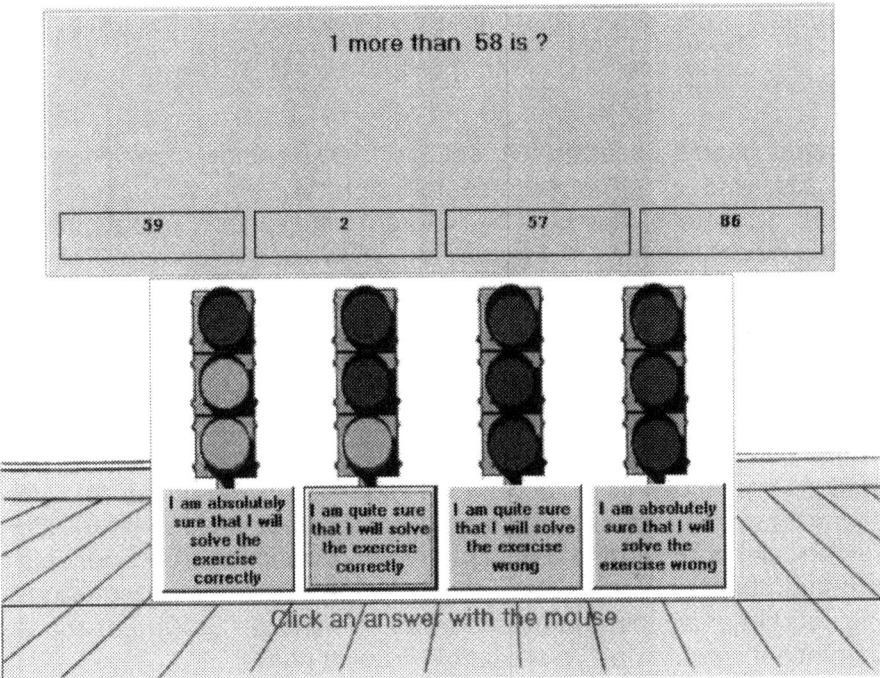

The mathematical problem solving tests consisted of the Kortrijk Arithmetic Test(Kortrijkse Rekentest, KRT) (Cracco et al. 1995) and the Arithmetic Number Fact Test (Tempo Test Rekenen, TTR) (De Vos, 1992). The KRT is a test for procedural calculation and number system knowledge. All children in the procedural disability group (PRD-group) and in the group of children with a combined disability (CoD-group) had scores below $-2SD$ on the KRT. The psychometric value of the KRT has been demonstrated on a sample of 3,246 Dutch-speaking children. The Arithmetic Number Fact Test (Tempo Test Rekenen, TTR) (de Vos, 1992) is used as a test on 200 arithmetic number-fact problems. Children have to solve as many number-fact problems as possible out of 200 in 5 minutes. All children with a semantic memory disability (SMD-group) and children with a combined disability (CoD-group) had scores below $-2SD$ on the TTR. This test has been standardized for Flanders on 10,059 children (Ghesquière & Ruijssenaars, 1994).

As reading tests the One Minute Test (Een Minuut Test, EMT, Brus & Voeten, 1999) was used. The EMT is as a test of reading fluency for Dutch-speaking people, validated for Flanders on 10,059 children (Ghesquière & Ruijssenaars, 1994), measuring the capacity of children to read correctly as many words as possible. All children with reading learning disabilities (RLD-group) and combined reading and mathematics disabilities (MRD) had below −2SD on the EMT.

Procedure

The contribution is based on four studies. In a first study cognitive skills were assessed in 310 average intelligent children with or without learning disabilities in grade 3. Children with specific mathematics learning disabilities (MLD) in grade 3 (n=50) were compared with low-performing peers (BAP) (n=132) and age-matched peers without learning disabilities (NoD3) (n=138). For more information, we refer to Desoete, Roeyers, & Buysse (2000).

In a second study three cognitive skills were assessed in 113 average intelligent children with or without learning disabilities in grade 3. Children with mathematics learning disabilities due to problems with semantic memory in grade 3 (SMD) (n=14) were compared with children with procedural mathematics learning disabilities (PRD) (n=19), children with mathematics learning disabilities and problems with both memory and procedural calculation (CoD) (n=40) and age-matched peers without learning disabilities (NoD3) (n=40). For more information, we refer to Desoete and Roeyers (2001).

In a third study all cognitive en metacognitive skills were assessed in 200 children with or without learning disabilities in grade 3. Children with mathematics learning disabilities due to problems with semantic memory in grade 3 (SMD) (n=31) were compared with children with procedural mathematics learning disabilities (PRD) (n=34), children with a mathematics learning disabilities and problems with both memory and procedural skills (CoD) (n=30) and age-matched peers without learning disabilities (NoD3) (n=105). For more information, we refer to Desoete and Roeyers (2002a).

In a fourth study metacognitive skills were assessed in 437 average intelligent children with or without learning disabilities in grades 2 and 3. Children with specific mathematics learning disabilities in grade 3 (MLD) (n=62) were compared with peers with specific reading disabilities (RLD) (n=53), children with combined reading and mathematics learning disabilities (MRD) (n=72), age-matched peers (NoD3) (n=130) and younger children (NoD2) (n=120) matched at mathematical problem-solving level. For more information, we refer to Desoete and Roeyers (2002b).

Results

Study 1

In order to answer our research question on the relation between cognitive skills and mathematics in children with mathematics learning disabilities, in study 1 a multivariate analysis of variance (MANOVA) was conducted on 310 third-graders, with cognitive skills as dependent variables and belonging to one of the mathematical ability groups (MLD, BAP, NoLD3) as a factor. The MANOVA revealed a significant main effect for the mathematical performance groups at the multivariate level ($F(14, 622) = 32.42$, $p < .0005$).

On the univariate level we found significant differences on all cognitive parameters. Post hoc Tukey analyses revealed differences between the three groups of children on mental representation tasks, procedural calculation tasks and on language related tasks. For Means and Standard Deviations see Table 1.

Table 1 Cognitive skills in children with and without mathematics learning disabilities in grade 3

	NoD3 n=138	BAP n=132	MLD n=50	$F(2, 317)$
COGNITION	M (SD)	M (SD)	M (SD)	
NR-tasks	99.57a (1.69)	97.41 (8.48)	95.06b (15.42)	6.05*
S-tasks	87.65a (11.04)	67.65b (20.19)	66.30b (21.40)	55.85**
P-tasks	69.20a (17.29)	51.59b (13.79)	40.80c (14.12)	78.48**
L-tasks	93.48a (13.27)	80.00b (24.59)	64.80c (32.47)	33.59**
V-tasks	87.54a (22.17)	37.73b (30.93)	25.20c (26.74)	158.86**
C-tasks	87.97a (19.41)	37.73b (28.35)	33.60b (28.70)	166.93**
R+N-tasks	65.98a (21.85)	39.81b (20.77)	35.45b (20.24)	66.40**

** p < .0005   * p<.005   abc posthoc analyses
Note. NR, S, P, L, V, C and R+N tasks max 100 points (measured with EPA)
NoD3= children without learning disabilities, BAP = below averabe performing children on mathematical problem-solving tasks, MLD = children with mathematics learning disabilities.

Study 2

In order to investigate of the cognitive skills and mathematics is the same in all subtypes of mathematics learning disabilities, the above mentioned cognitive skills were assessed in 113 children with and without mathematics learning disabilities in grade 3. A MANOVA was conducted with cognitive skills (V, L and P) as dependent variables and belonging to one of the mathematical ability groups (SMD, PRD, CoD and MA3) as a factor. The MANOVA revealed a significant main effect for the mathematical performance groups at the multivariate level ($F(9, 261)=25.23$, $p<.0005$). On the univariate level we found significant differences on all cognitive parameters. For Means and Standard Deviations see Table 2.

Table 2 Cognitive skills in children with and without mathematics learning disabilities in grade 3

	NoD3. n=40	PRD n=19	SMD n=19	CoD n=40	$F(3,195)=$
COGNITION	M (SD)	M (SD)	M (SD)	M (SD)	
P-task	67.25a (15.07)	53.23b (15.08)	73.93a (14.96)	34.00b (16.02)	39.18*
L-task	86.00a (22.28)	83.53a (26.20)	88.57a (26.85)	53.50b (33.71)	11.06*
V-task	74.00a (22.28)	18.82b (21.36)	82.88a (28.13)	16.00b (21.34)	66.90*

* $p < .0005$ abc posthoc analyses
Note. P, L and V max 100 points (measured with EPA2000)
NoD3= children without learning disabilities, PRD = children with procedural mathematical disabilities, SMD = children with semantic memory disabilities, CoD = children with combined procedural and semantic memory disabilities.

Children with combined procedural and semantic memory mathematics learning disabilities in particular failed on the language prerequisite to solve word problems. Children with isolated mathematics automatization disabilities (the semantic memory group) or children with isolated procedural disabilities did not have problems solving language tasks. In addition, several children with a specific mathematics learning disability were found to have less developed mental representation skills. Only the children with an automatization disability (semantic memory deficit) did not fail on and even had high scores on these mental representation tasks. Finally, several children with a procedural or a combined mathematics learning disability had problems with procedural skills, using several bugs.

Study 3

In order to confirm the differences between the subtypes of mathematics learning disabilities, a third study was conducted with a larger group of children ($n=200$) with and without mathematics learning disabilities. A MANCOVA was conducted with all cognitive skills (NR, S, K, P, L, M, C, N and R) and the metacognitive skills (Pr, Ev) as dependent variables, intelligence as covariate and belonging to one of the mathematical ability groups (SMD, PRD, CoD and NoD3) as a factor. The MANCOVA revealed a significant main effect for the mathematical performance groups ($F(33, 546)=2.37$, $p<.0005$) and for the covariant factor of intelligence ($F(11, 185)=2.94$, $p<.005$). On the univariate level we found significant differences on all cognitive and metacognitive parameters, with expectation of the tasks where children had to deal with irrelevant information (R). For Means and Standard Deviations we refer to Table 3.

Table 3 (Meta)cognitive skills in children with/without mathematics learning disabilities in grade 3

	NoD3 n=105	PRD n=34	SMD n=31	CoD n=30	F(3,195)=
COGNITION	M (SD)	M (SD)	M (SD)	M (SD)	
NR-task	88.00a (16.78)	82.35a (24.00)	82.58a (23.52)	71.33b (22.70)	4.29*
S-task	90.76a (13.88)	86.35a (14.09)	86.88a (13.30)	78.13b (16.56)	6.49**
K-task	74.09a (18.99)	60.29b (23.42)	59.03b (23.00)	47.67b (23.15)	15.36**
P-task	78.69a (15.62)	67.79b (20.27)	66.40b (12.69)	54.36c (19.67)	19.17**
L-task	89.59a (18.29)	74.96b (26.13)	74.11b (25.37)	78.00 (25.51)	5.46**
V-task	49.06a (32.34)	39.03a (22.48)	38.71a (22.47)	32.67b (20.67)	3.45*
C-task	70.16a (26.17)	52.45b (27.41)	47.58b (35.56)	45.00b (28.16)	9.89**
R-task	41.05 (24.69)	37.79 (18.06)	50.81 (26.21)	36.67 (24.33)	2.38
N-task	59.05a (21.07)	48.68 (16.44)	57.42a (26.70)	47.33b (18.56)	4.68*
METACOGNITION					
Pr-task	67.81a (8.82)	57.63b (9.43)	67.20a (12.28)	59.72b (11.16)	11.92**
Ev-task	69.87a (10.70)	61.09b (9.39)	66.51a (11.67)	57.09b (14.66)	11.35**

* $p < .005$, ** $p < .0005$ abc posthoc analyses
Note. NR, S, K, P, L, V, C, N, Pr and Ev max 100 points (measured with EPA2000) NoD3= children without learning disabilities, PRD = children with procedural mathematics disabilities, SMD = children with semantic memory disabilities, CoD = children with procedural and semantic memory disabilities.

Children with combined procedural and semantic memory mathematics learning disabilities failed significantly more on NR, S, K, P, M, C and N cognitive tasks and on the Pr and Ev metacognitive tasks than the children in the other groups. Children with isolated mathematics automatization disabilities (the semantic memory group) and children with an isolated procedural disability failed on K, P, L and C tasks. Children with an isolated semantic memory disability did not have lower metacognitive scores than the age-matched group of children without learning disabilities. Children with an isolated procedural disability did also fail on the Pr and Ev tasks compared with the children without learning disabilities.

Study 4

In order to answer our research question on the relation between prediction and evaluation skills and mathematics in children with mathematics learning disabilities, in our final study ($n=437$) several MANOVA's were conducted to investigate whether metacognitive skills were general, person-related characteristics of several learning disability subtype groups or domain-specific skills. A first multivariate analysis of variance (MANOVA) was conducted with prediction and evaluation skills, as measured by EPA2000, as dependent variables and belonging to one of the five mathematical ability groups (NoD2, NoD3, MLD, RLD, MRD) as a factor. The MANOVA revealed a significant main effect for the groups at the multivariate level ($F(8, 862)=40.21$, $p<.0005$). No differences were found between children with a specific mathematics learning disability or combined mathematics learning disabilities and mathematical performance-matched younger children. Furthermore, children with reading disabilities did not have significantly lower prediction and evaluation scores than age-matched. For Means and Standard Deviations we refer to Table 4.

We further analyzed whether third-grade students with mathematics learning disabilities had problems with prediction and evaluation on easy tasks (P1, E1), tasks designed for grade 2 (P2, E2), age accurate tasks (P3, E3) and difficult tasks (P4, E4). A second multivariate analysis of variance (MANOVA) was therefore conducted with P1, P2, P3 and P4 as dependent variables and belonging to one of the five mathematical performance groups as a factor. The MANOVA revealed a significant main effect for the mathematical performance groups at the multivariate level ($F(16, 1311)=26.32$, $p<.0005$). Children with specific or combined mathematics learning disabilities did worse than age-matched children on the easy tasks (P1). No difference was found between mathematical performance-matched younger children and children with specific or combined mathematics learning disabilities on the P2, P3 and P4 tasks. A third MANOVA was conducted with E1, E2, E3 and E4 as dependent variables and belonging to one of the five mathematical performance groups as a factor. Children with specific or combined mathematics learning disabilities did worse than mathematical performance-matched younger children on the easy evaluation tasks (E1). No significant differences were found on evaluation tasks designed for grade 2, evaluation tasks designed for grade 3 and evaluation tasks designed for grade 4, between the three groups of children. For Means and Standard Deviations we refer to Table 4.

Table 4 Metacognitive skills in children with and without learning disabilities

METACOGNITION	NoD2 n=120 M (SD)	NoD3 n=130 M (SD)	MLD n=62 M (SD)	RLD n=53 M (SD)	MRD n=72 M (SD)	
Pr	64.79b (9.62)	79.27a (8.16)	61.90b (11.59)	76.30a (9.14)	61.21b (8.80)	$F(4, 432)=$ 74.79*
P1	83.25b (9.17)	92.97a (7.88)	72.76c (17.73)	88.88a (9.79)	77.62c (9.99)	49.27*
Pk	56.43a (17.07)		47.83b (17.76)		48.40b (14.54)	$F(2, 251)=$ 7.96**
Pp	51.65a (27.62)		41.74b (24.71)		44.25 (22.44)	3.72*
Ev	64.12b (9.92)	79.77a (6.79)	62.90b (12.34)	77.17a (7.54)	60.63b (11.17)	$F(4, 432)=$ 79.79*
E1	84.87b (9.08)	94.08a (5.64)	79.20c (10.11)	91.73a (7.39)	80.91c (7.92)	57.84*
Ek	59.04a (18.51)		50.87b (20.75)		51.49b (15.70)	$F(2, 251)=$ 5.79*
Ep	47.74a (22.41)		39.35b (22.06)		35.11b (19.59)	7.95**

* $p < .005$, ** $p < .0005$ abc posthoc analyses
Note. Pr, P1, Pk, Pp, E, E1, Ek en Ep max 100 points (measured with EPA2000)
Pr= prediction on all tasks, P1= prediction on easy tasks, Pk= prediction on number knowlege tasks, Pp= prediction on procedural calculation tasks, Ev= evaluation on all tasks, E1= evaluation on easy tasks, Ek= evaluation on number knowlege tasks, Ep= evaluation on procedural calculation tasks, NoD2= children without learning disabilities in grade 2 (performance matched), NoD3= children without learning disabilities in grade 3 (age matched), MLD = children with mathematics learning disabilities in grade 3, RLD = children with reading learning disabilities in grade 3, MRD = children with combined reading and mathematics learning disabilities.

In addition, we investigated whether the prediction and evaluation skills in children with specific or combined learning disabilities differed from those of younger children matched on mathematical performance on numeral and operation symbol comprehension (Ps, Es), number system knowledge (Pk, Ek), mental arithmetic (Pm, Em), procedural calculation (Pp, Ep) and word problems (Pw, Ew). A fourth MANOVA was conducted with Ps, Pk, Pm, Pp and Pw and as dependent variables and belonging to the mathematical performance group of second-graders, third-graders with mathematics learning disabilities or third-graders with combined reading and mathematics learning disabilities as a factor. The MANOVA revealed a significant main effect for the mathematical performance groups at the multivariate level ($F(10, 402)=2.12$, $p<.05$). Post-hoc analyses revealed better prediction performance for younger children matched on mathematical performance than for children with specific mathematics learning disabilities on number knowledge (Pk), mental arithmetic (Pm) and procedural calculation tasks (Pp). Furthermore, young children matched on mathematical performance did better than children with combined learning disabilities on prediction about number knowledge (Pk) and word problem (Pw) tasks. A fifth MANOVA was conducted with Es, Ek, Em, Ep and Ew as dependent variables and belonging to one of the mathematical performance groups as a factor. The MANOVA revealed a significant main effect for the mathematical performance groups at the multivariate level ($F(10, 494)=4.79$, $p<.0005$). Post-hoc analyses revealed significantly better evaluation scores for young children matched on mathematical performance on number knowledge (Ek) and procedural calculation tasks (Ep) compared with children with specific and combined mathematics learning disabilities. For Means and Standard Deviations we refer to Table 4.

Discussion

Our four studies underlined the importance of *three cognitive and two metacognitive skills* to differentiate children with mathematics learning disabilities from children with age adequate mathematical performances. We summarized the skills in Figure 3. Children with mathematics learning disabilities were found to differ from children without mathematics learning disabilities on linguistic aspects (L) of mathematical problem-solving, tasks depending upon mental representation (V) and on procedural calculation (P) skills (study 1, 2 and 3). Moreover prediction (P) and evaluation (E) skills did also differentiate between children with mathematics learning disabilities and peers without learning disabilities (study 4).

Figure 3
Especially important cognitive and metacognitive skills to be assessed in children with mathematics learning disabilities

Before the task Metacognition	During the task Cognition	After he task Metacognition
Prediction skill (Pr) Pp Pl Pv P1 Pk	*Cognitive skills* Procedural calculation (P) Language comprehension (L) Visualization (V)	*Evaluation skill (Ev)* Ep - - E1 Ek

Note . Pr = prediction, Ev = evaluation, P = procedural calculation, L = language comprehension, V = visualization, P1 = prediction on easy tasks, Pk = prediction on number system knowledge tasks, Pp = prediction on procedural calculation tasks, Pl = prediction on lanuage comprehension tasks, Pv = prediction on visualization tasks, E1 = evaluation on easy tasks, Ek = evaluation on number system knowledge tasks, Ep = evaluation on procedural calculation tasks

L-skills

Some children can solve tasks in a number problem format (e.g., 38 + 5 = _) but fail when this problem is presented in a sentence (e.g., 5 more than 38 is _) (L-tasks in Figure 3). Especially children with mathematics learning disabilities due to a combination of procedural and semantic memory disabilities failed on the language prerequisite to solve word problems (study 2 and 3). Children with an isolated semantic memory disability or children with isolated procedural disability did not have problems solving L-tasks in study 3, but failed on these tasks in study 2.

V-skills

Several children with a mathematics learning disability answer '43' to tasks as '38 is 5 more than _', '46 is 3 less than _' and '86 is half of _'. Especially, children with a procedural mathematics learning disability were found to have less developed visualization or mental representation skills (V-skills in Figure 3). Children with a semantic memory deficit did not fail (study 3) on and even had high scores on these mental representation tasks (study 2). These findings support the idea that children with a procedural disability use blind calculation techniques depending on a simple translation of keywords in an instruction. This mathematics disability group might therefore depend too little on a mental representation (V) of problems. It is important to assess those skills in order to detect if a child uses such techniques and if a treatment has to be tailored upon this weak cognitive skill or if this skill can be used to compensate for other weak cognitive skills (for example problems with context skills or relevance skills).

P-skills

Problems with procedural calculation skills (P in Figure 3) give mistakes as 38+5 = 88 or 813. This kind of mistakes is called 'bugs' (Van Lehn, 1990). Several children with a procedural disability might answer '43 to tasks as '23+2 _', '21+2= _' and '93-5= _'. It is obvious that measuring procedural skills is important in the approach of children with mathematics learning disabilities (study 2 and 3).

Pr-skills

Prediction (Pr see Figure 3) guarantees for children thinking about the learning objectives, proper learning characteristics and the available time. Moreover, children estimate or predict the difficulty of a task and use that prediction metacognitively to regulate engagement, related to outcome and efficacy expectation. The ability to predict makes children relate problems to other problems, develop intuition about the prerequisites required for doing the task and distinguish between apparent and real difficulties in mathematical problem-solving (Lucangeli et al., 1998). A majority of children with mathematics learning disabilities are found to have less accurate prediction skills than peers without learning disabilities (study 4). Moreover, younger children outperformed all children with mathematics learning disabilities on prediction on tasks designed for first grade students (so called 'easy tasks') (P1) (see Figure 2). Furthermore, children with specific mathematics learning disabilities were found to have less accurate predictions on number system knowledge (Pk) and procedural calculation (Pp) (see Figure 2). In addition, children with combined learning disabilities were found to have less accurate predictions on word problems depending upon language related (Pl) and visualization (Pv) tasks (see Figure 2) (study 4).

Ev-skills

The 'evaluation' skill (Ev see Figure 2) makes children evaluate their performance and compare task performance with other people and use the final result in locating the error in the solution process (Lucangeli et al., 1998). Prediction and evaluation skills differentiated between average and above-average mathematical problem solvers and between students with a mathematics learning disability (Desoete, Roeyers, Buysse, & De Clercq, 2001). In study 4, a majority of the children with mathematics learning disabilities was found to have less accurate evaluation skills than peers without learning disabilities. In addition, children with mathematics learning disabilities revealed to have especially problems estimating their chances of success on the 'easy tasks' (Ev 1 see Figure 3). Finally, children with mathematics disabilities did worse than younger children, matched at the level of mathematical problem-solving, on the evaluation on number knowledge (Ek see Figure 3) and procedural calculation tasks (Ep see Figure 3) (study 4).

However not all children with mathematics learning disabilities had the same amount of cognitive or even metacognitive problems. Especially children with a semantic memory disability might have a different cognitive and metacognitive profile (study 3). These findings reveal that it is important to assess cognition and metacognition in children with mathematics learning disabilities, since these skills seems to be 'often' but 'not always' impaired. In the case of impaired cognitive skills, these skills have to be explicitly learned and automatized (Desoete, Roeyers, & De Clercq, 2003). In the case of age adequate cognitive skills, these skills can be used to assist or compensate other deficient skills. Moreover our findings suggest that a general standardized cognitive or metacognitive intervention on all children with mathematics learning disabilities certainly would be an overconsumption of therapeutic energy, since not all children lack those skills.

One of the most challenging questions that arise from the data in our chapter is what implication the above-described results have for the assessment of children with mathematics learning disabilities. Several issues in the field of mathematical problem-solving have been presented. Firstly, we argued to be careful about the *diagnosis* of 'mathematics learning disability'. Secondly a *conceptual framework on mathematical problem-solving* was presented depending upon several cognitive and metacognitive skills. As cognition, mathematical problem-solving depends on numeral comprehension and production, operation symbol comprehension and production, number system knowledge, procedural calculation, language comprehension, context comprehension, mental visualization, selecting relevant information and number sense. Furthermore also metacognitive skills (prediction and evaluation skills) appear to be important for mathematical problem-solving (Desoete, Roeyers, & De Clercq, 2004). In addition, we stressed that although metacognition seems to be involved in learning, there remain several conceptual problems related to the disjoint meanings of metacognitive constructs. Nevertheless, metacognitive skills were found able to differentiate elementary-school children with mathematics learning disabilities from those with moderate mathematical performances and from subjects with above-moderate mathematical skills (Desoete, Roeyers, & Buysse, 2001). Thirdly, striking problems emerged in the assessment of metacognition (Desoete, Roeyers, & De Clercq, 2002a). Therefore an indirect computerized dynamic assessment *instrument* was developed for third-grade children with and without mathematics learning disabilities (Desoete, Roeyers, & De Clercq, 2002b). Fourthly, we stressed the importance of a cognitive and metacognitive *assessment* procedure in children with mathematics learning disabilities. Our results indicate that relevant cognitive and metacognitive skills have to be assessed, especially (but not only) if things go wrong in mathematical problem-solving. As to cognition, this means measuring procedural calculation, language comprehension and mental visualization skills. Furthermore, a measurement of prediction and evaluation skills seems indicated. Moreover, additional measurement of number reading, operation symbol comprehension, number knowledge, dealing with context information, dealing with irrelevant clues and number sense skills can be useful in order to assist or compensate weak cognitive skills in children with mathematics learning disabilities.

Despite the consistency of findings, confirming the importance of metacognitive skills, the results should be interpreted with caution. As described our studies of mathematical problem-solving were guided by the cognitive and metacognitive approach. Consequently, no implications for a motivational, behavioural or emotional approach could be drawn from the results of our studies. Moreover, our studies only included participants with an average intelligence in grade 3. So we cannot ground large conclusions on children with above or below average intelligence or on younger or older children. In addition, several lines for future research can be drawn. On the one hand there is no doubt that in many respects more in-depth research is needed as to metacognition and cognition in third-grade children. On the other hand cognition and metacognition has to be researched in younger and older children and in children with below or above average intelligence. We think that the research data derived from such studies could improve our understanding of the mechanism of metacognitive regulating behaviour.

To sum up, a majority of the average intelligent children with mathematics learning disabilities in grade 3 were found to show inaccurate cognitive and metacognitive skills. It may therefore be advisable to assess these skills and focus on these skills in young children with mathematics learning disabilities.

References

Boekaerts, M. (1999). Metacognitive experiences and motivational state as aspects of self-awareness. Review and discussion. *European Journal of Psychology of Education, 14,* 571-584.

Borkowski, J.G. (1992). Metacognitive Theory : A Framework for Teaching Literacy, Writing, and Math Skills. *Journal of Learning Disabilities, 25,* 253-257.

Brown, A. (1987). Metacognition, executive control, self-regulation, and other more mysterious mechanisms. In F. Reiner & R. Kluwe (Eds.), *Metacognition, motivation, and understanding* (pp. 65-116). Hillsdale, NJ: Erlbaum.

Brus, B.T., & Voeten, M.J.M. (1999). *Een Minuut Test* [One Minute Test]. Lisse: Swets & Zeitlinger.

Campbell, J.I.D (1998). Linguistic influences in cognitive arithmetic: comment on Noel, Fias and Brysbaert (1997). *Cognition, 67,* 353-364.

Carr, M., & Biddlecomb, B. (1998). Metacognition in Mathematics from a constructivist perspective. In D.J. Hacker, J. Dunloksy & A.C. Graesser (Eds.), *Metacognition in educational theory and practice* (pp. 69-91). Mahwah, NJ: Erlbaum.

Carr, M., & Jessup, D.L. (1995). Cognitive and metacognitive predicators of mathematics strategy use. *Learning and Individual Differences, 7,* 235-247.

Cawley, J.F., & Miller, J.H. (1989). Cross-sectional comparisons of the mathematical performance of children with learning disabilities: Are we on the right track toward comprehensive programming? *Journal of Learning Disabilities, 23,* 250-259.

Collet, M. (2003). *Diagnostic Assessment of the understanding of the base-ten-system.* Paper presented at the Symposium 'Current Issues in Assessment of Learning Disabilities' of the congress van de European Federation of Psychologists Associations (EFPA). Vienna: 10th of July 2003.

Cracco, J., Baudonck, M., Debusschere, A., Dewulf, B., Samyn, F., & Vercaemst, V. (1995). *Kortrijkse Rekentest* [Kortrijk Arithmetic Test]. Kortrijk: Revalidatiecentrum Overleie.

Cross, D.R., & Paris, S.G. (1988). Development and instructional analyses of children's metacognition and reading comprehension. *Journal of Educational Psychology, 80,* 131-142.

De Clercq, A., Desoete, A., & Roeyers, H. (2000). EPA2000 : A multilingual, programmable computer assessment of off-line metacognition in children with mathematical learning disabilities. *Behavior Research Methods, Instruments, & Computers, 32,* 304-311.

Dehaene, S. (1997). *The Number Sense.* Pinguin books Ltd.: London.

Desoete, A., & Roeyers, H. (in press). Cognitive building blocks in mathematical problem solving in grade 3. *British Journal of Educational Psychology.*

Desoete, A., & Roeyers, H. (2001). Het enigma van de rekenstoornis. Procedurele, talige en representatiedeficieten bij achtjarigen met rekenstoornissen. [The enigma of the mathematics learning disability. Procedural, linguistic, and representation deficits in eight-year olds with mathematics learning disabilities.] *Significant. Electronisch Wetenschappelijk Tijdschrift voor Klinische Research en Reviews voor Revalidatie en Psychosociale Hulpverlening, 1,* 18 pp.

Desoete, A., & Roeyers, H. (2002a). (Meta)cognitie bij kinderen met een automatisatiestoornis bij Rekenen [(Meta)cognition in children with an automatisation disability in mathematics]. *Tijdschrift voor orthopedagogiek, kinderpsychiatrie en klinische kinderpsychologie, 27,* 128-143.

Desoete, A., & Roeyers, H. (2002b). Off-line metacognition. A domain-specific retardation in young children with learning disabilities? *Learning Disability Quarterly, 25,* 123-139.

Desoete, A., Roeyers, H., De Clercq, A; (2003). Can off-line metacognition enhance mathematical problem solving? *Journal of Educational Psychology, 95,* 188-200.

Desoete, A., Roeyers, H.,& De Clercq, A. (2004). Children with mathematics learning disabilities in Belgium. *Journal of Learning Disabilities, 37,* 50-61.

Desoete, A., Roeyers, H., & Buysse, A. (2000). Achtjarigen, waarbij rekenen nooit routine wordt. Rekenstoornissen in Vlaanderen: aard en prevalentie van de problematiek [Eight year olds, where mathematics never becomes routine. Mathematics learning disabilities in Flanders: sort and prevalence of the problems], *Tijdschrift voor Orthopedagogiek,10,* 430-441.

Desoete, A., Roeyers, H., & Buysse, A. (2001). Metacognition and mathematical problem solving in grade 3. *Journal of Learning Disabilities, 34,* 435-449.

Desoete, A., Roeyers, H., Buysse, A., & De Clercq, A. (2002). Dynamic assessment of metacognitive skills in young children with mathematics learning disabilities. In D. Van der Aalsvoort, W.C.M. Resing & A.J.J.M. Ruijssenaars (Eds.), *Learning Potential Assessment and Cognitive Training* (pp 307-333). JAI Press Inc/Elsevier Science Ltd.: England.

Desoete, A., Roeyers, H.,& De Clercq, A. (2002a). The measurement of individual metacognitive differences in mathematical problem solving. In M. Valcke, D. Gombeir & W.C. Smith (Eds.). *Learning Styles. Reliability & Validity Proceedings of the 7th annual ELSIN Conference Ghent University, Belgium* (pp. 93-102) Academia Press Scientific Publishers: Gent.

Desoete, A., Roeyers, H.,& De Clercq, A. (2002b). Assessment of off-line metacognitive skills in young children with mathematics learning disabilities. *FOCUS. On Learning problems in mathematics, 24 (2),* 53-69

De Vos, T. (1992). *Test voor het vaststellen van het rekenvaardigheidsniveau der elementaire bewerkingen (automatisering) voor het basis en voortgezet onderwijs. Handleiding.* [Test to assess the arithmetic level of elementary calculations (automatization) in elementary and secundary education] Nijmegen: Berkhout.

Donlan, D. (1998). *The development of mathematical skills.* UK: Psychological Press.

Geary, D. (2003). Learning disabilities in arithmetic: problem-solving differences and cognitive deficits. In L. Swanson, K.R. Harris & S. Graham (Eds.) *Handbook of learning disabilities* (pp. 199-212). The Guilford Press: New York.

Geary, D. (2004). Mathematics and Learning Disabilities. *Journal of Learning Disabilities, 37,* 4-15.

Ghesquière, P., & Ruijssenaars, A. (1994). *Vlaamse normen voor studietoetsen Rekenen en technisch lezen lager onderwijs.* [*Flemish norms for tests: Arithmetic and technical reading elementary school.*]Leuven: K.U.L.-C.S.B.O.

Hacker, D., Dunlosky, J., & Graesser, A. (Eds.) (1998). *Metacognition in educational theory and practice. The educational psychology series.* Mahwah, NY: Erlbaum.

Jacobs, J.E., & Paris, S.G. (1987). Children's Metacognition about reading: Issues in definition, measurement, and instruction. *Educational Psychologist 22,* 255-278.

Kavale, K.A., & Forness, S.R. (2000). What Definitions of Learning Disability Say and Don't Say. A Critical Analysis. *Journal of Learning Disabilities, 33,* 239-256.

Lucangeli, D., & Cornoldi, C. (1997). Mathematics and Metacognition: What is the Nature of the Relationship? *Mathematical Cognition, 3,* 121-139.

Lucangeli, D., Cornoldi, C., & Tellarini, M. (1998). Metacognition and learning disabilities in mathematics. In T.E. Scruggs & M.A. Mastropieri (Eds.), *Advances in learning and behavioural disabilities* (pp.219-244). Greenwich: JAI Press Inc.

McCloskey, M., Macaruso, P. (1995). Representing and using numerical information. *American Psychologist, 50,* 351-363.

Meltzer, L., Roditi, B., Houser, R.F.,& Perlman, M. (1998). Perceptions of academic strategies and competence in students with learning disabilities. *Journal of Learning Disabilities, 31,* 437-451.

Montague, M. (1997). Cognitive Strategy Instruction on Arithmetics for Students with Learning Disabilities. *Journal of Learning Disabilities, 30,* 164-177.

Montague, M. (1998). Research on Metacognition in Special Education. In T.E. Scruggs & M.A. Mastropieri (Eds.), *Advances in learning and behavioural disabilities* (pp.151-183). Greenwich: JAI Press Inc.

Mora, J., & Saldana, D. (1995). *Metacognitive assessment : An Intervention Oriented Instrument.* Paper presented at the VIIth European Conference on Developmental Psychology, Krakow.

Noel, M.P. (2000). La dyscalculie développementale : Un état de la question. In M.. Meseti,& X. Seron. *Neuropsychologie des troubles du calcul et du traitement des nombres* (pp. 59-84). Solal: Marseille.

Rittle-Johnson, B., Siegler, R.S., & Alibali, M.W. (2001). Developing conceptual understanding and procedural skill in mathematics: An iterative process. *Journal of Educational Psychology, 93,* 346-362.

Rourke, B.P., & Conway, J.A. (1997). Disorders of Arithmetics and Mathematical Reasoning: Perspectives from Neurology and Neuropsychology. *Journal of Learning Disorders, 30,* 34-45.

Shalev, R..S. Manor, O., Kerem, B., Ayali, M., Badichi, N., Friedlander, Y.., & Gross-Tsur, V. (2001). Developmental dyscalculia is a familial learning disability, *Journal of Learning Disabilities, 34,* 59-65.

Siegler, R.S. (1989). 'How domain-general and domain-specific knowledge interact to produce strategy choices.' *Merrill-Palmer Quarterly, 35,* 1-26.

Simons, P.R.J. (1996). Metacognition. In E. De Corte & F.E. Weinert (Eds.), *International Encyclopedia of Developmental and Instructional Psychology* (pp. 436-444). Oxford: Elsevier sience LTD.

Sowder, J. (1992). Estimation and number sense. In: D.A. Grouws (Ed.), *Handbook of research on arithmetics teaching and learning. A project of the National Council of Teachers of Arithmetics* (pp. 371-387). New York: Simon & Schuster Macmillan.

Swanson, H.L. (2000). Issues facing the field of learning disabilities. *Learning Disability Quarterly, 23,* 37-49.

Sweller, J. (1994). Cognitive Load Theory, learning difficulty and instructional design. *Learning and Instruction, 4,* 295-312.

Tobias, S., & Everson, H. (2000). Assessing metacognitive knowledge monitoring. In G. Schraw, & J.C. Impara (Eds.), *Issues in the measurement of metacognition* (pp. 147-222). Lincoln, NE: Buros Institute of Mental Measurements.

Van Lehn, K. (1990). *Mind bugs. The origins of procedural misconceptions.* Cambridge: MA: Massachussets Institute of Technology.

Veenman, M.V.J., Wilhelm, P., & Beishuizen, J.J. (2004). The relation between intellectual and metacognitive skills from a developmental perspective. *Learning and Instruction, 14*, 89-109.

Veenman, M.V.J., Prins, F.J., & Verheij, J. (2003). Learning Styles: Self-reports versus thinking aloud measures. *British Journal of Educational Psychology, 73*, 357-372.

Verschaffel, L. (1999). Realistic mathematical modeling and problem solving in the upper elementary school: Analysis and improvement. In J.H.M. Hamers, J.E.H. Van Luit & B. Csapo (Eds.), *Teaching and learning thinking skills. Contexts of learning.* (pp. 215-240). Lisse: Swets & Zeitlinger.

Winne, P.H.,& Perry, N.E. (2000). Measuring self-regulated learning. In M. Boekaerts, P.E. Pintrich,& M. Zeidner (Eds.), *Handbook of self-regulation* (pp. 531-566). San Diego: Academic Press.

Wong, B.Y.L. (1996). Metacognition and Learning Disabilities. (pp. 120-139). In. B.Y.L. Wong (Ed.), *The ABC's of Learning Disabilities.* California: Academic Press.

Acknowledgements: *This research was supported by the Stichting Integratie Gehandicapten (SIG), the Arteveldehogeschool Gent (studierichting logopedie) and the Centrum ter Bevordering van de Cognitieve Ontwikkeling (CeBCO), to whom the authors extend their thanks.*

5
THE RELATIONSHIP OVER TIME BETWEEN ACADEMIC PERFORMANCE AND BEHAVIOUR PROBLEMS IN YOUNG CHILDREN

Els Gadeyne, Pol Ghesquière & Patrick Onghena

Introduction

Even in the seventies and the eighties, several studies confirmed experiences that had been made in the field regarding the comorbidity of learning disabilities (LDs) and behaviour problems (BPs) in children (for reviews, see for example Bender & Smith, 1990; Kavale & Forness, 1996). More recently, Rock, Fessler and Church (1997) have stated that between 24 and 52% of the children with learning disabilities suffer from social, emotional and behavioural problems. Of the children experiencing serious emotional disturbance, about 38 to 75% are also learning disabled. These co-occurrences are clearly above the expected rate if LDs and BPs were independent. The group of children having both learning and behaviour problems seems extremely vulnerable to a variety of poor outcomes onto adulthood (Rock et al., 1997).

Having a closer look at the type of problem behaviour that is exposed by children with learning disabilities, the literature points out that it are especially attention problems and externalising problem behaviour (Ghesquière, Grietens, & Hellinckx, 1998; Hinshaw, 1992; Jorm, Share, Matthews, & Maclean, 1986; Sanson, Prior, & Smart, 1996; Shalev, Auerbach, & Gross-Tsur, 1995). Externalising problem behaviour refers to actions that are disturbing to the child's environment, such as disruptive classroom behaviour or aggressive behaviour. Problems regarding social competencies are often reported as well in children with learning disabilities. However, these problems are rarely studied from the scope of behaviour problems. They are mostly labelled in terms of social perception, social acceptance, or social skills (Bryan, 1989; Nabuzoka & Smith, 1995; Shridar & Vaughn, 2001; Vaughn, Hogan, Kouzekanani & Shapiro, 1990; Vaughn, McIntosh, Schumm, Haager, & Callwood, 1993a). Findings on internalising problem behaviour, such as withdrawn or depressed behaviour, are somewhat mixed. Some research suggests that it is mainly concurrent with arithmetic disabilities (Prior, Smart, Sanson, & Oberklaid, 1999; Shalev et al., 1995). Reading and spelling disabilities on the other hand are not mainly related to a specific type of BPs, but can co-occur with any manifestation of BPs (Haager & Vaughn, 1995; Prior et al., 1999; Sanson et al., 1996; Willcutt & Pennington, 2000).

When it becomes clear that different types of behaviour problems appear to be associated with learning disabilities, one wants to find out how these co-occurrences come into being. Rourke and Fuerst (1991, 1995) reviewed the literature to find evidence for the three following hypotheses: 1) LDs are causing BPs, 2) BPs are causing LDs, and 3) LDs and BPs are both being caused by one or more common factors. Other authors, like Morrison and Cosden (1997) or Sanson et al. (1996), add a fourth, a fifth or even a sixth pathway, which in our opinion can be viewed as combinations of the previous ones: 4) LDs and BPs are affecting each other simultaneously, 5) or circular, 6) or in combination with other risk factors.

In their reviews, Hinshaw (1992) and Cornwall and Bawden (1992) conclude that most of the studies point into the direction of externalising BPs - particularly ADHD - being present (long) before academic achievement is formalised and thus before a specific reading disability or underachievement becomes prominent (see also more recent studies like Fergusson & Lynskey, 1997; Rabiner & Coie, 2000). In general, BPs seem to be a better predictor of LDs rather than the reverse (Prior et al., 1999). This relates to our causal hypotheses 2 and 3. A reading disability or reading underachievement on itself for example does not have to lead to any secondary BPs (cf. hypothesis 1; Cornwall & Bawden, 1992; Fergusson & Horwood, 1992; Fergusson & Lynskey, 1997; Klicpera & Schabmann, 1993; Sanson et al., 1996).

Looking at specific manifestations of BPs, attention problems show to be directly related to and predictive of LDs when relevant variables in the child and it's environment are taken into account (Rabiner & Coie, 2000). Externalising problem behaviour seems to be indirectly related to/predictive of LDs through its high comorbidity with ADHD (Beitchman & Young, 1997; Frick et al., 1991; Smart, Sanson, & Prior, 1996). The findings on internalising problem behaviour causing LDs are less abundant and not equivocal (Hinshaw, 1992). In their meta-analysis, Horn and Packard (1985) found internalising problem behaviour, together with attention problems, to be the best single behavioural predictors for reading achievement (see also Vaughn, Zaragoza, Hogan & Walker, 1993b, for reading as well as mathematics). Other studies though do not show the predictive value of internalising problem behaviour (McGee, Williams, Share, Anderson, & Silva, 1986; Prior et al., 1999; Vaughn et al., 1990).

Reviewing the literature thus far, we noticed that the existing research chiefly focuses on reading disabilities or dyslexia, and sometimes lacks a proper refinement of BPs as well. Second, with regard to the problem of prediction, most of the studies are cross-sectional, and hence not appropriate to make causal inferences. Of the longitudinal studies, the majority started when a sample of children with learning disabilities could be identified, say in third grade. Yet, it is interesting to start assessing the behaviour *before* academic learning becomes formalised in the primary school years. It should enable the researcher to detect whether behaviour problems already existed at the very beginning or even prior to failing primary school experiences of children, and to see how children evolve from then on in both areas. Thus we set up a longitudinal study to assess the *dynamic* relationships between learning and behaviour problems over a period of time. Specifically, we aimed to address the issue of refinement of the co-occurrence of LDs and BPs, and the issue of prediction. We wanted the study to start at kindergarten age at the latest. Here, no selection of children with learning problems or disabilities could be made yet. Since the study had to make an early start, and about two years were available for data collection, we focussed on young children. For practical and statistical reasons, we did not compose a subset of children with LD a posteriori either, but analysed the whole range of academic achievement and behaviour in their predictive and concurrent interrelationships. Literature points out that when studying the whole range of academic achievement (Rabiner & Coie, 2000), when studying LDs as a continuous variable (Fergusson & Lynskey, 1997), or when comparing specific learning disabled children with low achieving children (Ghesquière et al., 1998; Gresham, MacMillan & Bocian, 1996; Haager & Vaughn, 1995; Hinshaw, 1992; Smart et al., 1996; Tur-Kaspa & Bryan, 1995; Vaughn et al., 1990), mostly similar findings on comorbidity issues are obtained. Indeed, to date, it is not clear whether learning disabilities should be seen as one end of an academic performance continuum, or rather as a qualitatively distinct learning profile or disprofile. Although we felt supported in our approach by the literature, we must obviously remain cautious to extend our findings to the field of specific learning disabilities.

The research questions related to the issues above were formulated as follows:
1. Are behaviour problems a better predictor of low academic achievement in young children than the other way around? And does this hold for different academic skills?
2. Are attention problems and externalising behaviour problems the most important single precursors of learning problems in the behavioural domain? Does this hold for different academic skills as well? And what is the meaning of internalising behaviour problems and social behaviour problems in relation to academic achievement?

Method

Participants

Participants were 268 children who started third kindergarten in September 1998, and finished their second grade in 2001, at the end of our study. The children were recruited from 11 regular schools in the region Leuven - Tienen - Diest in Flanders, Belgium. The area is more or less rural, and very few children were foreign. Schools were randomly selected within the area. When the schools agreed to participate, the parents of all children residing in third kindergarten were asked for written consent. As a result, full or nearly full classes of children together with their parents and teachers were involved. Boys and girls were equally represented in the sample. The longitudinal design encompassed four waves: February-March in third kindergarten, December-February in first grade, May-June in first grade, and January-February in second grade. Although undoubtedly relevant to the topic, children who had to repeat a grade in the course of the investigation and those who made the transition to special education were not withheld in the study. They could not perform the same curriculum-based academic tests in the same wave as the other children, and we expect their individual academic progress and behaviour is influenced by more complex processes (e.g. the reference group they use to evaluate their achievement, the way they cope with grade retention or referral).

Measures

(Pre-)academic achievement. In the first wave, two tests for pre-academic skills that are widespread in the Netherlands were administered to groups of around 8 children at a time in third kindergarten. The first test measures pre-academic reading and spelling skills ('Language for Kindergarteners', Cito, 1996), the second one pre-academic math skills ('Sequencing', Cito, 1992). Due to time limitations, we only administered the second half of both tests, since these items are most closely related to reading, spelling and mathematical abilities in primary school. Our language construct is then composed of auditory analysis, sequencing and synthesis, of rhyming, and of familiarity with written language. The math construct is made up of comparing amounts, counting amounts, and familiarity with digits. An Alpha Coefficient of .89 respectively .81 is reported for the total administration forms halfway third kindergarten.

In the first and second grade, reading, spelling and math tests out of a Flemish fully standardised pupils monitoring system were administered to the children (Dudal, 1997, 1998, 2000, 2001). In the scope of this article, the reading achievement score will not be used. Its measure is statistically spoken less strong, and it is well correlated to spelling achievement. Spelling and math tests were administered to whole classes. In the spelling test, correct writing of letters (for halfway the first grade), words, and sentences was subsequently administered. For practical reasons, we had to make a selection of about half of the items out of the mathematical test, covering mainly classic calculating problems like ordering numbers, simple number work, algebraic problems, and simple calculations under time pressure. A KR20 coefficient of .92 is reported as a measure of internal consistency for the spelling as well as the mathematics test.

Behaviour problems. At each of the four waves, the parent and the teacher form of the Child Behavior Checklist (Achenbach, 1991a, 1991b) were presented to both parents and to the teacher of every child. In the problem behaviour part, 120 items concerning behavioural and emotional problems are to be rated on a three-point scale. Processing the answers results in eight syndrome scales: Withdrawn Behaviour, Somatic Complaints, Anxious/Depressed, Social Problems, Thought Problems, Attention Problems, Delinquent Behaviour, and Aggressive Behaviour. The first three syndromes can be combined into a score for Internalising Problem Behaviour; the last two compose a score for Externalising Problem Behaviour. Finally, also a Total Problem Score is calculated, composed of all marked problem items. In the present study, the raw scores on Internalising, Externalising, Attention Problems and Social Problems according to both parents or according to teachers were used. Achenbach discriminates between attention problems and externalising problem behaviour, which distinction was of particular interest to us. The syndrome of Thought Problems was left out here, because it only occurs at a very low rate. The instrument's reliability and validity is demonstrated in different ways (e.g. test-retest reliability, internal consistency, interrater consistency, long-term stability, external validity; Achenbach, 1991a, 1991b).

Data analysis

The data were analysed using the structural equation modelling program LISREL, version 8.30, providing maximum likelihood estimates of the model parameters (Jöreskog & Sörbom, 1999). This modelling technique allowed for the simultaneous analysis of the complex relationships between behaviour and achievement for several waves of data-collection. Due to school absences and no-return of parent questionnaires, depending on the variables under analysis the sample varied between 198 and 263 subjects.

The strategy advised by Jöreskog (1993) was used for model construction. The measurement model is created step by step, before the structural model is tested. In the presentation of the results, only the final models with the best measurement and structural relationships are discussed. The selection of goodness-of-fit indices reported underneath each model is indicative of model fit, model comparison, and model parsimony (Hox, 1999; Schumacker and Lomax, 1996).

Results

In the models presented beneath, the sensible and statistically relevant relationships between learning and behavioural variables over the four moments in time are depicted. Spelling and mathematical performance were analysed separately. For the behaviour variables, the behaviour as observed by teachers and the behaviour as observed by parents was studied successively. Indeed, the home and school behaviour of a child, or the perception of this behaviour through the eyes of the adults in question do not necessarily fully correspond to one another. Since behaviour as observed by the teachers appeared more strongly related to achievement than behaviour as observed by the parents, only these models are depicted here. The main differences with the parents' models will be pointed out at the end of the section. The teachers' models however have a drawback in that the measurement part as well as the structural relationships between the behaviour constructs turned out to be weaker than those of the parents' models, due to the single observed measure for behaviour. This also affected the overall fit indices. Nevertheless, our main interest goes to the connections between achievement and behaviour. Except for the behaviour measure, all other constructs bear upon at least two observed variables, and revealed no further difficulties in their measurement. By consequence, we will omit the measurement part in the models as to draw the reader's attention to the central issues of the study.

Figure 1 depicts the final models relating externalising problem behaviour to spelling and mathematics in the course of the four waves. We will explain it in detail, to make the reader familiar with the meaning of the models. In the middle of third kindergarten, there is no statistically significant connection between the presence of externalising problem behaviour as recorded by the teacher and pre-academic language abilities. The presence of externalising problem behaviour in third kindergarten however appears to be related to poor spelling achievement in the middle of the first grade, as is shown by the leftmost arrow. The fairly small simultaneous correlation between externalising and spelling in the middle of the first grade (it is -.11) can be explained by this former predictive relationship, and is therefore not added to the diagram. A similar process takes place between the constructs for externalising and spelling between halfway the first grade and the end of first grade, be it that the simultaneous correlation between spelling and externalising at the end of the first grade has increased a bit, up to -.21. Comparing the end of the first grade to the middle of the second grade, we see a somewhat different picture. We do not find a relationship in time between externalising and spelling, but both constructs show a simultaneous negative correlation of -.19 in the middle of the second grade. This correlation cannot be fully accounted for by the former interrelations between externalising and spelling, but exists in addition to them. All significant relationships point into the expected direction, since numbers with negative signs represent a relation between a high behaviour problem score and a poor academic achievement score. All numbers in the diagram that accompany arrows or curves are t-values, representing the strength of a relationship, unrelated to the scale of the measures. The numbers underneath the diagram represent statistically significant simultaneous correlations between the behaviour and the achievement construct right above. Below the model, a series of goodness-of-fit statistics is reported.

The model representing mathematical achievement and externalising problem behaviour according to the teachers does not show as many and as strong relationships. Only one predictive relationship turns out to be significant, and it points in the opposite direction: poor pre-academic mathematical abilities seem to have an impact on the presence of externalising problem behaviour in the middle of the first grade.

Figure 1
Longitudinal relationships between externalising problem behaviour according to the teachers and spelling (left) res. mathematics (right)

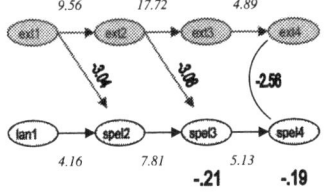
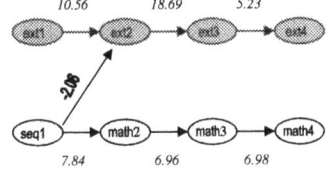

N=251, χ^2=139.78, df=94, p=.002, RMSEA=.044   N=263, χ^2=138.07, df=98, p=.005, RMSEA=.040
NFI=.93, NNFI=.97, CFI=.97, GFI=.93, AGFI=.91   NFI=.92, NNFI=.97, CFI=.98, GFI=.94, AGFI=.91

Legend. ext=externalising problem behaviour; lan=pre-academic language achievement; spel=spelling achievement; seq=pre-academic sequencing achievement; math=math achievement. Numbers accompanying arrows represent significant t-values; numbers underneath the ellipses represent significant correlations between the two latent variables right above.

The relationships between internalising problem behaviour and spelling (see Figure 2) are fewer and weaker than the ones between externalising problem behaviour and spelling. Connections between internalising problem behaviour and math on the other hand are more pronounced as far as the teacher's behavioural judgement is concerned. The directions of the predictive relationships are the same as in the models with externalising behaviour. One can also notice that sometimes concurrent relationships are not significant - like in the model with spelling -, while predictive relationships do exist.

Figure 2
Longitudinal relationships between internalising problem behaviour according to the teachers and spelling (left) res. mathematics (right)

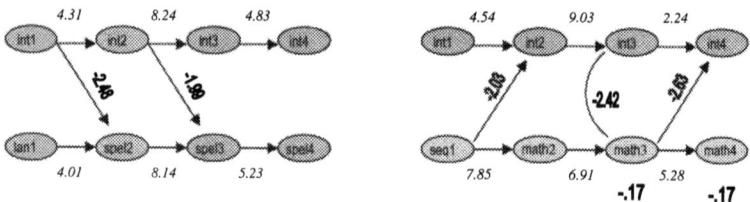

N=251, χ^2=125.75, df=97, p=.026, RMSEA=.034   N=263, χ^2=172.57, df=97, p=.000, RMSEA=.055
NFI=.92, NNFI=.98, CFI=.98, GFI=.94, AGFI=.92   NFI=.87, NNFI=.92, CFI=.94, GFI=.92, AGFI=.89

Legend. int=internalising problem behaviour; lan=pre-academic language achievement; spel=spelling achievement; seq=pre-academic sequencing achievement; math=math achievement. Numbers accompanying arrows represent significant t-values; numbers underneath the ellipses represent significant correlations between the two latent variables right above.

Next, we find multiple and strong concurrent and predictive relationships between spelling and attention problems according to teachers, and the connections only seem to get stronger over time (see Figure 3). At the end of the first grade for example, we find a concurrent correlation of -.39. The connection between mathematics and attention problems according to the teachers is as strong as the one between spelling and attention problems, but points into the opposite direction once more.

Figure 3
Longitudinal relationships between attention problem behaviour according to the teachers and spelling (left) res. mathematics (right)

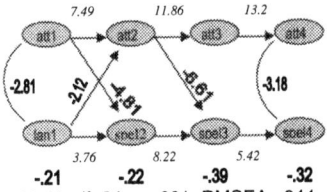 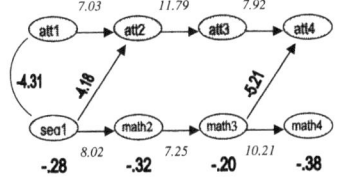

N=251, χ^2=140.41, df=94, p=.001, RMSEA=.044
NFI=.92, NNFI=.96, CFI=.97, GFI=.93, AGFI=.91

N=263, χ^2=215.79, df=98, p=.000, RMSEA=.068
NFI=.87, NNFI=.90, CFI=.92, GFI=.91, AGFI=.87

Legend. att=attention problem behaviour; lan=pre-academic language achievement; spel=spelling achievement; seq=pre-academic sequencing achievement; math=math achievement. Numbers accompanying arrows represent significant t-values; numbers underneath the ellipses represent significant correlations between the two latent variables right above.

Finally, after attention problems, social problems according to the teachers are related second best to spelling and math achievement, as can be seen in the concurrent and predictive relationships in Figure 4.

Figure 4
Longitudinal relationships between social problem behaviour according to the teachers and spelling (left) res. mathematics (right)

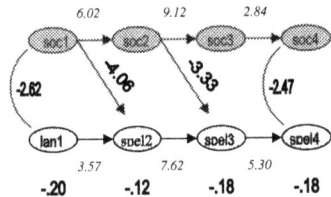 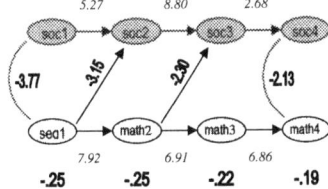

N=251, χ^2=131.77, df=93, p=.005, RMSEA=.041
NFI=.92, NNFI=.96, CFI=.97, GFI=.94, AGFI=.91

N=263, χ^2=120.96, df=95, p=.037, RMSEA=.032
NFI=.91, NNFI=.98, CFI=.98, GFI=.95, AGFI=.92

Legend. soc=social problem behaviour; lan=pre-academic language achievement; spel=spelling achievement; seq=pre-academic sequencing achievement; math=math achievement. Numbers accompanying arrows represent significant t-values; numbers underneath the ellipses represent significant correlations between the two latent variables right above.

In the models with the four behavioural ratings according to the parents, the concurrent as well as the predictive relationships are fewer and less strong. However, the existing connections always point in the same direction as in the teachers' models, and the overall fit-measures are somewhat better. This latter fact is due to the stronger measurement models (the behaviour constructs bear upon two indicators now, namely the judgement of mothers and fathers).

Discussion

To conclude, we can state that in young children from regular schools, some behaviour problems are clearly connected to academic achievement. The literature on learning disabilities suggests that the presence of behaviour problems seems to be a better predictor of learning problems than the other way around. However, these findings are mainly based on studies with reading disabled or dyslexic children. Our own results can confirm this viewpoint with regard to children with spelling problems. Going from third kindergarten to the middle of the first grade, and going from the middle to the end of the first grade, the presence of internalising, externalising, attention as well as social behaviour problems is predictive of low spelling achievement. Low spelling achievement on itself is not such a good predictor of subsequent behaviour problems. For internalising and externalising behaviour problems, no concurrent connections with spelling exist, but only predictive ones. For attention behaviour problems and social behaviour problems, concurrent and predictive connections are present simultaneously. Opposite to our expectations in hypothesis one however, poor pre-academic and academic math abilities are associated with increased behaviour problems over time. They do not seem to be affected by previous behaviour problems themselves. The strength of the relationships between behaviour problems and spelling respectively mathematics is more or less comparable.

Second, both academic skills are related the most to attention problems, and second most to social problems. Our study thus partly confirms the second hypothesis, since in addition to attention problems social problems rather than externalising behaviour problems are single best related to language as well as math subjects. In our study of the literature though, the social dimension was studied more in terms of social acceptance or social skills than in terms of social behaviour problems. Although judged an important area with regard to learning disabilities, few authors tried to rank it next to other behavioural domains.

Third, influences in time between learning and behaviour prove to add to potential concurrent connections. So their relationship changes over time, and is truly interactive of nature. We observed the biggest impact at the transition from kindergarten to primary school, but later effects were detected as well, and concurrent relations between learning and behaviour remain at least more or less stable throughout the three school years of interest.

Fourth, we find that teachers' views on behaviour problems in their pupils differ from those of the parents, and their observations are more relevant to the academic achievement of the children.

Fifth, since attention problems and social problems are already related to both pre-academic spelling and math achievement in the first wave of our study, it is impossible to say what causal mechanisms are responsible for them being connected.

Do children already have some feeling of school failure in their early kindergarten years, which results in poorer attention levels and problems with peers? Do early behaviour problems impede on the achievement of pre-academic goals in a significant way? Or should we look for child- or environment-related mechanisms causing both problems at the same time in the early years of life?

Last, our findings on the role of different kinds of behaviour problems in relation to academic achievement are quite in line with research findings on young children with specific learning disabilities. Indeed, children with learning disabilities form a part of our research sample, so they can be partly responsible for the outcomes. Still, we consider the results to be indicative of the continuum view on learning disabilities, at least with regard to behavioural functioning. Yet, several issues like child- and environmental covariates must be sorted out before clear causal statements are truly permitted.

Next to the conclusions, there are some methodological caveats to be considered. Because the report of both parents on the child's behaviour was used in the analyses, children of whom only one parent filled out the questionnaire or only one parent is present at home were not included in the analysis. This might cause selective drop-out, and could thereby be part of the explanation why behaviour as observed in the (two-parent) home is less related to academic achievement than behaviour as observed by the teachers, where no such drop-out is present. We verified this hypothesis by comparing the teacher-behaviour models with the mother-behaviour models (instead of with the parent-behaviour models). The relationships between behaviour problems and academic achievement did not ameliorate at all in the latter models. Thus the possibility of selective drop-out in view of the research interests is not supported.

Another issue pertains to the absence of a multivariate normal distribution of variables. In our study, there was no satisfying solution to this problem. Normalisation procedures did not succeed for all variables, and distribution-free estimation techniques require a much larger sample size. Since our main attention went to the parameter estimators, we decided to rely on normal distribution estimation techniques anyway, but one should be very cautious in interpreting other statistics.

Bibliography

Achenbach, T. M. (1991a). *Manual for the CBCL/4-18 and 1991 Profile*. Burlington, VT: University of Vermont, Department of Psychiatry.

Achenbach, T. M. (1991b). *Manual for the Teacher's Report Form and 1991 Profile*. Burlington, VT: University of Vermont, Department of Psychiatry.

Beitchman, J. H., & Young, A. (1997). Learning disorders with a special emphasis on reading disorders: a review of the past 10 years. *Journal of the American Academy of Child and Adolescent Psychiatry, 36*, 1020-1032.

Bender, W. N., & Smith, J. K. (1990). Classroom behavior of children and adolescents with learning disabilities: a meta-analysis. *Journal of Learning Disabilities, 23*, 298-305.

Bryan, T. (1989). IQ and learning disabilities: a perspective from research on social factors. *Journal of Learning Disabilities, 22*, 480-481.

Cornwall, A., & Bawden, H. N. (1992). Reading disabilities and aggression: a critical review. *Journal of Learning Disabilities, 25*, 281-288.

Dudal, P. (1997). *Leerlingvolgsysteem lezen: Toetsen 1-2-3. Basisboek* [Pupil's Monitoring System for Reading Grade 1-2-3]. Leuven: Vrije PMS-Centra & Garant.

Dudal, P. (1998). *Leerlingvolgsysteem spelling: Toetsen 1-2-3. Basisboek* [Pupil's Monitoring System for Spelling Grade 1-2-3]. Leuven: Vrije PMS-Centra & Garant.

Dudal, P. (2000). *Leerlingvolgsysteem wiskunde: Toetsen 1. Basisboek* [Pupil's Monitoring System for Mathematics Grade 1]. Leuven: Vrije Centra voor Leerlingenbegeleiding & Garant.

Fergusson, D. M., & Horwood, L. J. (1992). Attention deficit and reading achievement. *Journal of Child Psychology and Psychiatry, 33*, 375-385.

Fergusson, D. M., & Lynskey, M. T. (1997). Early reading difficulties and later conduct problems. *Journal of Child Psychology and Psychiatry, 38*, 899-907.

Frick, P. J., Kamphaus, R. W., Lahey, B. B., Loeber, R., Christ, M.-A. G., Hart, E. L., & Tannenbaum, L. E. (1991). Academic underachievement and the disruptive behavior disorders. *Journal of Consulting and Clinical Psychology, 59*, 289-294.

Ghesquière, P., Grietens, H., & Hellinckx, W. (1998). Prevalence of problem behavior in a general population sample of children with learning problems. *International Journal of Child & Welfare, 98*, 26-42.

Gresham, F. M., Mac Millan, D. L., & Bocian, K. M. (1996). Learning disabilities, low achievement, and mild mental retardation: more alike than different? *Journal of Learning Disabilities, 29*, 570-581.

Haager, D., & Vaughn, S. (1995). Parent, teacher, peer, and self-reports of the social competence of students with learning disabilities. *Journal of Learning Disabilities, 28*, 205-215, 231.

Hinshaw, S. (1992). Externalizing behavior problems and academic underachievement in childhood and adolescence: causal relationships and underlying mechanisms. *Psychological Bulletin, 111*, 127-155.

Horn, W. F., & Packard, T. (1985). Early identification of learning problems: a meta-analysis. *Journal of Educational Psychology, 77*, 597-607.

Hox, J.J. (1999). Principes en toepassing van structurele modellen [Principles and applications of structural models]. *Kind & Adolescent, 20*, 200-217.

Jöreskog, K. G. (1993). Testing Structural Equation Models. In K. A. Bollen & J. S. Long (Eds.), *Testing Structural Equation Models* (pp. 294-316). Newbury Park: Sage

Publications.
Jöreskog, K., & Sörbom, D. (1999). *Lisrel 8.30 and Prelis 2.30 (February 2000)*. Chicago: Scientific Software International, Inc.
Jorm, A. F., Share, D. L., Matthews, R., & Maclean, R. (1986). Behaviour problems in specific reading retarded and general reading backward children: a longitudinal study. *Journal of Child Psychology and Psychiatry, 27*, 33-43.
Kavale, K. A., & Forness, S. R. (1996). Social skill deficits and learning disabilities: a meta-analysis. *Journal of Learning Disabilities, 29*, 226-237.
Klicpera, C., & Schabmann, A. (1993). Die Häufigkeit von emotionalen Problemen und Verhaltensauffälligkeiten im Unterricht und der Zusammenhang mit Lese- und Rechtschreibschwierigkeiten: Ergebnisse einer Längsschnittuntersuchung. *Praxis Der Kinderpsychologie Und Kinderpsychiatrie, 42*, 358-363.
Lomax, R. G. (1989). Covariance Structure Analysis: extensions and developments. *Advances in Social Science Methodology, 1*, 171-204.
McGee, R., Williams, S., Share, D. L., Anderson, J., & Silva, P. A. (1986). The relationship between specific reading retardation, general reading backwardness and behavioural problems in a large sample of Dunedin boys: a longitudinal study from five to eleven years. *Journal of Child Psychology and Psychiatry, 27*, 597-610.
Morrison, G. M., & Cosden, M. A. (1997). Risk, resilience, and adjustment of individuals with learning disabilities. *Learning Disability Quarterly, 20*, 43-60.
Nabuzoka, D., & Smith, P.K. (1995). Identification of expressions of emotions by children with and without learning disabilities. *Learning Disabilities Research and Practice, 10*, 91-101.
Ordenen [Sequencing]. (1992). Arnhem: Cito.
Prior, M., Smart, D., Sanson, A., & Oberklaid, F. (1999). Relationships between learning difficulties and psychological problems in preadolescent children from a longitudinal sample. *Journal of the American Academy of Child and Adolescent Psychiatry, 38*, 429-436.
Rabiner, D., & Coie, J. D. (2000). Early attention problems and children's reading achievement: a longitudinal investigation. *Journal of the American Academy of Child and Adolescent Psychiatry, 39*, 859-867.
Rock, E. E., Fessler, M. A., & Church, R. P. (1997). The concomitance of learning disabilities and emotional/behavioral disorders: a conceptual model. *Journal of Learning Disabilities, 30*, 245-263.
Rourke, B. P., & Fuerst, D. R. (1991). *Learning Disabilities and Psychosocial Functioning. A neuropsychological perspective.* New York: The Guilford Press.
Rourke, B. P., & Fuerst, D. R. (1995). Cognitive processing, academic achievement, and psychosocial functioning: a neurodevelopmental perspective. In D. Cicchetti & D. J. Cohen (Eds.), *Developmental Psychopathology. Volume 1: Theory and Methods* (pp. 391-423). New York: John Wiley & Sons, Inc.
Sanson, A., Prior, M., & Smart, D. (1996). Reading disabilities with and without behaviour problems at 7-8 years: prediction from longitudinal data from infancy to 6 years. *Journal of Child Psychology and Psychiatry, 37*, 529-541.
Schumacker, R.E., & Lomax, R.G. (1996). *A beginner's guide to structural equation modelling.* Mahwah, N.J.: Lawrence Erlbaum Associates.Shalev, R. S., Auerbach, J., & Gross-Tsur, V. (1995). Developmental dyscalculia, behavioral and attentional aspects : a research note. *Journal of Child Psychology and Psychiatry, 36*, 1261-1268.
Shridar, D., & Vaughn, S. (2001). Social functioning of students with learning disabilities. In D.P. Hallagan & B.K. Keogh (Eds.), *Research and global perspectives in*

learning disabilities (pp. 65-91). Mahwah, N.J.: Lawrence Erlbaum Associates.

Smart, D., Sanson, A., & Prior, M. (1996). Connections between reading disability and behavior problems: testing temporal and causal hypotheses. *Journal of Abnormal Child Psychology, 24,* 363-383.

Taal voor Kleuters [Language for Kindergarteners]. (1996). Arnhem: Cito.

Tur-Kaspa, H., & Bryan, T. (1995). Teachers' ratings of the social competence and school adjustment of students with LD in elementary and junior high school. *Journal of Learning Disabilities, 28,* 44-52.

Vaughn, S., Hogan, A., Kouzekanani, K., & Shapiro, S. (1990). Peer acceptance, self-perceptions, and social skills of learning disabled students prior to identification. *Journal of Educational Psychology, 82,* 101-106.

Vaughn, S., McIntosh, R., Schumm, J.S., Haager, D., & Callwood, D. (1993a). Social status, peer acceptance, and reciprocal friendships revisited. *Learning Disabilities Research and Practice, 8,* 82-88.

Vaughn, S., Zaragoza, N., Hogan, A., & Walker, J. (1993b). A four-year longitudinal investigation of the social skills and behavior problems of students with learning disabilities. *Journal of Learning Disabilities, 26,* 404-412.

Willcutt, E. G., & Pennington, B. F. (2000). Psychiatric comorbidity in children and adolescents with reading disability. *Journal of Child Psychology and Psychiatry and Allied Disciplines, 41,* 1039-1048.

Acknowledgements: *The present study was supported in part by the Foundation for Learning Disabilities, Flanders, Belgium.*

PART II

INTERVENTION AND INSTRUCTION METHODS

6
EARLY LITERACY INTERVENTION: WHO BENEFITS AND WHO DOES NOT?

Helen Whiteley, Chris Smith, Mark Godwin and Suzanne Oakley

Introduction

There is an abundance of evidence linking phonological processing skills to success in learning to read. These skills include phonological awareness, phonological short-term memory and ease of access to phonological information from long-term memory. For example, many years of research have shown that the ability to decode print is closely linked to an ability to segment and manipulate the sounds within spoken words (e.g. Bradley & Bryant, 1983; Muter, Hulme, Snowling & Taylor 1997; Seymour 1997). This field of evidence underpins the Phonological Processing Deficit (PPD) hypothesis of dyslexia (e.g. Stanovich 1988, 1998), which predicts that reading difficulties will be associated with deficits in phonological processing skills.

Research into the links between phonological processing and literacy development has led to the publication of several early screening packages (e.g. The Cognitive Profiling System (CoPS) (Singleton & Thomas, 1994); the Dyslexia Early Screening Test (DEST) (Nicolson & Fawcett, 1996)) and early intervention packages (e.g. Sound Linkage (Hatcher, 1994); Launch into Reading Success (Ottley & Bennett, 1997)). The development of early screening tools for use with pre-readers to identify those 'at-risk' of reading difficulties allows the possibility of avoiding failure and all that goes with it.

On the basis of data from group comparisons, there is substantial evidence for the effectiveness of interventions based upon the systematic development of phonological awareness skills, especially when coupled with the training of literacy skills (e.g. Hatcher, Hulme & Ellis, 1994). However, within a group of children for whom learning to read poses significant difficulties, there inevitably will be a number of children for whom the intervention has little effect. These children are described as 'treatment resisters' and are a recognised cause for concern (Blachman, 1994; Torgesen & Davis, 1996). An alternative term adopted here by the authors is 'non-beneficiaries'.

Very few intervention studies have considered both children who are successful following training and those who fail to succeed. Most work in this area has been carried out by Torgesen and his colleagues. Torgesen, Morgan & Davies (1992), for example, found that 30% of their at-risk group showed no measurable growth in phonological awareness following an 8 week training period.

To date, reading research has been successful in providing help for many children experiencing, or at-risk of experiencing, reading problems. However, the existence of non-beneficiaries poses an, as yet, unresolved challenge to the field. While the PPD hypothesis continues to reflect the predominant view in the field that phonological processing difficulties are the key factor underlying literacy problems, alternative theories expand this view in ways which may aid our understanding of why some children fail to benefit from purely phonological interventions. One theory offering this potential is the Dyslexic Automatisation Deficit (DAD) Hypothesis (Nicolson & Fawcett, 1995).

The DAD hypothesis attempts to account for not only phonological problems in dyslexia, but also a range of non-phonological problems which often accompany dyslexic difficulties, e.g. distractibility and clumsiness. Nicolson and Fawcett propose that developmental dyslexia reflects problems with the automatisation of a range of skills including phonological, motor and balance skills. This raises the possibility that while some children may have predominantly phonological skills deficits, others may have a broader range of difficulties across both primitive skills and phonological processing skills. The DAD hypothesis raises the possibility that children with a range of deficits may appear as non-beneficiaries when purely phonological interventions are used.

The key aim of the project reported here is to identify the characteristics which differentiate non-beneficiaries from those children who do benefit from solely phonologically based interventions. A better understanding of the characteristics of non-beneficiaries will support the development of more effective tools for early screening and intervention.

This paper reports the first two years of the project which is a three-year longitudinal study. Children were screened in Reception class (minimum age 4:6) to identify those at-risk of literacy problems. Matched groups of at-risk and not at-risk children were identified and detailed cognitive-linguistic profiles were compiled for each child. A fifteen week phonologically based intervention was implemented with all of the at-risk children (in school Year 1). Following this, all children were assessed to ascertain their progress with reading and spelling. A group of beneficiaries and non-beneficiaries were identified and their profiles were examined to identify any characteristics which may distinguish between the two groups.

Method

Participants

All children participating in this study were in Reception class and attended schools in the Blackpool Education Authority. Twelve schools (432 children) were visited for the initial screening procedure. Ninety children were identified as At-risk and a Control group of ninety children was identified from the same schools. The At-risk and Control group children were matched for age, eligibility for free school meals, general ability (measured by Raven's Coloured Matrices) and all children were from the autumn intake. The At-risk group comprised 52 boys and 38 girls and the Control group 47 boys and 43 girls.

Design

A longitudinal design was adopted with children being followed through from Reception class to the end of school Year 2 (this chapter reports on work up to the end of school Year 1). It should be noted that, although children were assigned to one of two groups: At-risk (of literacy difficulties) or Control (not at-risk of difficulties), *the entire* At-risk group received the intervention. This study was not designed primarily to test the effectiveness of the intervention used: the primary aim was to identify beneficiaries and non-beneficiaries following the use of an established intervention.

Materials

The Dyslexia Early Screening Test (DEST, Nicolson & Fawcett, 1996) was used to identify children at-risk of literacy problems. This comprises ten subtests: rapid naming, bead threading, phonological discrimination, postural stability, rhyme detection, digit span, digit naming, letter naming, sound order and shape copying. Raven's Coloured Progressive Matrices was used to match At-risk and Control children on general non-verbal ability (Raven, 1962).

Pre- and post-intervention assessment measures were: the Wide Range Achievement Test (WRAT3) (Wilkinson, 1994) to measure reading and spelling; the Graded Nonword Reading test (Snowling, Stothard, & McLean, 1996); the Phonological Abilities Test (PAT: 8 subtests comprising rhyme detection, rhyme production, word completion (syllables and phonemes), phoneme deletion (beginning and end), speech rate and letter knowledge) (Muter, Hulme & Snowling, 1997).

Cognitive-linguistic profiling measures were: Rapid Naming (RAN) Tests for Objects, Colours, Letters and Numbers (Denckla & Rudel, 1976); the Wide Range Assessment of Memory and Learning (WRAML, Sheslow & Adams, 1990); the Test of Word Knowledge (TOWK, Wiig & Secord, 1991).

The intervention package used was the Launch Into Reading Success (LIRS, Ottley & Bennett, 1997). This involved daily sessions of twenty minutes over a period of 15 weeks. The package focuses on the systematic development of phonological awareness skills through game-like activities. These are followed by activities which link the sounds in words to their representative printed letters.

Procedure

Twelve schools were visited. Whole classes of Reception children were screened individually using the DEST and the Raven's Coloured Matrices. Children were identified as at-risk of literacy problems or not at-risk on the basis of their DEST scores and were assigned to At-risk and Control groups accordingly. The children in the two groups were matched for Raven's score and age within schools. When they moved into Year 1, all children completed a series of profiling measures and pre-assessment tests as listed under the Materials section. In Year 1 Term 2, all of the At-risk children took part in the LIRs intervention programme for a period of 15 weeks for 20 minutes on each school day. The intervention package was delivered by research workers to groups of a maximum of six children.

In Year 1 Term 3, all children were reassessed with the WRAT reading and spelling, Nonword reading and PAT measures to establish their progress. Measures of progress were used to identify beneficiaries and non-beneficiaries within the At-risk group.

Results

Of the 432 children screened with the DEST, 90 (20.8%) were identified as at-risk of literacy difficulties. Analyses comparing the performance of the At-risk group and the Control group on the 10 DEST subtests confirmed highly significant differences on all the subtests except the postural stability test which did not significantly differentiate between the two groups.

Pre-intervention assessment measures confirmed significant differences between the At-risk and Control groups. The Control group scored more highly on WRAT reading, WRAT spelling, Nonword reading, and all PAT measures except rhyme production and rhyme detection. The relatively good performance of the At-risk group on measures of rhyme most likely reflects the current focus on rhyme activities in classroom teaching practice.

Cognitive-linguistic profiling measures also revealed a clear pattern of differences between the At-risk and the Control groups pre-intervention. The At-risk group was slower and less accurate on each of the four RAN tasks, the WRAML and the TOWK.

Seventy-five children completed the 15 week intervention. (Because Blackpool schools have a high transience rate, 15 At-risk children had moved to different schools between the start and end of the intervention.) Post-intervention assessment measures demonstrated a continuing advantage for the Control over the At-risk children on WRAT reading and spelling, Nonword reading and all PAT measures, including rhyme detection and rhyme production where a greater improvement by the Control group took them ahead of the At-risk group. Profiling measures were not repeated at this stage of the study.

An assessment of progress for the At-risk and Control groups revealed significant improvements in WRAT reading and spelling, Nonword reading and in all PAT measures for each of the At-risk and Control groups.

Whilst the At-risk group as a whole had benefited, it was clear that a number of individuals within the group had failed to make any real progress. In order to identify beneficiaries and non-beneficiaries within the group, changes in performance on WRAT standard reading scores were taken as a primary indicator of progress and changes in WRAT standard spelling scores were taken as a secondary indicator. Overall, 25 (33%) of the 75 At-risk children were classed as non-beneficiaries and 47 as beneficiaries. Just three children could not be classed as either beneficiaries or non-beneficiaries due to very mixed profiles.

Analyses comparing beneficiaries and non-beneficiaries at Time 1 revealed no differences for WRAT reading, WRAT spelling, Nonword reading, all PAT measures, Raven's Matrices, all WRAML measures and TOWK measures. The only significant differences between the groups of beneficiaries and non-beneficiaries were on the DEST subtests of phonological discrimination (mean for beneficiaries = 5.02 out of 9 correct and for non-beneficiaries = 3.84, t=2.608, p=0.011) and postural stability (mean for beneficiaries =2.28 and for non-beneficiaries = 3.72 where a higher score indicates less stability, t=2.488, p=0.015) and on the total score for the RAN object naming test (mean time for beneficiaries = 129.74 seconds and for the non-beneficiaries = 98.64 seconds, t=2.85, p=0.006) where, surprisingly, non-beneficiaries were more efficient. Absences did not predict non-beneficiaries (many had no absences).

Discussion

This study was designed to examine the characteristics which differentiate between children who benefit and children who fail to benefit from a typical phonologically-based literacy intervention. The At-risk group made significant improvement overall on all of the assessment measures of WRAT reading and spelling, Nonword reading and all of the PAT subtests.

Consistent with previous research (e.g. Torgesen et al., 1992) an examination of individual profiles within the At-risk group revealed a number of children (33% in this instance) who had made little or no progress in spite of the intensity of the intervention. An examination of absence data confirmed that the lack of progress could not simply be explained in terms of poor attendance at school. Further analysis revealed interesting differences between the groups of beneficiaries and non-beneficiaries. Not surprisingly, and consistent with the PPD hypothesis (Stanovich, 1988; 1998), the non-beneficiaries as a group performed more poorly on the test of phonological discrimination (from the DEST). This test requires children to listen to pairs of words and decide whether they are exactly the same, for example, *bad* and *dad*, *cub* and *cup*. A poor performance on this test suggests that the non-beneficiaries had even more severe problems with analysing speech into its constituent sounds than the remainder of the At-risk group. Thus, it may be that the non-beneficiaries have such severe deficits in phonological processing skills that they are unable to benefit from the small group intervention implemented here in spite of its relative intensity. It may be that for these children only one-to-one intervention taken at an even slower pace will be effective in addressing their literacy problems.

The second factor which discriminated between beneficiaries and non-beneficiaries as a group was postural stability, a subtest of the DEST which is designed to measure balance skills. This test is based on the proposal that specific reading difficulties have their origin in problems with the automatisation of a range of skills (Nicolson & Fawcett, 1995). The finding that non-beneficiaries are significantly poorer on postural stability than are the beneficiaries is consistent with the DAD hypothesis and suggests that perhaps the non-beneficiaries have a deficit in primitive skills (balance) in addition to their severe problems in the phonological domain. If this is the case, then a purely phonologically-based intervention would be unlikely to be effective.

The final factor which differentiated between the beneficiaries and the non-beneficiaries was the Rapid Naming for Objects (RAN). Whilst it was anticipated that non-beneficiaries would have poorer phonological processing and postural stability than beneficiaries, the RAN finding was contradictory to expectations. In line with previous findings (e.g. Denckla & Rudel, 1976), the At-risk group was significantly less efficient on all RAN measures than the Control group. Within the At-risk group, however, the non-beneficiaries were *more* efficient when asked to name a series of objects as quickly as possible. It is argued that the RAN tasks reflect speed of lexical access with good performance reflecting rapid access to lexical codes (Wolf & O'Brien, 2001). Although the non-beneficiaries were more efficient than the beneficiaries on the RAN Object naming, it is important to note that this superior performance was restricted to object naming and also that the At-risk group as a whole were significantly poorer on all RAN tests than the Control group. At this stage it is not possible to draw any conclusions about this pattern on the RAN. Further work will examine whether the advantage of non-beneficiaries on object naming reflects a visual/holistic learning style which may have impeded their ability to profit from the phonologically-based intervention. A visual learning style may have played a causal role in the children's reading problems; alternatively, it may reflect the adoption of a compensatory strategy as a consequence of severe phonological processing problems.

In summary, the most salient characteristics which distinguished between children who benefited and children who did not benefit from a phonologically based, 15-week daily intervention, were postural stability (DEST), phonological discrimination (DEST) and rapid naming of objects (RAN). While the first two findings sit well with previous research and theories of reading problems, the latter finding was unexpected and only further research will clarify exactly what role this factor may have to play in children's reduced ability to benefit from phonologically-based intervention. Further work in the current project will address this issue. Examinations of individual profile data for beneficiaries and non-beneficiaries will also be conducted to establish any salient profiles within the groups. This work will contribute to the identification of factors which can be used in the early detection of children at-risk of literacy difficulties and, in particular, which may be used to identify those in need of an intervention which tackles more than just phonological skills.

References

Blachman, B.A. (1994). What we have learned from longitudinal studies of phonological processing and reading, and some unanswered questions: A response to Torgesen, Wagner and Rashotte. *Journal of Learning Disabilities, 27 (5),* 287-291.

Bradley, L., & Bryant, P.E. (1983). Categorising sounds and learning to read: a causal connection. *Nature, 301,* 419-421.

Denckla, M.B. & Rudel, R.G. (1976). Naming of object drawings by dyslexic and other learning disabled children. *Brain & Language, 3,* 1-15.

Hatcher, P.J. (1994). *Sound Linkage: An Integrated Programme for Overcoming Reading Difficulties.* London: Whurr.

Hatcher, P.J., Hulme, C. & Ellis, W. (1994). Ameliorating early reading failure by integrating the teaching of reading and phonological skills: The phonological linkage hypothesis. *Child Development, 65,* 41-57.

Muter, V., Hulme, C. & Snowling, M. (1997). *Phonological Abilities Test.* The Psychological Corporation Limited: London.

Muter, V., Hulme, C., Snowling, M. & Taylor, S. (1997). Segmentation, not rhyming, predicts early progress in learning to read. *Journal of Experimental Child Psychology, 65 (3),* 370-396.

Nicolson, R.I. & Fawcett, A.J. (1995). Dyslexia is more than a phonological disability. *Dyslexia, 1,* 19-36.

Nicolson, R.I. & Fawcett, A.J. (1996). *The Dyslexia Early Screening Test.* The Psychological Corporation: London.

Ottley, P. & Bennett, L. (1997). *Launch into Reading Success.* The Psychological Corporation: London.

Raven, J.C. (1962). *Coloured Progressive Matrices.* H.K. Lewis: London.

Seymour, P.H.K. (1997). Foundations of orthographic development. In C.A. Perfetti, L. Rieben, & M. Fayol, (Eds.) *Learning to Spell: Research, Theory and Practice Across Languages.* LEA: London.

Sheslow, D. & Adams, W. (1990). *WRAML: Wide Range Achievement of Memory and Learning.* The Psychological Corporation: London

Singleton, C. & Thomas, K. (1994). Computerised screening for dyslexia. In C. Singleton (Ed), *Computers and Dyslexia.* Dyslexia computer resource centre, University of Hull.

Snowling, M. J., Stothard, S.E. & McLean, J. (1996). *Graded Nonword Reading Test.* Thames Valley Test Company: UK.

Stanovich, K.E. (1988). Explaining the differences between the dyslexic and the garden-variety poor reader. The phonological-core variable-difference model. *Journal of Learning Disabilities, 21* (10), 590-604.

Stanovich, K.E. (1998). Refining the phonological core deficit model. *Child Psychology and Psychiatry, 3* (1), 17-21.

Torgesen, J.K., Morgan, S.T. & Davis, C. (1992). Effects of two types of phonological awareness training on word learning in kindergarten children. *Journal of Educational Psychology, 84,* 364-370.

Wiig, E.H. & Secord, W. (1991). *TOWK: Test of Word Knowledge.* The Psychological Corporation: Kent, UK.

Wilkinson, G.S. (1994). *WRAT3: Wide Range Achievement Tests.* The Psychological Corporation: Kent, UK.

Wolf, M. (1997). A provisional, integrative account of phonological and naming-speed deficits in dyslexia: Implications for diagnosis and intervention. In B.A.

Blachman (Ed.), *Foundations of Reading Acquisition and Dyslexia.* LEA: London.

Wolf, M. & O'Brien, B. (2001). On issues of time, fluency and intervention. In A. Fawcett (Ed.), *Dyslexia: Theory and Good Practice.* Whurr: UK.

Acknowledgements: *The project currently being conducted by the authors is supported by a grant from the National Lottery Charities Board (grant number RB217511). The authors wish to thank Blackpool Education Authority and all of the participating schools for their helpful support throughout this project.*

7
INTERVENTION APPROACHES FOR LEARNING PROBLEMS IN LITERACY IN AUSTRALIA

*Christina E. van Kraayenoord, Mary Rohl
and Judith Rivalland*

Introduction

Governments in many countries around the world are concerned about the literacy achievements of their citizens with calls for the development of literacy standards, outcomes and benchmarks of performance. For example in Australia, the Commonwealth Government announced in 1991 that *"all children would read and write by Grade 3"* (Department of Education and Employment, 1991), and in 1998 the Commonwealth, state and territory Ministers endorsed the right of "literacy for all" and announced the goal *"... that every student should be numerate and be able to read, write and spell at an appropriate level"* (Department of Employment, Education, Training and Youth Affairs, 1998, p. 9).

In Australia these calls have lead to the introduction of mandated testing and in countries such as the United States (US), there has been an increase in the use of testing with associated claims that such measures will improve accountability of education systems and teachers as they strive to reach the goals of improved achievement. In Australia, standardized tests of reading, spelling and writing have been mandated by state and territory governments in Grades 3, 5 and 7. Student performances are reported in comparison to benchmarks and recorded for the parents on their child's Student Report Card. In many states and territories school performances are also published in newspapers in the name of being accountable to the public (van Kraayenoord, 2003).

At the same time as these initiatives are occurring in Australia and elsewhere around the globe, there have been calls for an examination of reading instruction and renewed debate about how students should be taught. In the US some of the questions related to reading instruction have been reduced to questions related to the Great Debate (Chall, 1967; Anderson, 1998). In Australia there has been a much broader discussion with examinations of how literacy itself (rather than just reading) is conceptualized. These discussions about how literacy can be understood have led to other discussions about the skills that need to be developed given the different conceptualizations, the purposes and audiences for literacy, as well as discussions about how literacy might be taught and assessed (Comber, 1998; Luke & Freebody, 1999; Turbill, 2002).

One of the results of the emphasis on assessment, in particular testing, has been the renewed attention on those students who do not do well in literacy. Commonly in English-speaking countries worldwide, students who struggle to acquire literacy knowledge and skills and who perform poorly on such tests are students with learning problems, those with disabilities, indigenous students, and those for whom English is a second or third language. With respect to students with learning problems in Australia, these students may be referred to as students with learning difficulties or learning disabilities, although the most commonly used term is learning difficulties.

An examination of the US literature in relation to the provision of literacy instruction for these groups reveals a number of emphases and associated developments. First, there has been an emphasis on the prevention of learning problems in literacy with attention being given to preschool programs and to enhanced instruction in the first year of schooling (Gaffney, 1998; Klesius & Griffith, 1996: Mandel Morrow & O'Connor, 1995; Pressley, et al., 2001). Second, there has been an emphasis on intervention for those who do not respond to the preventive efforts and initial instruction (Hiebert & Taylor, 2000; Lyons & Beaver, 1995; Morris, Ervin & Conrad, 1996; Pikulski, 1994).

In contrast to the US, there has been little research in Australia related to the nature of literacy instruction for students at-risk of learning problems or those with learning problems. It was in this context that in 1998, the Commonwealth government of Australia called for proposals for an Australian-wide study of policies and practices related to students with learning problems to be undertaken. A team of academics from four universities tendered for and was awarded the contract. One aim of the study was to "map" the programs and strategies used to teach and intervene in literacy in Australian classrooms with students with learning problems. The researchers were asked to focus on students at the primary and middle years levels of schooling. In essence this meant that the researchers were asked to provide a national picture of how primary and middle school students with learning problems were supported in schools. The study, entitled: "Mapping the Territory - Primary Students with Learning Difficulties: Literacy and Numeracy" was conducted by Louden, Chan, Elkins, Greaves, House, Milton, Nichols, Rohl, Rivalland and van Kraayenoord (2000).

Participants and data collection strategies

Several data collection strategies were used to obtain information related to nine issues identified by the researchers in the larger study. In this section reference is made to the participants and data collection strategies used to examine one of the issues, namely that of the programs and strategies employed to provide teaching and intervention support to those with learning problems in literacy.

The first group of participants consists of key individuals and policy officers in the state, Catholic, and independent school system authorities in each state and territory of Australia. Twenty-four interviews were undertaken. The interviews were conducted either face-to-face or by telephone. Participants were asked to comment on a number of issues referred to in an interview proforma sent to the participants prior to the interview. Participants were specifically asked to identify the programs and strategies that they included in their official handbooks and guidelines for teachers and/or that they were aware were being used in schools to support students with learning problems in literacy. Some interviews were tape-recorded and later transcribed, while others were recorded in long-hand by the researchers. All interview data were then coded by two of the researchers, Rivalland and House. In coding the interview data themes mentioned across the interviews and the specific details of the various programs and strategies were identified. Further information regarding the coding and analysis procedures for these interviews can be found in Rivalland and House (2000, Volume 2 of Louden, et al., 2000).

The second data collection strategy involved obtaining documents, such as curriculum handbooks, syllabi, and teacher guidebooks developed by the education system authorities in each state and territory. These documents were systematically examined to identify the various programs and strategies used in teaching and intervention. Further details regarding the document analyses can be found in Rivalland and House (2000, Volume 2 of Louden, et al., 2000).

The third data collection strategy was the construction of a series of school case studies. The case studies were undertaken in 20 schools in five states, namely New South Wales, Queensland, South Australia, Victoria and Western Australia. School selection was guided by the tender brief and by the belief that the case studies should represent some aspect of excellence in their provision for children with learning problems. Recommendations came from school systems, professional colleagues of the researchers, and from among the team of researchers. The final set of 20 case study schools was also selected to represent a cross-section of school systems, locations, school sizes, and the socio-economic circumstances of school communities (For further details see Volume 3 of Louden, et al., 2000).

Each case study represented the equivalent of approximately one week of full-time data collection in a school. The data collection involved classroom observations and other teaching observations (e.g., individual tutoring) of selected students with learning problems, document collection, and interviews with the principals, classroom teachers, Support Teachers-Learning Difficulties, parents and the students themselves. Written field notes, verbatim notes, and transcripts of interviews were developed. Case studies were written to a common format and the first draft of each case study was reviewed by another member of the research team. Each case study was then revised by the individual researcher(s)/author(s) and returned to the schools to check for accuracy.

In constructing the information reported in the results section below we have drawn on all three data sources.

Results

In this section of the chapter we report the findings of our investigation concerned with the range and nature of the teaching and intervention approaches related to literacy offered in schools. We refer to: complexity and making choices, and to first, second, and third wave teaching.

Complexity and making choices

Our findings exposed the very complex and diverse ways in which the different education systems supported students who have difficulty with literacy. Most state or territory education systems provided specific curriculum documents which gave guidance to teachers and all systems also suggested the use of a range of programs and approaches for teaching and intervention. Australian teachers have choice in selecting the programs and approaches for working with students in literacy; however in our study we found that often whole schools or grade levels (e.g., junior school) adopted a particular program.

First wave teaching

In the report *"Mapping the Territory"* Louden et al. (2000) used the phrase "waves of teaching" and it is important to understand the nature of the related terms: first, second and third wave teaching. First wave teaching refers to literacy instruction offered to all students in the first few years of schooling and will be discussed next.

In examining the case study schools the majority of teaching in the first years of schooling emphasised structured explicit teaching of literacy, as many teachers and administrators saw this as a means of helping to prevent literacy problems. Three well-known programs observed as part of first wave teaching were: The Early Years Literacy Program (Crevola & Hill, cited in Hill, 1997), School-Wide Early Language and Literacy (SWELL) (Center, Freeman & Robertson, 1998), and First Steps which was developed by the Education Department of Western Australia (www.ecurl.com.au/src/Firststep/backgrnd.html). These three programs or derivations of them are commonly found in many Australian classrooms. They are discussed briefly below.

The Early Years Literacy Program

The Early Years Literacy program is a whole school literacy program developed in the state of Victoria and which has spread throughout Australia. It is based on the work Crevola and Hill (1998) and Hill and Crevola (1998) and has several essential features, namely a daily focused two hour literacy session, planned home/school liaison, an early years' school coordinator and a whole school commitment. During the literacy session, activities include reading to, and writing with students, language experience, shared reading and writing, guided reading and writing, and independent reading. Following a three-step process these activities move from whole-class teaching to small group work with a teacher or independently, and then back to whole-class sharing of what has been learned.

School-Wide Early Literacy and Language

School-Wide Early Language and Literacy (SWELL) was developed in New South Wales (Center & Freeman, 1997) and focuses on beginning reading (Kindergarten to Year 3 in the New South Wales school system). Based on the US program Success for All (Slavin, et al. 1994) SWELL is a highly structured program that uses explicit teaching of sequenced skills, in particular phonemic awareness and phonological skills. During the first three to six months the Emergent Literacy Program focuses on developing the essential prerequisites to reading. The next period, the Becoming Literate Program focuses on developing and extending the acquisition of literacy. The next stage is Towards Literacy Competence which focuses on the teaching of listening and reading comprehension activities. Lessons in the three stages involve modelling and talk about the task, structured group work, whole class teaching and review. Typically the activities involve reading, writing, speaking and listening.

First Steps

First Steps was developed by the Education Department of Western Australia (www.ecurl.com.au/src/Firststep/backgrnd.html). It comprises professional development and materials that assist teachers in teaching reading, writing, spelling and oral language. First Steps provides developmental continua that identify indicators of progress in these areas. The indicators provide teachers with a tool to map students' progress and help them select appropriate teaching strategies. First Steps also suggests that teachers use a range of strategies which are selected as appropriate for learners at different levels of development and suited to the students' literacy needs. At one of the case study schools where First Steps was observed in use teachers employed teaching strategies such as: modelled writing, "have-a-go" (note)pads for spelling, genre frameworks, sentence frames, collaborative learning and various metacognitive strategies.

In addition, with respect to first wave teaching, our study found that schools were using commercial programs such as THRASS and Letterland. These are described below.

Teaching Handwriting Reading and Spelling Skills (THRASS)

The THRASS program *(www.thrass.com)* is used to teach phonics through a whole-picture key word method. The program focuses on teaching phonemes and graphemes used in word decoding and encoding in reading and writing. The teacher uses various resources (e.g., charts, audiotapes, CDs) to teach students skills including phonemic and graphemic awareness, segmenting and blending phonemes, naming letters, pronouncing phonemes, recognizing and using graphemes in spelling, developing whole-word awareness, and using word analogy skills.

Letterland

Letterland (www.letterland.com) is a system for teaching students to read, write and spell using pictograms. Teachers use Letterland materials, such as charts, cards, audiotapes, and videotapes to teach skills including phonemic awareness, sound-symbol associations, letter formation, blending and segmenting skills, and sentence building.

Many other schools had developed their own programs that were often eclectic in nature, and while some of these programs included commercial programs these played a relatively minor role in the total program. The schools that had created their own programs argued that they were better able to tailor their program for their own students and school community. Sometimes the literacy programs involved specific patterns of organization as well as particular content and delivery. For example, one case study school employed multi-age groups with several teachers and teacher aides.

Second wave teaching

In all of the case study schools there was some form of early intervention program for children whose literacy progress was of concern. This is known as second wave teaching. Many of these programs were devised by the schools themselves, although some programs comprised a "package", in that the program content and/or format were prescribed.

An examination of the school-developed programs indicated that many of them included an oral language component. This was particularly the case where there were students from non-English speaking backgrounds or who spoke Standard English as a second dialect. These children were mainly children of Aboriginal or Torres Strait Islander decent. Several of these programs also used an eclectic mix of Reading Recovery (see below) and First Steps (see above) with an emphasis on one-to-one teaching. Many of these school-created intervention programs delivered instruction with students organized into ability groups for parts of the lessons.

In each of the three Victorian case study schools, Reading Recovery formed part of the integrated whole school early literacy strategy. That is, Reading Recovery was seen as integral to the strategy which involved the Early Years of Literacy Program (see above) as first wave teaching. Some of the case study schools had adapted certain principles of Reading Recovery to suit their own particular needs and available resources.

Reading Recovery

Perhaps the most well-known early intervention for students with learning problems in literacy is Reading Recovery (Clay, 1993). Reading Recovery is used in all the states of Australia, although it is most widely used in New South Wales and Victoria. Reading Recovery is aimed at children who have the poorest performance in reading after one year of instruction. The program provides accelerated learning so that students can catch up with their peers who are performing at the average of their class. Typically this takes 12 to 20 weeks. If students do not achieve satisfactorily in the program they are removed and offered alternative support. The program is intensive with short lessons of 30 minutes daily.

Summary of first and second wave teaching

A feature of most of the literacy programs outlined in the study shows that they consisted of a wide variety of activities that involved the reading and writing of connected text. In most, but not all schools, the second wave teaching took the form of structured, small group or individual direct-teaching sessions which targeted letter and sight word recognition and oral language, with particular emphasis on phonological awareness.

While we observed programs in schools that had been nominated by education department sources as "successful", it is likely that some were more effective than others. However, the researchers had no evidence about this issue and it was not the aim of the study to compare them. As Wasik and Slavin (1993) point out, it is difficult to compare the effectiveness of programs when they differ in terms of reading models, tutorial methods, curricula, duration and integration with the regular classroom context, in addition to encompassing a diverse array of populations, procedures and outcome measures.

Third wave teaching

Most of the case study schools had put an emphasis on intervention in the first two years of schooling and devoted a significant proportion of the resources to identifying and teaching children who were seen as at-risk of developing literacy problems. The Reading Recovery program, which requires one-to-one teaching by highly trained teachers on a daily basis, tied up large amounts of some schools' resources for a few children. Other early intervention programs observed in two of our case study schools could only be resourced for a limited number of weeks. In many circumstances, the schools chose to put most of their limited resources into early years' classroom intervention and classroom literacy programs as they saw these emphases as the most effective use of resources.

This channeling of resources into the early years meant however, that in some schools there were few resources left over for those children who, in spite of good first wave teaching and intensive early intervention or second wave teaching, still required ongoing, intensive support. In some of the schools, whilst the progress of middle and upper primary school students with literacy problems was regularly monitored, specialised services were not always available.

This appeared to be the case in one of the Catholic schools and also at least one of the non-Catholic schools.

Further, in contrast to the clearly articulated early intervention programs which usually contained a balance between the teaching of skills and practice in the reading and writing of connected text, some of the support programs for middle and upper primary school students focussed on just one aspect of literacy, such as decoding.

Several schools used direct instruction packages such as Spelling through Morphographs and Corrective Reading which are both discussed briefly below.

Spelling through Morphographs

Spelling through Morphographs is produced by the SRA/McGraw Hill Company in the United States for students in Grades 4 and up (www.sraonline.com/index.php/home/ curriculumsolutions/di/9). It teaches students to spell multisyllabic words using morphographic patterns by focusing on prefixes, suffixes and word bases, as well as other spelling rules. Following a Direct Instruction approach the teacher uses the structured lessons and activities from a Teachers' Manual and students use workbooks to complete practice exercises.

Corrective Reading

Corrective Reading is also produced by the SRA/McGraw Hill Company in the United States and comprises a series of sequenced lessons for students in Grades 4 to 12 who are reading one or more years below grade level (www.sraonline.com/index.php/home/ curriculumsolutions/di/9). The intensive, highly structured, teacher-directed lessons focus on decoding and/or comprehension. The lessons in decoding include developing students' accuracy, automaticity and fluency, while those in comprehension concentrate on developing students' comprehension, vocabulary, and reasoning.

One school combined Corrective Reading with a less formal guided reading program based on the strategy described in the First Steps Reading Resource Book (Education Department of Western Australia, 1994). Two distinct withdrawal programs were offered in one school where THRASS (see below) was used. Other schools that had resources available for this older age group chose to use the resources to employ additional personnel to work in classrooms as in-class support. For example, a Learning Support Teacher in one school and "Literacy teachers" in two rural schools were used to work alongside the teachers in regular classrooms. These specialist teachers were often involved in teaching skills to a small group of students with learning problems. Another school was using a very different approach to assist learners with ongoing reading difficulties. Specifically, this school was using Reciprocal Teaching which is described below.

Reciprocal Teaching

Reciprocal Teaching (Palincsar & Brown, 1984) is used to help develop comprehension skills in reading. It is a metacognitive approach to teaching reading comprehension involving the use of four strategies: predicting, questioning, summarizing, and clarifying. In using this approach in the classroom, first, the students, in response to teacher-guided questions, predict what the text and subsections of the text will be about. Next, the students monitor their understanding of what they have read and again with the teacher's guidance generate questions and summarize their understanding of the text. Finally they clarify any misleading or complex sections of text. This cycle, using the four strategies, is repeated throughout the reading of the text. In addition to employing the strategies the teacher and the students discuss together how and when these strategies can be used during reading. They learn to take turns at leading the dialogue until eventually the students can undertake the dialogue in small groups without the teacher's presence.

Three of the case study schools had the resources for intensive provision of literacy intervention for the individual needs of students. At one of these schools there was a withdrawal class for children with learning disabilities which had ten pupils. The program in this school focussed on the use of direct instruction and the development of independent learning skills through metacognitive strategies. The program elements included a phonics program, sight word recognition and spelling. In a second independent school a specially trained teacher used the Hickey Multisensory Language Course (Augur & Briggs, 1993, now Combley, 2001). This is a sequenced program using a phonics approach to teach reading, writing and spelling based on material from the UK Dyslexia Institute. The third school was also an independent school for boys. In an education support unit in that school, children were on individual programs that included a variety of teacher-made and commercial materials.

Two issues

Two issues which emerged from the results are discussed in this section. They relate to third wave teaching and to program evaluation.

Comments about third wave teaching

The picture of ongoing support in the case study schools for students with ongoing learning problems in literacy engaged with third wave teaching was far more complex than that for first and second wave teaching. Nevertheless, some general observations can be made.

First, the resources available for supporting the students with ongoing learning problems were usually very limited so that schools were forced to make choices as to which students they could afford to support. Accordingly, the patterns of support for these students were extremely varied: some students were placed in withdrawal groups, some had in-class support and others were not able to have any support at all.

Second, in terms of program content there were differences that seemed to be based on both funding restraints and the schools' philosophy of literacy learning. Some students were enrolled in specific "package" programs that focussed on a particular aspect of literacy. Some students were enrolled in eclectic, highly structured programs that focussed on a number of literacy-related areas, in particular comprehension, metacognition and word level skills in both reading and spelling. Some programs had an emphasis on developing students' self-esteem and self-management. Of the three withdrawal programs supporting students with severe learning problems in the case study schools only one was in a government school and this was due to be closed. The other two programs were in independent schools. In spite of funding restraints, most of these support programs were run by extremely enthusiastic experienced and committed teachers. Many of these teachers, but not all of them, were highly qualified. We would argue that it is very important to have the highest qualified teachers working with these hardest to teach students with learning problems.

Program evaluation

Another finding based on data from the interviews, document collection, and the case studies related to the issue of formally evaluating and reporting on the use of these programs. The researchers found that across Australia many systems carried out program evaluation through documentation, reporting and comparison of individual students' progress, rather than through specific program evaluations. Schools themselves seldom undertook evaluations of the programs they implemented, except at the level of anecdote and individual students' progress or where the program was part of a formal research initiative undertaken by university researchers. The

Early Years Literacy program by Crevola and Hill (as cited in Hill, 1997) and the School-Wide Early Literacy and Language program by Center, Freeman and Robertson (1998) were two programs that had been initiated by university researchers and had been extensively evaluated.

The lack of program evaluation is a matter of considerable concern. Program evaluation is important particularly when schools adopt new programs and make resource allocations to specific programs and approaches. In addition to teacher judgements, program evaluations should make good use of comparisons within schools from year to year and comparisons between schools serving similar children and communities.

Conclusions and implications

This chapter has reported findings of an Australian study that examined the programs and strategies used to teach and intervene in literacy for students with learning problems in Australian classrooms.

The findings indicated that state and territory education system authorities in Australia have afforded schools and teachers with considerable freedom in the selection of literacy programs and approaches to teaching and intervention. We would argue that this has led to considerable variety which is a healthy signal for promoting the literacy achievement of children with learning problems. Specifically schools and school districts are not locked into one approach and therefore, teachers are able to choose programs that are best suited to the students' individual needs and the local school and/or community contexts. This contrasts with recent developments in the US where politicians and policy makers in some states (e.g., California) have directed and legislated that only specific forms of instruction are permissible (McGill-Franzen, 2000).

The findings in our study also suggested that effective first wave (regular class teaching) and second wave early intervention literacy programs and strategies were well established in the case study schools in our project. However, one of the challenges for schools and school systems in Australia is for the enhanced provision of third wave support for children with learning problems in literacy. Such support would require Commonwealth, state and territory government recognition and resource support.

In spite of good first wave and second wave teaching some students continue to have persistent problems in literacy. Schools in Australia need to maintain the intensity of effort currently devoted to first and second wave literacy teaching and increase the intensity of effort devoted to third wave teaching for these children. In addition, improved third wave teaching will require the development of well-researched intervention programs.

If the Australian Commonwealth government's goals related to the literacy abilities of its citizens are to be realised, then there will need to be a greater emphasis on supporting students with learning problems in literacy. Changes to teacher education and a new emphasis on the professional development of teachers, funding to support schools to evaluate their programs, and new studies to enhance the support given to students with severe and persistent learning problems in literacy are required.

References

Anderson, R.C. (1998). Introduction: Reflections on literacy education. In J. Osborn & F. Lehr (Eds.). *Literacy for all: Issues in teaching and learning* (pp. 1- 8). New York: The Guilford Press.

Augur, J., & Briggs, S. (1993). *The Hickey Multisensory Language Course.* London: Whurr.

Center, Y., Freeman, L. & Robertson, G. (1998). An evaluation of School-Wide Early Language and Literacy (SWELL) in six disadvantaged schools. *International Journal of Disability, Development and Education, 45*(2), 143-172.

Chall, J. (1967). *Learning to read: The great debate.* New York: McGraw Hill.

Clay, M. M. (1993). *Reading Recovery: A guide book for teachers in training.* Portsmouth, NH: Heinemann.

Comber, B. (1998). "Coming ready or not!": Changing what counts as early literacy. *Keynote address to the Seventh Australia and New Zealand Conference on the First Years of School. New Approaches to Old Puzzles – Reconceptualizing the Early Years of School,* Canberra, 13-16 January 1998. Retrieved 12 December 2001 from http://www.schools.ash.org.au/litweb/ barb2.htm

Combley, M. (Ed.) (2001). *The Hickey Multisensory Language Course* (3rd ed.). London: Whurr.

Corrective Reading. Direct Instruction, SRA. Retrieved 12 December 2001 from http://www.sraonline.com/index.php/home/curriculumsolutions/di/9.

Crevola, C.A., & Hill, P.W. (1998). Evaluation of a whole school approach to prevention and intervention in early literacy. *Journal of Education for Students Placed At Risk, 3,* 33-156.

Department of Education and Employment. (1991). *Australia's language: The Australian language and literacy policy.* Canberra, ACT: Australian Government Printing Service.

Department of Employment, Education, Training and Youth Affairs. (1998). *Literacy for all: The challenge for Australian schools.* Canberra, ACT: Author.

Education Department of Western Australia. (1994). *First Steps reading resource book.* Melbourne: Longman.

First Steps. Retrieved 12 December 2001 from http://www.ecurl.com.au/src/Firststep/-backgrnd.html.

Gaffney, J.S. (1998). The prevention of reading failure: Teach reading and writing. In J. Osborn & F. Lehr (Eds.). *Literacy for all: Issues in teaching and learning* (pp. 100-110). New York: The Guilford Press.

Hiebert, E. H., & Taylor, B. M. (2000). Beginning reading instruction: research on early intervention. In M. Kamil, P.B. Mosenthal, P.D. Pearson, & R. Barr (Eds.), *Handbook of reading research*, Vol III (pp. 455-482). Mahwah, NJ: Lawrence Erlbaum Associates, Publishers.

Hill, P.W. (1997, October). The literacy challenge in Australian primary schools. *Paper presented at the APPA/ACPPA National Conference*, Sydney.

Hill, P.W., & Crevola, C. A. M. (1998). Characteristics of an effective literacy strategy. *Unicorn, 24*(2), 74-85.

Klesius, J.P., & Griffith, P.L. (1996) Interactive storybook reading for at-risk learners. *The Reading Teacher, 49*, 552-560.

Letterland. Retrieved 12 December 2001 from http://www.letterland.com.

Louden, W., Chan, L.K.S, Elkins, J., Greaves, D., House, H., Milton, M., Nichols, S., Rohl, M., Rivalland, J. & van Kraayenoord, C. (2000). *Mapping the Territory; Primary students with learning difficulties: Literacy and Numeracy*, Vol. 1-3. Canberra: Commonwealth of Australia, Department of Education, Training and Youth Affairs. Retrieved 12 December 2001 from http://www.dest.gov.au/schools/literacyand numeracy/publications/mapping/index.htm

Luke, A., & Freebody, P. (1999). Further notes on the Four Resources Model. *Practically Primary, 4*(2), 5-8.

Lyons, C.A., & Beaver, J. (1995). Reducing retention and learning disability placement through Reading Recovery: An educationally sound, cost-effective choice. In R.L. Allington & S.A. Walmsley (Eds.), *No quick fix: Rethinking literacy programs in America's elementary schools* (pp. 116-136). New York: Teachers College Press.

Mandel Morrow, L., & O'Connor, E.M. (1995). Literacy partnerships for change with 'at-risk' kindergartners. In R.L. Allington & S.A. Walmsley (Eds.), *No quick fix: Rethinking literacy programs in America's elementary schools* (pp. 97-115). New York: Teachers College Press.

McGill-Franzen, A. (2000). Policy and instruction: What is the relationship? In M. Kamil, P.B. Mosenthal, P.D. Pearson, & R. Barr (Eds.), *Handbook of reading research*, Vol III (pp. 889-908). Mahwah, NJ: Lawrence Erlbaum Associates, Publishers.

Morris, D., Ervin, C., & Conrad, K. (1996). A case study of middle school reading disability. *The Reading Teacher, 49*(5), 368-377.

Palincsar, A.S., & Brown, A.L. (1984). The reciprocal teaching of comprehension-fostering and comprehension-monitoring activities. *Cognition and Instruction, 1*, 117-175.

Pikulski, J.J. (1994). Preventing reading failure: A review of five effective programs. *The Reading Teacher, 48*(1), 30-39.

Pressley, M., Allington, R.L., Wharton-McDonald, R., Collins Block, C., & Mandel Morrow, L. (2001). *Learning to read: Lessons from exemplary first-grade classrooms*. New York: The Guilford Press.

Slavin, R.E., Karweit, N.L., Wasik, B.A., Madden, N.A., & Dolan, L.J. (1994). Success for All: A comprehensive approach to prevention and early intervention. In R.E. Slavin, N.L. Karweit, & B.A. Wasik (Eds.), *Preventing school failure* (pp.175-205). Boston: Allyn and Bacon.

Spelling through Morphographs. Direct Instruction, SRA. Retrieved 12 December 2001 from http://www.sraonline.com/index.php/home/curriculumsolutions/di/9.

Teaching Handwriting Reading and Spelling Skills (THRASS). Retrieved 12 December 2001 from http://www.thrass.com.

Turbill, J. (2002, February). The four ages of reading philosophy and practice: A framework for examining theory and practice. *Reading Online*. Retrieved on 4

February 2002 from http;// www.readingonline.org/international/turbill4/index.html

van Kraayenoord, C.E. (2003). Literacy assessment. In G. Bull & M. Anstey (Eds.). *The literacy lexicon* (2nd ed., pp. 273-287). Frenchs Forest, NSW: Prentice Hall.

Wasik, B.A. & Slavin, R.E. (1993). Preventing early reading failure with one-to-one tutoring: A review of five programs. *Reading Research Quarterly, 28*(2), 179-201.

8
DEVELOPMENT OF READING COMPREHENSION OF LEARNERS WITH DYSLEXIA BY MEANS OF A TECHNIQUE OF IMAGING

Cecilia Bouwer and Vasti Jordaan

Introduction

When recognition of words in written text is delayed or blocked - which frequently happens when individuals have a specific reading impairment (dyslexia) - the text becomes fragmented and the message tends to disintegrate. Fortunately, understanding a passage in print rests on far more than the sum of the meanings of the words constituting the text.

It is argued that strength-based learning support for reading comprehension in a constructivist vein (i.e. negotiating meaning by means of holistic, interactive processing which utilises each learner's unique base of knowledge, skills and abilities in idiosyncratic ways) renders positive results even with learners with dyslexia. Imaging as one method of supporting the development of reading comprehension, certainly meets these requirements.

Inclusive education constantly seems to pose new challenges to many teachers, changing individual learners with special educational needs entering their classroom, utilising their particular strengths and contending with their particular barriers to learning in a unique way. Inclusive education is about striving to achieve optimal learning by all learners in the class, also those with impairments and other forms of learning problems. To this end, it is the responsibility of the school to make adaptations to meet the educational needs of all its learners, instead of expecting the learner to adapt to the standards or style of instruction of the school. The teacher is often hard put to devise an appropriate form of support to optimise the particular strengths of the learner with an impairment.

Learners with dyslexia generally have phonological and/or visual processing deficits (Everatt, 2002; Goswami, 1998; Singleton, 2002; Snowling, 1996; Turner, 1997) contributing to their problems with decoding and word recognition. They thereby tend to stumble over and/or 'lose' words from printed text. Consequently, the text frequently becomes fragmented to the extent where the meaning of a sentence, paragraph and eventually the full passage might disintegrate. Learners with a learning impairment do not automatically apply active learning strategies, such as the monitoring skills of metacognition and the questioning/prediction of events (Burke, 1997). Therefore, learning support to these learners should include a distinctly holistic and meaning-based component that focuses on the enhancement of thinking skills.

We have argued elsewhere (Bouwer & Jordaan, 2002) that the learning problems of a learner with dyslexia could actually be intensified by inappropriate reading development strategies, especially those which focus exclusively or inordinately on the bottom-up processes of word recognition. An overly strong process-orientation to reading could be essentially unproductive, since an emphasis on decoding could be teaching to the weaknesses of the learner with dyslexia instead of to the intact abilities and also endorses word-by-word reading at the expense of whole-text.

Especially in the mainstream classroom, adaptable, chiefly non-specialist group procedures are called for, to enhance self-development and self-regulation of the reading comprehension skills of learners with dyslexia. The technique of imaging might be one option to consider in this regard.

The research reported in this chapter examined the feasibility and some effects of the utilisation of a conscious process of imaging to improve the reading comprehension of learners with dyslexia. A brief contemplation of reading comprehension provides the theoretical framework, followed by a discussion of imaging as a technique to support reading comprehension. We then look at the impact of dyslexia on reading comprehension. After reporting the process and findings of the study, we conclude with a brief discussion.

Reading comprehension

Comprehension is so integral to reading, that Pike, Compain and Mumper. (1997) state reading and comprehension to be synonymous. It is virtually impossible to look at reading outside the context of meaning-making. We should think of reading as an integrative mode of communication - vitally intra-active as well as interactive (Bouwer, 2004). It is intra-active, in that the reader is constantly cross-referencing a vast amount and range of his or her own abilities, knowledges and skills to access the text, and makes semantic sense and personal meaning of it. It is interactive, in that the reader is conducting a dialogue with the text in an endeavour to process the sense intended by the author and uses the information of the printed text to construct meaning (Brand-Gruwel, Aarnoutse & Van den Bos, 1998; Moore & Wade, 1998; Shanker & Ekwall, 1998).

The communication of thoughts and emotions between the writer and the reader results from the reader's construction of meaning through integrating his or her prior knowledge with the information presented in the text. In this regard, Manzo and Manzo (1995) draw a valuable distinction between reconstructive reading (understanding the author's intended meaning) and constructive reading (personalising and building on the author's message).

In processing running text, readers use three sources of information, namely semantic, syntactic and graphophonic information (Pike et al., 1997; Sampson, Sampson & Van Allen, 1995).
- *Semantic* information is regarded as pivotal. It involves the reader's knowledge of meanings in the language of the text, and his or her associations with relevant experiences and existing content knowledge, which together form the frame of reference to construct the personal meaning of the text.
- *Syntactic* knowledge carries the processing of the statements, besides enabling readers constantly to monitor their reading and backtrack to clarify confusion when a word is misread.
- *Graphophonic* information underpins the decoding process, affording the reader access to each word in the text.

Reading from running text holds obvious advantages since it enables one to utilise the three information systems described above to the optimum. Presenting learners with isolated words to recognise and/or decode, such as in word lists or on flash cards, actually casts them adrift from their various bases of meaning (Bouwer, 2004). In being required to focus only on the structural characteristics of the word (the sequence and form of letters and the sound-symbol relationship in the orthography of the language of the text), they have to do without much supportive information that can be derived from text.

Few symbols, sounds and words are by themselves pivotal to comprehension of the full text. In fact, most readers are constantly losing some detail information from text for a variety of reasons, such as orthographic and/or syntactic complexity, unfamiliarity of words and pronunciation, and cultural/experiential context. Added to these reasons, are problems such as poor visual discrimination and the phonological processing errors demonstrated by many learners with dyslexia. Readers at all levels of proficiency are therefore constantly, albeit mostly unconsciously, performing acts of closure with regard to both decoding and comprehension, by applying their phonological, linguistic and semantic/world knowledge to supplement the information which they derive from the text.

When word recognition is delayed, jumbled or blocked, the text can become fragmented and the message can disintegrate unless learners have conscious controls in place to scaffold and self-regulate their understanding (Bouwer & Jordaan, 2002). The greater the word recognition problems, the more words are closed by means of inferencing and/or sheer guessing (Goodman, 1988; Stanovich, 1980). The guessing will obviously increase at the expense of constructive inferencing – and will, in fact, become wilder - when the reader is unable to maintain textual coherence for any reason, such as processing and knowledge deficits, a working memory overload and even reading instruction which is flawed by an extreme focus on word-by-word reading or a lexical approach.

For Vygotsky, in true keeping with his theory of the Zone of Proximal Development, effective mediation for reading development focused on learners' strengths rather than on their errors (Hellier, 1994). In many of the helping professions, we are presently noting a movement away from the earlier deficit and discrepancy models. Instead of focused yet mostly fruitless efforts to 'fix' deficits by means of 'remediation', interventions are increasingly favouring a strength-based and largely preventive approach which is directed more holistically and constructively towards mobilising and enhancing those resources, abilities and skills which are available to the person(s) in difficulty (Lewis & Doorlag, 1999). Proponents of interactive models have become increasingly interested in the reader's personal strategies of monitoring and fixing reading problems as they occur. Such strategies are often found to be unique to an individual since they are derived from assorted cognitive strengths with regard to readers' processing of meaning and print (Bouwer, 2004). In accordance with the shift to a strength-based approach, the primary aim of reading support then should be the improvement of learners' skills to negotiate print by learning to apply active strategies constantly to check their reading (Burke, 1997).

One such strategy is to image textual content. Imaging would fit in well with the outcomes-based approach in education, where learning is increasingly directed at self-discovery. If imaging could be made to support learners with dyslexia as well as learners who do not have special reading education needs, it would have considerable worth in inclusive education.

Imaging for reading comprehension

We could probably stimulate the potential of most learners to read with understanding by teaching them to form a habit of consciously creating multisensory, dynamic images of textual content. The hope represented by this helpline has been described as making one's world 'visible' (Mills, 1993).

To image while one is reading, entails forming mental images of the printed text. It is a natural way of transforming the words in print into meaning-filled concepts. At a low or unmediated level, arising from the learner's existing lexicon by way of association, the imaged scene may be but sparsely filled, perhaps more like a single object on an otherwise blank page, with the amount and quality of definition depending on the focus and word knowledge of the individual and the amount of information actually utilised. Learners with an attention deficit disorder may, on the other hand, spontaneously branch off into confabulation and fill the 'page' with details not mentioned in the text at all.

Quite obviously, then, imaging does not per se ensure a coherent reconstruction of the text, let alone the construction of new understanding or knowledge. It is relatively easy to image familiar, real objects mentioned in text, especially in static form and in visual terms, but the strategy should be established as a habit and should then be extended. First, educators should mediate how to richly integrate information from all the other sensory modalities when imaging and, in doing so, reconstruct the content of the text in relational and interactional terms. Even more importantly, learners should be supported to construct their own understanding and augment their word knowledge through imaging. They must learn to do this by drawing on their own experiences (since textual associations with personal schemata form the framework for understanding) and linking with all possible textual information to infer meaning. Words that we don't know admittedly can blur and distort our understanding, but – as in spoken language – we acquire many new words quite naturally in reading when exposed to them repeatedly within the meaningful context of printed text. According to Shepard (in Hodes, 1990), imaging is indeed relevant to the higher order thinking skills at the confluence of concrete presentations with related association processes at the abstract conceptual level.

The imaging process and its potential value in interpreting, reasoning and recall of printed information is succinctly described by a learner's remark, "I make movies when I read." (Sadoski, Goetz & Olivarez, 1990). The reader creates the scene while imaging the content as the text is being decoded, interacting with his/her stored knowledge, values and beliefs for the deep structures of meaning (Rieber, 1995).

Imaging is hypothesised to be an essential cognitive strategy in various thoughts and problem solving processes which link inner language to images and verbal language (Burke, 1997). Images are formed in the working memory as part of the long-term visual memory which stores and organises information and facilitates recall

(Silverman, 1995). Research has indicated that imaging the concrete meaning of words and paragraphs stimulates interest and is a powerful predictor of reading comprehension and retention of content (Burke, 1997).

Since images rely strongly on individual experiences and are usually formed individually, they are mostly unique. Information may be restructured differently by each reader, being influenced by cultural and environmental factors such as the quality and quantity of perceptual stimulation, language acquisition and frame of experience. Such differences then contribute to varying quality and richness of the images. There is little danger of 'incorrect' responses being derived from one's schemata. So, within the parameters of their own experiences, learners easily feel they are achieving success (Machiels-Bongaerts, Schmidt & Boshuizen, 1995; Mills, 1993).

Training in imaging can lead to improved retention while studying, by enabling learners to form associational structures in formerly unstructured domains of information (Richardson, 1995; Rieber, 1995; Solvberg & Valas, 1995). According to Edelstein (in Hodes, 1990), visually orientated recall strategies facilitate the integration of information, resulting in higher order metacognitive thinking and the acquisition of abstract concepts. Creating multi-sensorial images adds richness and nuance to the imaged comprehension, which in turn supports higher order cognitive skills such as prediction, inferencing and evaluation.

The hemispheres of the brain function as a coordinated unit in processing information (Fryburg, 1997; Mazzoni & Nelson, 1998). Silverman (1995) argues that creating an image when processing a concept or fact, anchors the information in both hemispheres. This improves the potential for meaning-full understanding and retention. When one is reading with comprehension, the hemispheres of one's brain also function in integrated fashion, thereby integrating cognitive and affective processes in a meaning-based response to the textual content (Truscott, Walker & Gambrell, 1995). It follows that a strategy of imaging reciprocally and holistically supports the integration of sensory and perceptual information with the verbal message and could effectively link images to the typically liniar information in academic text.

The skill of effective imaging does not develop automatically. It needs to be acquired and practised systematically and in accordance with the learner's abilities as well as the demands of the task. Learners below age eight have difficulty imaging without assistance, probably because of the abstract nature of the task (Oakhill & Patel, 1991). Learners master the technique more successfully between ages ten and twelve, although age has not emerged as the strongest factor for successful imaging (Solvberg & Valas, 1995). The questions remain as to whether learners with dyslexia could be supported to master the techniques of imaging for enhanced reading comprehension, how to effectively provide such learning support, and whether imaging will have sufficient effect on their reading performance to merit the effort.

Before reporting our study addressing this challenge, it is necessary briefly to contemplate the particular difficulties regarding reading comprehension experienced by learners with dyslexia.

The reading comprehension problems of learners with dyslexia

It is an established fact that the reading problems of some learners are strongly related to neuro-developmental factors (Knight & Hynd, 2002). As mentioned earlier, severe decoding and word recognition difficulties, variously related to deficits in phonological and visual processing, are noted by and large as characteristic of learners with dyslexia. However, Frith (2002) convincingly argues for a three-level description of contributing factors, i.e. in terms of a biological (neuro-developmental), cognitive (processing) and behavioural (product) component, and this approach provides a more understandable frame when looking at the reading comprehension problems of learners with reading impairment.

Although their comprehension of printed text is typically better than their word recognition (Turner, 1997), some learners with dyslexia tend to process what they read only superficially, and need to reread sections of the text repeatedly for better understanding. Chiappe, Hasher and Siegel (2000) suggest that their working memory is often unable to support the load and/or the time required for them laboriously, word-by-word, to translate print into speech, thereby causing them to lose track of the coherence and meaning of the text. Learners with dyslexia may further experience difficulty integrating old and new information. Many tend to display a lack of engagement with text and make little effort to solve the puzzles that crop up due to their virtually endless misreadings (Brand-Gruwel, Aarnoutse & Van den Bos, 1998; Shanker & Ekwall, 1998).

Also caused by dysfunctions in the central nervous system, attention deficit disorder with/without hyperactivity (ADHD) often occurs in comorbidity with other learning impairments. In reading, both the processes of decoding and comprehending printed text are obviously impacted upon by the associated lack of impulse control, selective attention deficits attributable to internal and/or external distractibility and an inability to sustain attention which characterise ADHD (Fryburg, 1997; APA, 1994; Green & Chee, 1997). Once more, the effect is a loss of coherence, preventing the reader at all levels to access meaning.

The research

Design

A predominantly qualitative small-group single case study was conducted in the form of a series of learning support sessions on imaging, looking at the participation of the group as well as each member individually. During action-researched sessions of learning support, the facilitator endeavoured to accommodate the subjects' unique learning needs and their lifeworld, inter alia the influence of factors such as the disposition, language proficiency, living environment and possible experiential limitations. A pretest-posttest assessment was made of the subjects' reading comprehension, using the Diagnostic reading test, Afrikaans First Language for Grades 3 – 6 (HSRC, 1990). These results were analysed individually and mostly qualitatively for each participant.

Site and participants

The research was conducted at a South African special school for learners with specific learning impairments. The five learners in the intermediate phase (Grade 4 – 6) who had the most severe problems in reading comprehension were identified by means of formal and informal individual assessment. The participants were all boys, with Afrikaans as their home language and language of learning and teaching. They differed in terms of age and grade level as well as performance level and cognitive skills (see Table 1 and Figure 2), and they all displayed varying degrees of attention deficit disorder.

The impact of environmental disadvantage on performance is perhaps demonstrated by the fact that the group consisted entirely of so-called coloured learners, coming from a traditionally lower-income socio-economic community in the vicinity of the school. Although the language differences are not dialectic in their scope, the spoken (expressive) communications of community members frequently contain lexical items and expressions which are distinct from so-called standard Afrikaans in written form. Obversely, texts in standard Afrikaans could contain terms and expressions unfamiliar to the learners at the receptive level of language usage.

Research question

As indicated earlier, the research addressed the question as to whether and how mastery of techniques of conscious imaging for enhanced reading comprehension could be facilitated to benefit learners with dyslexia in the intermediate school phase. We investigated how the strategy of imaging in reading should perhaps be adapted to have effect with these learners. We also needed to identify whether the degree of reading impairment could in a particular case be so severe as to prevent conscious imaging from being utilised successfully.

Method

Research

The technique of conscious imaging was formatively evaluated and adapted for use with learners with dyslexia, by means of action research and systematic participative observation. Ten learning support sessions of one hour each, one per week, were presented. The sessions were audiotaped and fieldnoted in detail. During each session, data were also collected on 15 criteria formulated to evaluate the degree of progress by learners with dyslexia in mastering the imaging technique.

Each session was refined and personalised for the learners individually, after reflecting on the dynamics and outcomes of the previous session. Verbal and non-verbal behaviours, responses and interactions were taken into consideration and care was taken not to absolutise either achievement or cross-comparisons at the cost of learners' individual experiences of participation in the meaning(s) of printed text.

To increase credibility of the findings and conclusions, interpretation of the qualitative descriptions on the participation and achievement of each learner was triangulated with a largely qualitative analysis of a pretest-posttest assessment of the subjects' reading comprehension which had been administered at the presumed reading level of each, using the Diagnostic reading test, Afrikaans First Language for Grades 3 – 6 (HSRC, 1990) and also by means of semi-structured interviews with the learners' therapists and teachers. The focus of the study was on examining the progress of each learner by means of intrapersonal comparison. The case study design, the unique nature of reading impairment and the environmental factors at play will allow some transfer of the research, findings and interpretation, but obviously will prevent broad generalisation.

Learning support sessions: facilitation of imaging skills

Requiring some skill in construction and abstraction, the process of controlled imaging differs from the spontaneous flow of unexpected images. For purposes of improved reading comprehension, it was essential to get the learners to involve as many senses as possible in forming detailed, dynamic images. Three components of imaging were attended to in the learning support sessions: imaging (pictures experienced as in a film), somatic responses (subjective feelings and emotions attached to the images), and ascribing meaning (forming ideas which contribute to understanding of the content). Learners with dyslexia appear inclined to function at the concrete level, so the facilitator needed to accommodate the cognitive level of functioning of each learner, while driving for growing powers of inferencing, editing and dealing with ideas. The steps of facilitation to master the technique of imaging when reading were the following (Bagley & Lavin, 1988; Burke, 1997):

- Create an atmosphere of trust, which is non-evaluative and non-judgemental.
- Point out the advantages and necessity of imaging in everyday life.
- Facilitate understanding of the procedure, rationale and purpose of imaging in simple, logical steps.
- Model (talk through) the strategy so that the learner is readily able to identify the various steps.
- Practise the skills with appropriate text at the learner's present level of comprehension.
- Give immediate feedback concerning the use of the imaging technique and its effectiveness.
- Encourage learners to generalise imaging techniques and apply these to other learning areas.

Each session began with an explanation of the rationale and nature of the particular content featuring in the session. Then followed a relaxation exercise and the session task, which entailed practising the skills of imaging and applying these individually, to contribute to better reading comprehension of the particular text. Each session contained a form of physical activity, such as drawing or mime, to provide the learners with a medium by means of which they were able to express their experiences of imaging in a concrete way. Figure 1 contains a broad summary of the participative behaviour per learner, with the purpose of showing the nature of reflection performed in the course of the research.

Results

The qualitative and quantitative outcomes of the study are summarised in Figure 1 (learners' participative behaviour and researcher's reflective planning), Table 1 (pretest and posttest results), Figure 2 (pretest and posttest observations of cognitive strategies for decoding, word recognition and reading comprehension), and Table 2 (mastery of the imaging technique). The data all supplement one another and the progress of each learner may be traced most richly and insightfully by means of constant cross-referencing through the figures and tables. Limited space allows little more than a cursory overview of the general trends suggested by the data. The focus will be primarily qualitative, i.e. on participative and achievement behaviours more than on scores.

The observations and reflections contained in Figure 1 (in Method, above) serve largely as a backdrop for the results in Tables 1 and 2 and Figure 2, providing some insight into each learner's participation in each session and the facilitator's personalised interventions. Learner 1, the youngest in the group, experienced severe difficulties during the earlier sessions, especially on account of impulsive and distractible behaviour. A turning point was apparently reached in Session 8, when he gained some measure of insight in the technique of imaging. During Sessions 9 and 10, he demonstrated increasing success, focus and commitment, even practising metacognition and sustaining attention. The behavioural and emotional problems of Learner 2 were finally beginning to resolve towards the end - but not before these had impacted heavily on the group, as reflected in observations regarding Learner 3 (Session 2) and Learner 5 (Session 6) in Figure 1, as well as in the shifts in the Total % criterion scores surrounding the period of his absence and return (Table 2, Sessions 1 through 8). Learner 3 was the first to master the technique of imaging for enhanced comprehension (Session 4) and, given his age and his criterion-scores in the early sessions (Table 2), he made the best progress, although his lack of emotional and cognitive control remained problematic to the end. Learner 4 had the most severe learning problems in the group, especially in visual-motor integration, attention and language, but with individual accommodations he started making progress as early as Session 2. He appeared to gain confidence as well as some independence in the final sessions. Learner 5, the senior learner in the group, demonstrated understanding of the imaging technique from the outset. His progress involved applying the principles of imaging more richly, and truly engaging with text to achieve emotional resonance while also expanding his concepts. Certainly most notable, he transferred the skill to his process of learning for a test in a content area to good effect.

Table 1 contains the pretest and posttest results, which give broad indications of the level of functioning of each of the 5 learners before and after participating in the learning support sessions in imaging. The varied number, levels and forms of the pretests are accounted for by the different levels of reading proficiency of the learners at the beginning of the research. Pretests were selected from the battery of the Human Sciences Research Council, the Diagnostic reading test, Afrikaans First Language for Grades 3 – 6 (HSRC, 1990), according to recommendations by the therapeutic team of the school. Posttests were selected from the same battery of reading tests with reference to each learner's performance on the pretests. A second posttest was administered where learners achieved 100% in the first posttest. All pretests and posttests contained separate texts to be read aloud and silently.

Figure 1: Behaviours of learners with a learning impairment, with resultant reflections on learning support sessions

Session		Learner 1	Learner 2	Learner 3	Learner 4	Learner 5
1	Observed Behaviour	Restless, unable to relax; impulsive; inadequate planning of sketch; visual-motor integration problems. Poor risk-taking behaviour, uncertain, frequently erases work. Totally unfamiliar with concept of imaging; limited lexicon to express thoughts.	Total task refusal – distracts group members, disrupts activities.	Positive attitude; visual processing difficulties (spatial, 2/3 dimension) affect performance especially re abstract thoughts; verbal description is more complete.	Has extreme difficulty focusing to 'register' internal image; ?concept of imaging is problematic; motor execution of tasks appears daunting.	Grasps concept; talks incessantly; asks about rationale for each aspect of session; enjoys task, is completely absorbed.
	Reflection	Requires much **guidance re task execution and encouragement** re emotional problems.	Quarrelled with members of group before session; appears negative with regard to facilitator, task and group.	Concentrates well on individual task, less so in group activity, same as in class. **Train to utilise technique of imaging to focus in class.**	Severe perceptual and learning problems; abstract concept of imaging ?vague. **Elicit alternative response mode and offer much support!**	Enjoys the session, grasps basic principles of imaging. **Manage dominance in age and skill.**
2	Observed Behaviour	Seems to enjoy session; talks constantly. Planning and execution are problematic.	Constantly clowns for attention, seeking alliance with group members; aggressive; no homework tasks performed.	Angry with Learner 2; anger has negative effect on his concentration and participation.	Visual-motor problems hamper drawing; meaningful verbal participation and increased detail with amanuensis.	Generally successful; distractibility hampers focus on internal images → loses details of information.
	Reflection	Requires **more structure**; give **positive support re self-discipline!**	Severe learning problems, poor risk-taking skills; **requires structure!**	Over-reaction – upset re everything → rejects task. ?Requires **empowerment to function as his own person in a group.**	Makes an effort to participate. Requires **detailed individual guidance, step-wise structure!**	Enjoys the session, grasps basic principles of imaging. **Focus on cognitive control for attention deficit?**
3	Observed Behaviour	Eyes itch during relaxation exercise, distracting him. Difficulties expressing thoughts in drawings as well as verbally persist. Positive intentionality.	Refuses to shut eyes for relaxation; opposes instructions, tries to conspire with group members – but his imaging suggests insight in the technique! No homework done.	Did not complete Session 2 homework (had not understood it). Strong intentionality; good concentration during individual task, less so in group activity.	Tried to do Session 2 homework, but was unsuccessful; displays insight into basic steps of imaging - detailed verbal description.	Participates wholeheartedly; utilises multi-sensory info → vivid descriptions of internal images; work habits vary according to interest level – lack of interest → work left incomplete / done carelessly.

145

4 Reflection	Emotional support seems effective. Visual-motor integration problems contribute to poor planning and difficulty in representation of images.	Behaviour ← ? affective lability. Yet his contributions are meaningful and suggest understanding of the technique. **Offer encouragement!**	Speeds through tasks. ?Is beginning to grasp principles of imaging. Concentration problem hampers efforts to focus on internal images.	Homework failure ← ?abstract nature of task / poor risk taking. **Provide encouragement!**	Internal images are enriched by multi-sensory info → **increase challenge per task.**
4 Observed Behaviour	Closes eyes very tightly to image, saying it helps him concentrate. Spontaneous and impulsive participation, completes task fast; motor execution is poor.	Failed to attend.	Describes image in detail, involving all senses; the image is an original composition derived from his schemata and enriched with new information.	Uncertain, constantly refers to work of others; partly grasps concept of imaging with individual support; slow ← problem integrating.	Restless during relaxation exercise – upset because of unpleasant incident at home; appears to grasp imaging technique; sings while working.
5 Reflection	Talks about other matters – distractible. **Beware of being too lenient / encouraging?** Enjoyed session.	Feels threatened / lack of interest? **Demonstrate concern!**	?Breakthrough; ?constructive imaging, incorporating the new information, enabled him to cut out distractions coming from the group.	Creative ideas, but limited language ability → verbalises with difficulty; guidance is processed meaningfully.	Becomes totally absorbed by imaging activity; creative! Singing ← internal distraction? **Encourage self-talk focused on tasks?**
5 Observed Behaviour	Giggles upon hearing birds during relaxation exercise; Focuses well while listening to story, enjoys it. Blurts out his image impulsively, talks in between, jokes with others, distracting them. Unable to read silently – sub-vocalises. Requires guidance to perform task.	Absent from school.	Listens to reading of text attentively, asking appropriate questions; first to complete task; successfully draws upon existing knowledge in cognitive frame and adds new information. Enjoys session.	Listens attentively to reading of text; but own reading is very slow, word x word → loses line of story, better risk-taking than in previous sessions, but needed step-by-step guidance.	Responds to L3's questions with insight; positive intentionality; hums while drawing; completes task in good time.
6 Reflection	Hyperactive, impulsive behaviour and distractions → quality of work fluctuated. **Provide guidelines for group conduct and control behaviour!** Enjoyed session.	Ill / personal problems? **Follow up!**	Speeds through work, the same as in class when he enjoys a task – needs to **develop cognitive control of emotions to curb over-reactions.**	With amanuensis, displays metacognition and understanding of technique; finds concrete presentation virtually impossible. **Give much support!**	Enjoys imaging activities, creative; "Is Jack (Beanstalk) white / brown?" Quality of work reflects emotional state. **Beware of neglecting him because he works well.**
6 Observed behaviour	Difficulty executing relaxation exercise on his own, distracted by people talking in next room. Talks incessantly. Requires learning support re word recognition and reading comprehension.	Exceedingly disruptive; seeks attention by talking, making noises, kicking wall & back chatting; yet completes task & creatively images *mountain of rice*.	Distracted by sounds from next-door, has difficulty doing relaxation exercise on his own due to attention deficit; draws creative inferences from text.	Distracted by sounds from next-door; leans heavily on support for technical reading and comprehension.	L2 upset him before session, wants to leave; aggressive, remains upset during relaxation activity, unable to focus. Does not participate in discussion. Work fast, poor quality in comparison with previous work.

7	Observed behaviour	Distractibility hampers functioning. Independent relaxation appears too difficult.	Behaviour and learning problems ?mutually reinforcing; ?call for help! **Positive reinforcement may support development of imaging skills.**	Hampered by poor concentration, but achieves imaging faster and more richly. **Attend to his development of cognitive control!**	Verbalises ideas more coherently and richly than in previous sessions - **profits by support**.	**Attend to impact of emotional condition on quality of work (emotional intelligence?).**
7	Reflection	Severely hyperactive, distracted and distracting behaviours. Impulsive remarks re task, digresses from theme, fails to wait his turn. Subvocalises.	Hyperactive, constantly wants to eat; impulsive, inappropriate remarks; subvocalises when reading; participation in discussion is seldom relevant.	Distracted by others' hyperactive behaviour; contributes well to group activity, but finds turn taking hard and is impatient with slower group members; shows elements of self discovery.	Reserved; has difficulty with abstraction of concepts.	Displays elements of self learning and self discovery; enjoys taking leadership of group, but fails to involve quiet members. Excited and distracted by others' hyperactive behaviour.
8	Observed behaviour	Behaviour influenced by group. Functions poorly in a group – requires **more individual structure!**	Personalised approach ignored / unnoticed; hyperactivity + learning problems complicate self-discovery & application of new concepts and skills. **Persevere being firm, accepting. Repeat instructions & explanations, but not explicitly directed at him.**	Displays growing insight and skill; should benefit from working in a (homogeneous) group if distractibility and impulsivity are brought under control.	Gets lost in group, too slow for them; poor risk-taking; benefits by **individual support, and own pace.**	Benefits by group discussion; gains self confidence by initiative in group; elements of self learning and self discovery; creative imaging. Attention deficit affects task execution.
8	Reflection	Fails to wait his turn, cries out responses impulsively; Talks incessantly about other matters. Demonstrates understanding of instructions, creative imaging.	Music has some calming effect; then opposes all instructions, yawns deliberately, seeks conflict with group members; performs task carelessly, yet description of image has rich and creative elements.	Having applied elements of imaging from an earlier text during the relaxation exercise, he reflects meaningfully on his metacognitive frame! Enjoys the session; quieter than usual.	While text is read by researcher, often loses place, but finds it again himself; verbal description is colourful & creative, but drawing doesn't represent internal image. Enjoys session.	Displays good understanding of technique; when working on his own, quality of work is better than in group.
9	Observed behaviour	Has partly mastered imaging technique despite hyperactivity and distractibility; enjoyed the sense of accomplishment.	Despite distractibility & behaviour problems, he demonstrates understanding of the technique; rare moments of enjoyment. **Avoid openly focusing personal attention on him!**	Demonstrates insight in techniques of imaging. Could this be utilised in any way to enhance either cognitive control or decoding?	Accommodation of pace permits him to demonstrate growing mastery of imaging technique. Show of immense pleasure and cooperation ← ?relief.	Emotionally stable, appears happy; wants to please facilitator, seeks approval; quality of work is influenced by state of mind. **Attend to cognitive control.**
9	Reflection	Focuses on task and completes it independently; at peace and cooperative. Verbal descriptions are more detailed than drawing. Sentences are concrete, language usage is limited.	Initially negative, but participates fully after relaxation exercise. Asks meaningful questions reflecting understanding of technique. Self-corrects drawing; quiet! Execution on concrete level, limited language.	Works eagerly, focuses on his own work; quickly and creatively completes task.	Reads text 3X on his own to achieve comprehension; requires encouragement to think constructively; concrete level of ideas; line of story is sparse; last to finish.	Motivated; metacognition - asks about spelling of difficult words; rich expression, using emotional references; more details in verbal description than in demonstration.

Reflection	Moments of creative imaging and enjoyment. **Cultivate the habit!**	Breakthrough / fluctuation ← ?affect /cognitive control; positive effect on group dynamics and own product. Persist in **subtle communications of encouragement and approval!**	No progress re cognitive control.	Creative and rich imaging. Enjoyed the session.
10 Observed behaviour	Creative imaging during relaxation exercise. Better control of impulsive behaviour, improved focus and quality in work - demonstrates metacognition! Sentences remain concrete and limited.	Definite signs of improved behaviour and concentration; line of story is intact; sentences are concrete and brief, but meaningfully enriched with sensory information.	Story is related in logical sequence & with emotional effects; language is rich.	Identifies own 'pebbles' successfully & corrects 2 errors while reading; coherent imaging, though on concrete level and with limited expression.	Absent.
Reflection	Frequency of imaging has increased. Metacognitive functioning clearly directs execution and enriches outcomes.	Direct effect of behaviour on outcome of imaging. Depends on, but also discomfited by, personal approval and encouragement.	Performance is still affected by learning problems & emotional instability.	Has made marked progress, but still requires encouragement and much individual learning support.	Absent

? preceding word/remark: consider the possibility
← : possible explanation, causal factor
→ : consequence
bold print: researcher's personal notes, to direct action

Table 1 Pretest and posttest results - scores for questions on texts read aloud and silently

L	M-T	Gr. 3 Form A PRETEST n	%	Gr. 3 Form B POSTTEST n	%	Gr. 4 Form A POSTTEST N	%	Gr. 4 Form B		Gr. 5/6 Form A		Gr. 5/6 Form B	
1 Gr. 4 10 yrs	L	10/15	67	18/18	100	2/5	40						
	S	8/10	80	4/10	40	refused	-						
	T	18/25	72	22/28	78	rest	-						

L	M-T			Gr. 3 Form B PRETEST N	%								
2 Gr. 5 11 yrs	L			Refused	-								
	S			1/10	10								
	T			1/28	3.5								
	M-T			POSTTEST N	%								
	L			16/18	88								
	S			5/10	50								
	T			21/28	75								

L	M-T			Gr. 3 Form B PRETEST n	%	Gr. 4 Form A POSTTEST n	%	Gr. 4 Form B PRETEST n	%	Gr. 5/6 Form A PRETEST N	%	Gr. 5/6 Form B POSTTEST n	%
3 Gr. 5 11 yrs	L			7/9	78	13/13	100	3.5/4	88	2/5	40	8/12	67
	S			10/10	100	7/9	78	6/8	75	7/10	70	7/8	88
	T			17/19	89	20/22	91	9.5/12	79	9/15	60	15/20	75

L	M-T	Gr. 3 Form A POSTTEST n	%	Gr. 3 Form B PRETEST n	%								
4 Gr. 5 12 yrs	L	18/19	95	6/9	67								
	S	5.5/7	79	7/10	70								
	T	23.5/26	90	13/19	68								

L	M-T					Gr. 4 Form A PRETEST n	%	Gr. 4 Form B POSTTEST n	%	Gr. 5/6 Form A POSTTEST n	%		
5 Gr. 6 13 yrs	L					5/7	71	13/13	100	10/11	91		
	S					7/8	88	8/9	89	7.5/9	83		
	T					12/15	80	21/22	95	17.5/20	88		

R: Respondent
M-T: Modes, Total
L: Reading aLoud
S: Reading Silently
T: Total

The data in Table 1 reflect gains in the total scores for reading comprehension of all the learners. However, a direct comparison of individual achievement is not possible because of differences in the levels of complexity (Grade 3 – Grade 5/6), the test forms (Form A and Form B) and the total number of items per test (4 – 19). Per learner, the grade level for the pretest and posttest was by and large kept constant, which caused a ceiling effect (100%) in some of the results of Learners 1, 3 and 5. Within-level improvement was attained by Learner 1 (Total 72 - 78%), Learner 2 (Total 3.5 - 75%) and Learner 4 (Total 68 - 90%), all of these at the level of Grade 3. Across-level improvement was attained by Learner 3 (up to 75%, Gr.5) and Learner

5 (80%, Gr.4 – 88%, Gr.5). In the pretests, all learners demonstrated better comprehension of the texts which they had read silently, excepting one text read by Learner 3 (Grade 4, Form B). In the posttests, the achievement pattern was reversed and all learners demonstrated better comprehension of the texts which they had read aloud, again excepting one text read by Learner 3 (Grade 5/6, Form B). The gains reflected in the posttest results were then understandably greater with regard to texts read aloud (ranging from 12% by Learner 3 at the Gr.4-level, to 33% by Learner 1 at the Gr.3-level) than texts read silently (ranging from 1% by Learner 5 at the Gr.4-level, to 18% by Learner 3 at the Gr.5-level). This finding of course excludes the results of Learner 2, on account of his pretest refusal.

Figure 2 provides a summary of the observations made during the pretest and posttest of the cognitive strategies which each learner applied with regard to decoding and word recognition (as an aspect of fluency), and reading comprehension.

The observation data in Figure 2 show that the learners gave more detailed responses and expressed their thoughts more richly both verbally and behaviourally in the posttest. In addition, some attempt appears to have been made to read more fluently. Although the learners still tended to read word-by-word, much sounding out of the words had been eliminated, with a distinct movement from grapheme-based to syllable-based word attack strategies. The technique of imaging, especially miming the content, was implemented with enjoyment. Three learners of the five, on their own initiative, repeated a reading before attempting to answer questions. On the downside, however, the learners' distractibility and their difficulties with eye movement control and silent reading were by and large recognised to persist.

Table 2 shows the observation scores per session on 15 criteria to assess mastery of the techniques of imaging. During every learning support session, the number of each learner was entered in the appropriate score-column reflecting his level of performance in respect of each criterion.

Figure 2:
Qualitative assessment, pretest and posttest - cognitive behaviours & reading comprehension

Learner	Pretest	Posttest
1 Gr. 4 10 yrs	Cognitive strategies for reading fluency: Reads word-by-word; sounds out and repeats words; substitutes and omits letter sounds; unable to read silently - subvocalises; tracks with finger; incorrectly (impulsively?) anticipates and adds words; little sign of metacognition. Reading comprehension: Negatively affected by anticipation and addition of words; impulsive, hasty task execution. Sometimes guesses – yet is hesitant to predict events.	Cognitive strategies for reading fluency: Positive intentionality, but impulsiveness and severe distractibility; reads word-by-word and repeats syllables; disregards punctuation; subvocalises and tracks with finger; poor risk-taking, but works enthusiastically when encouraged; gives up in more complex task – loses concentration and line of story. Reading comprehension: Forgets what he wanted to say; requires prompting to resort to imaging, but quality of responses improves when he complies; responds in brief, concrete sentences; substitutes words from text with synonyms; enjoys miming some responses.
2 Gr. 5 11 yrs	Cognitive strategies for reading fluency: Negative intentionality, emotional instability → displays anxiety and refuses task; reads word-by-word and sounds out words; substitutes letter sounds, makes numerous blending errors; reads in monotone; has a history of disciplinary problems, generally poor achievement and ineffective work habits. Reading comprehension: Virtually none; unable to respond.	Cognitive strategies for reading fluency: Initially refuses the reading aloud task, but settles down (confides he is sad due to problems at home) and even displays some spontaneity – it is a pleasure to work with him today, despite some slips in attention. Reads slowly, word-by-word and in a monotone, disregarding punctuation; repeats words, pauses before unfamiliar words; confuses and substitutes letter sounds; tires quickly, loses concentration in silent reading. Reading comprehension: Responds richly to passage read aloud; creatively utilises imaging; loses line of story, needs to be redirected (distracted by enjoyment of the imaging and miming mode of response?) Quality of responses to silent reading exercise is poorer than to reading aloud.
3 Gr. 5 11 yrs	Cognitive strategies for reading fluency: Repeats syllables and words; substitutes letter sounds, adds initial sounds; has difficulty analysing and synthesising parts of words; skips line in text; unable to read silently – subvocalises audibly; guesses / anticipates words wrongly; occasionally self-corrects; keeps eyes close to text, moves head, tracks with finger. Reading comprehension: Negatively affected by incorrect guessing of words; loses gist of story.	Cognitive strategies for reading fluency: Positive intentionality; repeats words and phrases; uneven reading speed; substitutes letter sounds, adds initial sounds; has difficulty analysing and synthesising words; subvocalises; reads in a monotone; distractible; keeps eyes close to text, moves head, tracks with finger; requests help with difficult words. Reading comprehension: Loses line of story due to repetitions, requests permission to read text aloud twice before attempting questions – and succeeds with all; utilises imaging when encouraged to do so and gives detailed responses; enjoys miming.
4 Gr. 5 12 yrs	Cognitive strategies for reading fluency: Severely distractible; severe word recognition difficulties; reverses letters and syllables, adds, omits and substitutes letter sounds, disregards punctuation; reads word-by-word and extremely slowly, pausing often; frequently repeats syllables and words; moves head and tracks with finger. Visual perception problems? Reading comprehension: Guesses most answers, fails to refer to text, unwilling to predict events.	Cognitive strategies for reading fluency: Severe learning and reading disability, poor risk-taking, but positive intentionality; distractibility; sounds out syllables; omits letter sounds and syllables; reads word-by-word at fair speed; pauses to subvocalise and repeat syllables and words; disregards punctuation; moves head and tracks with finger; applies miming when encouraged to do so. Reading comprehension: Participates enthusiastically and does his best; loses line of story; requests permission to read text twice before attempting questions; resorts to miming responses to compensate for his limited language; gives responses in brief and concrete statements; notably poorer quality of responses to text read silently than aloud.
5 Gr. 6 13 yrs	Cognitive strategies for reading fluency: Positive intentionality; frequently selfcorrects; reads word-by-word, omits and substitutes letter sounds (poor phonological skills), reverses and substitutes words; disregards punctuation and reads in a monotone; moves head, tracks with finger; distractible, constantly fidgets; task completion influenced by emotions. Reading comprehension: Keeps track of content despite fragmenting effect of problems and errors.	Cognitive strategies for reading fluency: Enthusiastic; reading speed fluctuates – begins fast, then slows down; lack of fluency, reads word-by-word, disregards punctuation, repeats letter sounds and parts of words; reverses letters; with difficult words: pauses before, subvocally sounds out syllables and frequently mispronounces them, but asks for correct pronunciation and meaning when he discovers that he is losing meaning; moves head and tracks with finger. Selfcorrects successfully, enjoys session. Reading comprehension: Requests permission to read the read-aloud text twice, deliberately focuses on imaging the second time; responses are rich and in full sentences; quality of work is influenced by emotions; loses concentration, changes the subject while answering the questions on the silent reading, quality of responses deteriorates; fidgets; teacher mentions that performance in history has improved – he says that he used imaging to learn for the test.

Table 2 Criteria of mastery for imaging by learners with a learning impairment: observations per session

11. Completed in set time (1 = No, 4 = Efficient)	2,4		2,3,4		2,4			4		2			4		4	1,2,3
12. Independent work (1=No, 4=Independent)	1,4	1,2	1,3	1,5	4	3,5	1,3		4	1,4	2		4	1,2,3,5	4	1,2,3
13. Metacognitive functioning (1 = Limited, 4 = Rich)	1,2,4	1,3	1,2	5	2,4	1,3	5	4	2,4,5		1,2,4	1,3,5		1,3,5	1,2	3
14. Intentionality (1 = Rejection, 4 = Enthusiasm)	2		1,2,3	4,5	2		1,4,5		5		1,2	1,3		2	1,4	1,2,3,4
15. Attention 1 = Frequent slips, 4 = Marked focus	1,3,4,5		2,3		1,3	1,3,4		1,4	2	1,3,4,5	2	3,4,5		1,2,5	1,2,4	3
TOTAL (Absent: Learner 2 in Sessions 4 & 5, Learner 5 in Session 10; Cr. n.a.: Criterion 9 in Session 7)	30	22	19	4	23	31	18	3	16	19	35	5	12	30	16	11
TOTAL %	40.0	29.3	25.3	5.3	30.7	41.3	24.0	4.0	21.3	25.3	46.7	6.7	20.0	50.0	26.7	18.3

(continued)													
					3		1,2,3	1,2,3		4		4	
			1,3,5	1,2,4		1,3,5	1,3,5	1,3			2,4	1,2,3,5	1,2,3,5
			1,3,5	1,2	3		1,3,4	1,2,3,4		4		1,2	1,2,3,4,5
		2		1,3,4	3					4	1,4		
			3,5		4,5			3,4,5	3			1,2,4	3
1	9	41	24	7	28	40	4	25	31				
1.3	12.0	54.7	32.0	9.3	37.3	53.3	6.7	41.7	51.7				

According to the data in Table 2, only 3 of the 15 criteria on the degree of mastery in imaging were possibly fully attained by Session 10 (No. 3, 4 and 14; scores were extrapolated for Learner 5, absent in Session 10, from his earlier progress). The 1-code (representing total failure) was never awarded in Sessions 9 and 10, and the 2-code (signifying some remaining difficulty) only 11 times, in comparison with 30 and 22 out of a possible 75 for the 1- and 2-codes in Session 1, and 23 and 31 out of a possible 75 for the 1- and 2-codes in Session 2. Extrapolating to Session 10 from the scores of Learner 5 for Session 9, two learners (Learners 3 and 5) could be taken to have achieved a 4-code (signifying good mastery) in Session 10 for all the criteria. Metacognitive Functioning (No. 13), Original Execution of Imaging (No. 7) and Flexible Transfer to a New Topic (No. 10) appear to have posed most difficulty for all the learners.

Discussion

Having attained the lowest scores in reading comprehension in a special school for learners with learning impairment, the participants were all contending with severe learning problems when they started receiving learning support to develop the strategy of imaging for reading comprehension. Figures 1 and 2 both show that attentional problems, impulsive behaviour, hyperactivity and perceptual problems in the visual and auditory domains were observed to impact heavily on their efforts to participate successfully in the learning support sessions. Affect further appears to have had a pervasive influence on the learners' progress, both positively and negatively, and would seem closely associated with experiences/feelings of self and of task. Breakthroughs in the mastery of the techniques of imaging, once achieved, appeared to make a considerable difference to performance (focus, commitment, application of techniques) and achievement. In this regard, the most notable change was in Learner 2, who improved from a refusal to read aloud in the pretest, to achieving 88% on the reading aloud text in the posttest (Table 1), and who had predominantly 1-codes on the criterion scores for imaging in Session 1, but went on to receive eight 3-codes and seven 4-codes in Session 10 (Table 2). Learner 4, the participant in the group who demonstrated the most severe reading impairments, also grew in confidence and independence, in addition to his firm progress in reading comprehension at the Gr.3-level (Table 1) and a consistent movement toward higher codes on the criteria for imaging (Table 2).

As stated earlier, a direct comparison of individual achievement in the pretests and posttests is not possible because of the variance in the levels of complexity (Grade 3 – Grade 5/6), the test forms (Form A and Form B) and the total number of items per test (4 – 19). Yet all of the five learners appear to have improved in reading comprehension from pretest to posttest (Table 1). The within-level improvement attained by the weaker learners (Learners 1, 2 and 4) suggests that they succeeded in gaining firm ground at the level of Grade 3, although this remained 1 to 2 grades below the norm; the across-level improvement of the stronger learners (Learners 3 and 5) actually brought both up to the standard of reading comprehension required for their grade. The ceiling effect (100%) in some of the posttest results of Learners 1, 3 and 5 (Table 1) might obviously mask a greater measure of improvement than suggested by the data. Reading silently appears to have supported comprehension during the pretest (Table 1), perhaps by releasing some powers of attention and memory for the processing of content information. The reversed pattern of achievement in the posttests, with learners now demonstrating better comprehension when reading aloud, leads one to suspect that the strategy of imaging actually supported the very decoding and recognition of words. This possibility is strengthened by the rather unexpected observation of a movement away from the sounding out of words to syllable-based word attack strategies (Figure 2).

Qualitatively, learners further demonstrated somewhat enhanced comprehension of print in the form of more detailed responses and more richly expressive language usage and behaviours during the posttest. Increased self-regulation may safely be inferred from the tendency of three learners to reread a passage before attempting to answer questions (Figure 2). This further suggests their growing confidence in their ability to break through into comprehending printed text and, perhaps, some development in their metacognitive skills. In this regard, the self-initiated and successful transfer of the imaging strategy by one learner (Learner 5) in preparing for a test in a content area is significant.

Behaviours associated with the strategy of imaging for understanding did not appear to develop consistently or at an even pace, although marked improvements were observed with regard to all of the criteria for imaging (Table 2). Constructive and creative thinking, together with flexible metacognitive control, might be the last to grow. Overall, the outcomes suggest that learning, not only reading had been enhanced during the support sessions and that imaging is a holistic, strength-based and adaptable reading comprehension technique for learners with dyslexia in the intermediate school phase, both when reading aloud and reading silently. The learners' deepened engagement with text as reflected in their participation and mastery of the technique of imaging in Table 2 appears confirmed by the posttest data in Table 1 and Figure 2.

Positive effects would appear attainable across the full grade and age range of learners in the intermediate phase (Gr.4-6, 10-13 years). Learners with dyslexia in the intermediate phase, even in Grade 4 (Learner 1), appear already to have the basic cognitive skills to implement imaging. Language problems as well as attention deficits proved to have a pervasive effect, but reading aloud with imaging seemed effectively to support comprehension. Although no attention was devoted to decoding skills, reading fluency moreover improved.

The effect of environmental disadvantage was observed in that subjects often had a limited or different experiential frame and vocabulary with which to form images. However, it was possible to make adjustments to accommodate the effect of environmental differences on the quality of the images formed. Although an inadequate culture of learning at home was generally evidenced, especially with regard to homework tasks and the nature of support rendered at home, the learners succeeded in mastering the technique adequately to utilise independent imaging when reading even without reinforcement at home.

A group size of five for learners with dyslexia appears manageable, although the variety of learning problems did complicate the learning support. With all the learners, attention deficits limited the quality and duration of focus on the images formed. However, they did seem increasingly to monitor their understanding, as demonstrated by the requests during the posttest to be permitted to repeat a reading. Modes of self-expression such as miming and discussion were preferred to those requiring fine visual-motor skills, such as drawing or cut-and-paste.

Limitations of the research

Interpretation of the data generated in this study obviously should not be generalised for a range of reasons, including the small sample-size and the individual nature of dyslexia.

The selection of discrete test materials for each learner restricts interpretation of the standardised reading assessment data to the qualitative level and has rendered the results largely incomparable. If Form A had been used consistently at the various grade levels during the pretest, some basis of comparison would at least have been possible.

Factors contributing to the improved reading comprehension results probably included a Hawthorne effect in the learners' positive relationship with the facilitator. Supporting the natural progression during this developmental phase from concrete to more abstract patterns of reasoning, may also have enhanced the results somewhat.

The lack of control data complicates evaluation of effect and the short duration of the intervention has further made it impossible to look systematically at transferring the skill to other reading activities and contexts.

Self reporting was one of the data collection techniques, especially for the criterion-data summarised in Table 2. Although commonly used when researching imaging, this may have been an unstable data source with learners with dyslexia. By nature of each subject's particular learning problems, abstracted imaging probably occurred at varying levels which was also difficult to recognise and/or assess. A cross-cultural element in the intervention (between the facilitator and learners from a socio-economically disadvantaged environment) may have further influenced the observation, description and coding of the learners' behaviour.

Regarding issues of a more practical nature, fatigue at the end of the school day (when sessions took place) probably affected results. The parents were difficult to contact, preventing the technique from being practised at home, and homework tasks were seldom performed.

Recommendations: teaching imaging to enhance reading comprehension

Focusing on internal images requires skills of concentration and creativity. With learners with dyslexia, the imaging technique should be practised step-by-step, first systematically introducing the senses in forming images and later integrating textual content into the procedure.

For readers with dyslexia, decoding difficulties complicate the task of simultaneously reading and imaging content. To internalise imaging as a reading habit, the technique should be revised regularly and explicitly generalised to all learning areas.

Since learners with dyslexia differ in their acquisition and application of imaging, it is advisable to personalise the learning support. In inclusive education, learners with dyslexia would probably benefit by focused (pull-out) learning support sessions. The technique could be facilitated with five learners with dyslexia at a time, accommodating the particular learning needs and cultural environment of each.

Conclusion

Given the awesome list of factors that could need addressing when a learner demonstrates a reading problem, we would do well to mind Manzo and Manzo's (1995) observation: *"Any method is potentially a special method when it is applied in response to an unattended need.*

Special does not need to mean exotic – though it can be; nor does it have to be specialised – which it also can be. However, it must always be thoughtful and provisional: if it doesn't work, change it, and if you find a match, light it!" (p. 345)

References

American Psychiatric Association. (1994). *Diagnostic and statistical manual of mental disorders* (4th ed.).Washington, DC: Author.

Bagley, M.T. & Lavin, C.L. (1988). *Reading through imagery.* New York: Trillium Press.

Bouwer, A.C. (2004). Reading and Writing. In Eloff, I & Ebersohn, L. (Eds.) *Keys to educational psychology* (pp. 83-118). Cape Town: Juta.

Bouwer, A.C. & Jordaan, V. (2002). The use of imaging to develop reading comprehension amongst learners with a learning disability. *Language Matters, 33*, 197-225.

Brand-Gruwel, S., Aarnoutse, C.A.J. & Van den Bos, K.P. (1998). Improving text comprehension strategies in reading and listening settings. *Learning and Instruction, 8* (1), 63-81.

Burke, M. (1997). *Does the teaching of active learning strategies improve the reading comprehension of learning disabled students?* Unpublished master's thesis, Kean College of New Jersey, Union, New Jersey.

Chiappe, P., Hasher, L. & Siegel, L.S. (2000). Working memory, inhibitory control and reading disability. *Memory and cognition, 28* (1), 8-16.

Everatt, J. (2002). Visual Processes. In G. Reid & J. Wearmouth (Eds.), *Dyslexia and literacy. Theory and Practice* (pp. 85-98). Chichester, West Sussex: John Wiley & Sons.

Frith, Frith, U. (2002) Resolving the Paradoxes of Dyslexia. In G. Reid & J. Wearmouth (Eds.), *Dyslexia and literacy. Theory and Practice* (pp. 45-68). Chichester, West Sussex: John Wiley & Sons.

Fryburg, E.L. (1997). *Reading and learning disability. A neuropsychological approach to evaluation and instruction.* Illinois: Charles C Thomas.

Goodman, K. (1988). The Reading Process. In P. Carrell, J. Devine & D. Eskey (Eds.), *Interactive Approaches to Second Language Reading* (pp.11-21). Cambridge: Cambridge University Press.

Goswami, U. (1998). *Cognition in children.* Hove: Psychology Press.

Green, C. & Chee, K. (1997). *Understanding ADHD.* London: Vermillion.

Hellier, C. (1994). Closing the gap: compensating for literacy delay in children with specific learning difficulties. *Support for Learning, 9* (4), 162-165.

Hodes, C.L. (1990). The induction, use and effectiveness of mental imagery as an instructional variable: A thesis in curriculum and instruction. (Doctoral dissertation, Pennsylvania State University, 1990). *Dissertation Abstracts International, vol. 5109A,* p.3017.

Human Sciences Research Council. (1990). *Diagnostic reading test. Afrikaans First Language. Grade 3 to Grade 6.* Pretoria: Author.

Knight, D.F. & Hynd, G.W. (2002). The Neurobiology of Dyslexia. . In G. Reid & J. Wearmouth (Eds.), *Dyslexia andLiteracy. Theory and Practice* (pp. 29-44). Chichester, West Sussex: John Wiley & Sons.

Lewis, R.B. & Doorlag, D.H. (1999). *Teaching special students in general education classrooms.* Upper Saddle River, NJ: Prentice-Hall.

Machiels-Bongaerts, M., Schmidt, H.G. & Boshuizen, P.A. (1995). The effect of prior knowledge activation on text recall: an investigation of two conflicting hypotheses. *British Journal of Educational Psychology, 65* (1), 409-423.

Manzo, A.V. & Manzo, U.C. (1995). *Teaching Children to be Literate. A Reflective Approach.* Orlando: Harcourt Brace & Company.

Mazzoni, G. & Nelson, T.O. (Eds.). (1998). *Metacognitive and cognitive neuropsychology. Monitoring and control processes.* London: Lawrence Erlbaum.

Mills, S. (1993). *For your imagination. Focused imaging. Instructional Strategies.* Canada: University of Regina.

Moore, M. & Wade, B. (1998). Reading strategies. A comparative study of ex-reading recovery students and peers. *Research in Education, 60,* 21-28.

Oakhill, J. & Patel, S. (1991). Can imagery training help children who have comprehension problems? *Journal of Research in Reading, 14* (2), 106-115.

Pike, K., Compain, R. & Mumper, J. (1997). *New Connections. An Integrated Approach to Literacy.* 2nd Ed. New York: Longman.

Richardson, J.T.E. (1995). The efficacy of imagery mnemonics in memory remediation. *Neuropsychologia, 33* (11), 1345-1357.

Rieber, L.P. (1995). A historical review of visualization in human cognition. *Educational Technology Research and Development, 43* (1), 45-54.

Sadoski, M., Goetz, E.T. & Olivarez, A. (1990). Imagination in story reading: The role of imagery, verbal recall, story analysis and processing levels. *Journal of Reading Behavior, 22* (1), 55-70.

Sampson, M., Sampson, M.B. & Van Allen, R. (1995). *Pathways to Literacy. Process Transactions.* Orlando: Harcourt Brace.

Shanker, J.L. & Ekwall, E.E. (1998). *Locating and correcting reading difficulties* (7th ed.). Upper Saddle River, NJ: Prentice Hall.

Silverman, L.K. (1995). *Effective techniques for teaching highly gifted visual-spatial learners.* Colorado: Gifted Development Center Denver.

Singleton, C. (2002). Dyslexia: Cognitive Factors and Implications for Literacy. In G. Reid & J. Wearmouth (Eds.), *Dyslexia andLiteracy. Theory and Practice* (pp. 115-130). Chichester, West Sussex: John Wiley & Sons.

Snowling, M.J. (1996). Developmental Dyslexia: An Introduction and Theoretical Overview. In M. Snowling& J. Stackhouse (Eds.), *Dyslexia, Speech and Language. A Practitioner's Handbook* (pp. 1-11). London: Whurr Publishers.

Solvberg, A.M. & Valas, H. (1995). Effects of mnemonic-imagery strategy on students' prose recall. *Scandinavian Journal of Educational Research, 39* (2), 107-119.

Stanovich, K.E. (1980). Toward an interactive compensatory model of individual differences in the development of reading fluency. *Reading Research Quarterly, 16,* 32-71.

Truscott, D.M., Walker, B.J. & Gambrell, L. (1995). Poor readers don't image, or do they? *Reading Research Report, 38,* 1-12.

Turner, M. (1997). *Psychological Assessment of Dyslexia.* London: Whurr Publishers.

9
EFFECTS OF DIFFERENT FORMS OF INSTRUCTION ON ACQUISITION AND USE OF MULTIPLICATION STRATEGIES BY CHILDREN WITH MATH LEARNING PROBLEMS

Evelyn H. Kroesbergen and Johannes E.H. van Luit

Introduction

This chapter focuses on how children with math learning problems learn multiplication, and particularly how they learn adequate strategy use. Most students easily learn the multiplication tables up to 10 x 10. However, some students really do not understand the meaning of the symbol "x" and, for example, that 5 + 5 is not the same as 5 x 5. These students have many difficulties remembering all of the multiplication facts. Almost every teacher will recognize a student such as Bob, a 9-year-old boy who participated in this study. Bob is in fourth grade and has had about two years of multiplication instruction. Due to considerable instruction and extra help, he now knows most of the multiplication tables, although he still makes many mistakes. One of the facts that he knows well is 2 x 4 = 8. However, when the teacher asks Bob to lay down '2 x 4' with blocks, he lays down one group of two blocks and one group of four blocks; he then starts to count and, when he arrives at six, thinks he must have made a mistake and starts counting again. Two times four really makes 6? He does not understand what is wrong. Bob is only one example of a student with serious math learning problems.

About 25 percent of students have difficulties learning math, and about five to ten percent have serious math difficulties (Rivera, 1997). These difficulties can manifest themselves in different ways and can have different causes. The difficulties can be explained by such student factors as intelligence, motivation, memory skills, metacognitive skills, or vocabulary. Another explanation may lie in the instruction; students with difficulties have special needs and therefore require special instruction (Carnine, 1997). Instruction should be adapted to the specific needs of students (Geary, 1994). In addition, special remedial teaching programs may be needed to teach and support students with learning problems. This chapter reports on a study in which two different teaching programs were offered to low performing students. Before describing the design and the results, however, we will first describe the problems encountered by children with math learning problems and how multiplication strategies can be taught in particular.

Children with math difficulties

Given that every student is unique and every student with math learning problems may encounter other difficulties, it is almost impossible to describe the typical student with math learning problems. Nevertheless, many similarities can be found within a group of such students. In fact, researchers have documented a number of specific mathematical deficiencies. For example, in the area of computation, students may exhibit deficits in the skills related to fact retrieval, problem conceptualization, speed of processing, and the use of effective calculation strategies (Rivera, 1997). Cawley and Miller (1989) have reported that the mathematical knowledge of students with serious learning problems tends to progress at a rate of approximately one year for every two years of school attendance. Most of the students with such learning problems also appear to reach a plateau during sixth or seventh grade and continue to encounter math difficulties throughout high school and into adult life.

Some of the students with math problems simply lag behind in the acquisition of procedural knowledge; others show developmental differences that do not necessarily disappear with age. Research suggests that the math deficiencies of students with learning problems emerge in the early years (Mercer & Miller, 1992; Schopman & Van Luit, 1996). An ability to form and remember associations, understand basic relationships, and make simple generalizations appears to be a basic cognitive skill needed to follow initial (formal) math instruction. More complex cognitive skills are needed when students progress to more complicated mathematical skills. In addition to this, the mastery of lower level skills is essential for the acquisition of higher level skills (Mercer & Miller, 1992). Stated concretely: Difficulties learning early numeracy during kindergarten may impede the learning of basic math skills during grade one and later (Schopman & Van Luit, 1996).

During first grade, students start with the learning of basic addition facts and progress to the learning of basic subtraction, multiplication, and division facts. These basic facts are necessary for the acquisition and understanding of higher level mathematical knowledge. Automaticity is also reached with lots of practice, but students with learning problems are often found to have many more problems with the development of such automaticity than their normal achieving peers (Schopman & Van Luit, 1996). Research shows, for example, that students with math difficulties must often calculate basic facts while other students simply know the facts directly (Pellegrino & Goldman, 1987). The development of long-term memory representations also proceeds more slowly or differently for children with math difficulties when compared to their peers (Geary, Brown, & Samaranayake, 1991). This leads also to difficulties in fact retrieval. In addition, such students continue to make more mistakes on basic skills than their peers.

Even when the students with learning problems master the basic computational skills, the problem-solving strategies they use may still differ from those of their peers. In general, students with learning problems have been found to use fewer and less adequate strategies than their normal-achieving peers (Geary et al., 1991; Rivera, 1997). The low math performance of many students can be explained by a lack of adequate strategies for the selection and processing of information and metacognitive deficiencies. Students with math learning problems can simply be overwhelmed by the memorization, strategies, vocabulary, and language coding required when the instruction is verbal, the introduction of concepts is rapid, and there is not sufficient time for review and practice. Such difficulties can then express themselves as an inability to acquire and apply computational, reasoning, and problem-solving skills (Rivera, 1997). The gap between the math achievement of students with learning problems and that of their classmates will only increase and become particularly apparent in the area of problem solving because the strategies needed for problem solving require not only mathematic competence but also linguistic competence (Carnine, 1997).

Math has a logical structure. Students construct simple relations first and then progress to more complex tasks. As the student progresses with the construction of different math tasks, the content and skills they have discovered are usually transferred as well (Mercer & Miller, 1992). However, students with math difficulties often fail to make the necessary connections between different problems and strategies. They do not automatically apply learned strategies to other situations, and the instruction for such students should therefore be adapted to their specific characteristics and needs.

Teaching multiplication strategies

For adequate problem solving, different types of knowledge are required. A distinction can be made between the more general metacognitive knowledge of students (or their awareness of the cognitive processes and strategies that they use to approach, organize, and evaluate the solution of a problem) and the more task-specific knowledge and strategies that they apply to solve a problem. Three components of metacognitive knowledge can be distinguished. To start with, students must have declarative knowledge: knowledge of the relevant quantitative concepts, operations, algorithms, and problem-solving strategies (Montague, 1992). Second, students must have procedural knowledge to apply their declarative knowledge: procedural knowledge means knowing how to apply learned skills to achieve certain goals. Third, students must have conditional knowledge, which enables them to select the appropriate strategies and apply these for the solution of specific tasks.

Students with learning problems are typically poor problem solvers. They show deficits in all types of knowledge (Montague, 1992). This means that they experience many difficulties with the learning of both general and specific math knowledge, tend to have insufficient information processing skills, do not apply information adequately, and experience troubles with the efficient organization of an approach to the problem-solving task (Case, Harris, & Graham, 1992). Instruction should therefore focus on these deficiencies, both on promoting automaticity and on acquiring adequate strategies. As Goldman (1989) states, the emphasis during instruction should lie on the procedures for solving problems. Students should be explicitly informed about the appropriate strategies for the solution of a given task. Most researchers state that students with learning problems need structured, teacher-direct instruction (Jitendra & Hoff, 1996), particularly when they have not had many learning experiences. In addition to this, of course, the instruction should involve activities to promote conceptual understanding.

With regard to strategy instruction, a distinction can be made between direct versus guided instruction (Goldman, 1989). Direct instruction is mostly used to teach task-specific strategies. Students are explicitly taught the steps for the solution of particular types of problems. The instruction is usually scripted and therefore structured step by step to insure mastery of a particular strategy before proceeding to the next type of problem. The focus of direct instruction when it comes to metacognitive knowledge is mainly on declarative knowledge (task-specific strategies), partly on procedural knowledge (how to apply task-specific strategies), and less on conditional knowledge (how to select strategies). Guided instruction, in contrast, is aimed at enabling students themselves to discover what multiplication is all about and just how multiplication problems can be solved. During guided learning, the learning process stands central and not the strategies or solution procedures that the teacher has in mind. In addition to this, the three components of metacognitive knowledge all play an important role in such instruction.

Research questions

The focus of this study is on students' acquisition and use of multiplication strategies. The emphasis is on the use of task-specific strategies for the solution of multiplication problems. For multiplication, a distinction can be made between such basic strategies as counting and repeated addition versus more advanced strategies such as splitting at five and doubling. However, the goal of teaching multiplication tables is always the automatization of multiplication facts. The central question in this study is therefore whether a differential effect of instructional method can be found for the strategies students apply during multiplication. For this purpose, the methods of direct versus guided instruction were compared. Our research question addresses the differential effects of the instructional methods immediately after intervention on both the test scores of the students (question 1) and the strategies used by the students (question 2). How the multiplication strategies used by the students develop during the intervention period in which the students received one of both instructional methods is shortly addressed based on video observations.

Method

Procedure and design

In order to measure the effects of different instructional methods, a quasi-experimental design containing two experimental conditions and one control condition was utilized. Pre- and post-test scores were calculated before and after instruction.

For a period of four to five months, the students in the experimental groups received twice weekly multiplication lessons with a duration of 30 to 45 minutes. Research assistants, trained and coached by the experimenter, conducted the lessons in small groups of four to six students each. To follow the development of the students, the research assistants kept a logbook for every lesson. In addition, 5 of the 30 lessons were videotaped. Given that the special instruction was undertaken during the time that the students would normally receive math instruction, the total amount of math instruction was comparable across the groups. On the days when the students in the experimental groups followed the regular math instruction in the class, they received the same instruction as their classmates with the exception of the multiplication instruction.

The students in the control condition took part in the regular mathematics curriculum, which included multiplication instruction.

Information on their mathematics instruction was obtained via a teacher questionnaire. The instruction that the control children received differed across schools but was always found to be somewhere between direct and guided instruction.

Participants

The participants in this study were students from elementary schools for regular and special education. The students were selected for low math performance on the basis of 1) their scores on a general mathematics test (below the 25th percentile) and 2) the opinion of the teacher. Further selection was conducted on the basis of two tests. The first test contained addition and subtraction problems up to 100. Students who scored below the 60% level on this test were excluded from the study as simply not ready to learn multiplication on the basis of repeated addition. The second selection test contained multiplication facts up to 100. Students who scored above the 50% level were excluded as already having a reasonable multiplication performance level.

Within each participating school, the students meeting the aforementioned criteria were assigned randomly to an experimental or control condition. Only one experimental condition was implemented per school. A total of 265 students from 24 schools were selected for inclusion in the study: 88 for Guided Instruction (GI), 87 for Direct Instruction (DI), and 90 for the Control condition (C). An overview of the descriptive information for the different groups is presented in Table 1. Multivariate analyses showed no significant differences across the three conditions for age or IQ but a significant difference for months of multiplication instruction received, $F(2,262) = 5.278$, $p = .006$. The students in the DI condition had, on average, received less multiplication instruction when compared to the students in the other conditions.

Table 1 Comparison of groups

Condition	N	Sex male	Sex female	Mean IQ (sd)	Education regular	Education special	Mean age (sd)	Experience (sd)[1]
Guided	88	55	33	87.3 (12.1)	42	46	9.8 (1.4)	11.0 (6.8)
Direct	87	45	42	88.4 (11.7)	44	43	9.4 (1.3)	8.2 (6.7)
Control	90	53	37	88.7 (12.3)	47	43	9.7 (1.3)	10.8 (6.0)
Total	265	153	112	88.1 (12.0)	133	132	9.7 (1.4)	10.0 (6.6)

[1] Experience: number of months that children had received instruction in multiplication before the intervention period

Materials

In order to gain insight into the solution procedures used by the students, they were given a paper-and-pencil test with a scratch paper to write down the strategy they used for every problem. In addition to this, each child was interviewed and asked to "think aloud" while they solved the given problems. Both the paper-and-pencil test and the interview test were conducted before and after the intervention period.

Paper-and-pencil test

The paper-and-pencil test contained 20 multiplication problems taken from the test items used to measure the mathematics levels of students in schools for special education in the Netherlands (Kraemer, Van der Schoot, & Engelen, 2000). Most of the problems were context problems: multiplication problems embedded in a short story that is recognizable for the students; the reader is referred to Figure 1 for an example of such a problem. Only four of the problems were bare math problems with no accompanying text or picture. The difficulty of the problems varied from 3 x 3 and 5 x 5 to 8 x 12 and 5 x 1.25. Only five of the problems were below 10 x 10. Two of the problems were actually division problems that could also be solved using multiplication strategies (e.g., "My aunt wants to paste 50 photos in an album. She wants to paste 5 photos on a page. How many pages will she fill?"). The students were also asked to write the solution procedure they used down on a scratch paper for each problem. The answers were scored as right or wrong, and the solution strategies used by each child recorded.

Figure 1
Example from the paper-and-pencil test

 Fred buys 5 bags.

Interview test

Ten bare problems from the multiplication tables up to twelve were used for the interview. The students were asked to "think aloud" while solving the problems. When only the answer was mentioned and not the solution strategy, the research assistant asked the student how he or she knew the answer and continued to question the student until the strategy was clear. The answers were scored as right or wrong, and the solution strategies used by each child recorded.

Instructional program

In this study, use was made of adapted versions of the multiplication part of the MASTER Training Program (Van Luit, Kaskens, & Van der Krol, 1993; see also Van Luit & Naglieri, 1999). The experimental programs consisted of a series of 25 multiplication lessons: 8 lessons on basic procedures; 11 lessons on multiplication tables; and 6 lessons on "easy" problems above 10 x 10. The emphasis in the lessons was on: (1) automated mastery of the multiplication facts as this knowledge is necessary for further learning and adequate problem solving, and (2) the use of strategies including metacognitive knowledge of how to apply strategies and how to select the most appropriate strategies. The teacher always kept the students' existing knowledge in mind and always proceeded at a tempo that fit the students. As already mentioned, the two experimental conditions reflect the use of two different forms of instruction: guided versus direct instruction.

Guided instruction. The lessons in the GI condition are always started with a review of the previous lesson. What the students do and say in this phase is taken as the starting point for the current lesson. When it appears that the students do not fully understand the tasks discussed in the previous lesson, the focus is again on these tasks. Otherwise, the teacher introduces the next topic (e.g., "Today we are going to practice with the table of 3"). During guided instruction, the discussion is always centered on the contributions of the children themselves, which means that topics and strategies other than those that the teacher has in mind may sometimes be addressed. Just as in the DI condition, the GI condition contains an introductory phase, a group practice phase, and an individual practice phase. However, in the GI condition, greater attention is devoted to the discussion of possible solution procedures and strategies than in the DI condition.

In the GI condition, much more space is provided for the individual contributions of the student. The main idea is that the teacher presents a problem and the children actively search for a possible solution by making a selection from their own repertoire or exploring new strategies. The teacher can encourage the discovery of new strategies by offering additional and/or more difficult problems. The teacher facilitates the learning process by asking questions and promoting the discussion of specific tasks and solutions by the students. The teacher never demonstrates the use of a particular strategy; this means that if none of the children discover a particular strategy, the strategy will not be discussed within the group. The teacher can, however, structure the discussions by asking the students to classify various strategies and posing questions about the usefulness of particular strategies, for example.

Direct instruction. The lessons in the DI condition are also always started with a repetition of what was done in the preceding lesson. When the students show sufficient knowledge of the preceding lesson, the teacher can proceed to the actual lesson. After a short introduction, the teacher explains how to solve the task in question and gives an example of a good solution strategy with the aid of concrete materials when necessary. After the presentation of one or two examples, several tasks are next practiced within the group with an emphasis on the use of strategies. The students then practice on their own, and the various strategies used to solve the tasks are discussed thereafter. During the practice phase, the children familiarize themselves with the kinds of tasks involved and establish connections to the mental solution of the problems. The goals of the final phase are control, shortening, automatization, and generalization.

The explicit teaching of new strategies is intended to help the students expand their strategy repertoires. When a new strategy is taught, it is always the teacher who tells the children how and when to apply the strategy. The children are then instructed to follow the example of the teacher. In the DI condition, there is little room for input from the children themselves (i.e., the children must follow the procedures the teacher teaches them). When a child applies a strategy that has not been taught, the teacher may observe that the particular strategy is certainly a possible strategy for solving the problem in question but that they are being taught a different strategy and then ask the child to apply the strategy being taught. The students in the direct instruction condition learn to work with a strategy decision sheet to help them choose the most appropriate strategy. The strategies taught in this condition are: reversal, splitting at five or ten, neighbour problem, doubling, saying the table, and repeated addition.

Observations. In the two experimental conditions, the students learned to use different strategies. In the GI condition, the students were encouraged to use those strategies familiar to them or the strategies they discover. Sometimes the students used the strategies of doubling or splitting at ten without actually knowing it or knowing the name of the strategy. The role of the teacher was then to name the particular strategy or strategies and stimulate the discussion of the use of different strategies. In other words, the students in this condition were already familiar with a number of strategies and encouraged to use the different strategies according to their own preferences. This means that certain strategies were learned in a different sequence than in the DI condition. All of the strategies explicitly addressed in the DI condition were spontaneously addressed in the GI condition, interestingly enough.

In the DI condition, the students also learn to use different strategies but only those dictated by the program and taught by the teacher. The teacher explains every strategy selected to be taught, which means that the students do not discover just how the strategy works on their own. In general, the students in the DI condition learned the strategies taught to them. However, it proved difficult for them to keep to the structure provided by the teacher and not use their own preferred strategies at times. For example, some of the students had considerable troubles with the number line while others did not see the benefit of using the splitting strategy and therefore did not learn much from the exercises concerned with this strategy. For a more detailed description of the lessons, the reader is referred to Kroesbergen (2002).

Coding of strategies

As already noted, the answers provided by the students on the paper-and-pencil test and the interview test were scored as right or wrong. In addition to this, the strategies the children used to solve the problems were coded. If the strategy (or strategies) used by a student was not apparent or completely unclear, this was coded as "unknown." When a student indicated that he "knew the answer out of his head" (on the scratch paper or during the interview), this was coded as "automatized." The following strategies were coded:
1. automatized;
2. reversal ($5 \times 6 = 6 \times 5$);
3. splitting at five or ten – addition ($8 \times 7 = 5 \times 7 + 3 \times 7$; $13 \times 5 = 10 \times 5 + 3 \times 5$);
4. splitting at five or ten – subtraction ($9 \times 7 = 10 \times 7 - 1 \times 7$);
5. doubling ($6 \times 4 = 3 \times 4 + 3 \times 4$);
6. neighbour ($8 \times 9 = 9 \times 9 - 1 \times 9$);
7. reciting aloud or writing down the multiplication table;
8. repeated addition;
9. use of concrete materials or drawing;
10. division;
11. and all possible combinations of such strategies.

For every student, the number of different strategies used was counted (strategy repertoire). For example, when a student used six times repeated addition, two times splitting at five, one time reversal and doubling, and one time reversal and repeated addition, his repertoire score was four as he used four different strategies.

In addition to the number of different strategies used, the relative frequency and efficiency of the students' strategy use was considered. To measure the efficiency of strategy selection, the strate-gies were assigned to one of the following five categories, based on the steps needed to solve the problem.
1. retrieval;
2. adequate solution requiring one step (e.g., reversing or splitting);
3. semi-adequate solution requiring two steps (e.g., reversal and splitting, splitting and adding: 7 x 4 = 5 x 4 + 4 + 4);
4. not very adequate solution requiring more than two steps (e.g., 4 x 8 = 8 x 4; 2 x 4 = 8; 8 + 8 = 16; 16 + 16 = 32);
5. repeated addition (more than two steps) or counting.

A mean efficacy score was then calculated for each student. For the example mentioned in connection with the number of different strategies used, the student's efficacy score would be 4.2 (6 x 5 + 2 x 2 + 3 + 5 / 10). A lower score means a higher efficacy.

Results

In order to compare the different methods of instruction, the test performances of the students in the different conditions were compared. Furthermore, the particular strategies and any changes in the strategies they use were examined. In addition to this, the differences between the two methods of testing (written versus oral) were considered.

In Table 2, the results for the pre- versus post-test performance of the students in the three conditions are presented. No significant differences were found between the three conditions, neither at pre-test or post-test. All of the groups improved significantly from pre- to post-test ($p < .05$), but the effect sizes differed with the DI group improving more on the paper and pencil test than the other two groups, $F(2,261) = 7.826$, $p = .001$. Further analyses revealed some differences between the students in regular versus special education. The students in special education performed better on the paper-and-pencil test, which is most likely due to the fact that these students are older and have had more multiplication instruction. When corrected for these differences, the effects of school type almost disappear. Given no further qualitative differences between the students from the two types of schools, the data were collapsed together for the remaining analyses.

Table 2 Means and standard deviations for test performance

Condition	Paper-and-pencil test (max. score 20)			Oral test (max. score 10)		
	pre-test	post-test	d	pre-test	post-test	d
GI	8.3 (5.1)	11.3 (5.0)	0.61	5.3 (3.1)	7.3 (2.4)	0.70
DI	7.3 (5.3)	12.1 (5.5)	0.89	4.2 (3.0)	6.5 (2.9)	0.76
C	8.5 (4.7)	11.0 (4.7)	0.53	5.1 (2.8)	6.6 (2.6)	0.57

Research question 2 concerns the strategy use (quality of problem solving) demonstrated by the students. First, the number of different strategies used by the students (their strategy repertoires) at pre- versus post-test were compared (see Table 3). The paper-and-pencil test showed the strategy repertoires of the students from the two experimental conditions but not those from the control condition to increase (GI: $t(1,87) = 3.051$, $p = .003$; DI: $t(1,86) = 5.064$, $p < .001$; C: $t(1,89) = 1.907$, $p = .060$). No differences between the GI and DI conditions were revealed by the written test. In the interview, however, the DI group used a smaller number of different strategies than the other two groups, both at pre-test and at post-test (pre-test: $F(2,262) = 7.610$, $p = .001$; post-test: $F(2,262) = 5.960$, $p = .003$). The differences also remained even after correction for age and months of instruction. However, no differences between the three groups were found for improvement from pre- to post-test, $F(2,264) = 1.811$, $p = .166$.

An overview of how many students in each condition used a particular strategy on at least one occasion (either in combination with another strategy or alone) is presented in Table 4. Significant changes in the use of strategies are observed for the experimental groups. At post-test, more students knew at least one of the problems out of their head than at pre-test (pp: $c2(1, N=175) = 22.185$, $p < .001$; o: $c2 (1, N=175) = 17.332$, $p < .001$). Also an increase in the use of the splitting strategy on the written test was found ($c2 (1, N=175) = 33.667$, $p < .001$). This was mainly due to the increased ability of the students to solve multiplication problems above 10 x 10 by "splitting at ten". Repeated addition was used less at post-test than at pre-test on the interview test ($c2 (1, N=175) = 4.719$, $p = .030$), presumably because the students have discovered more efficient strategies to use. The written test shows an increase in the students' use of "writing down the table" ($c2 (1, N=175) = 4.518$, $p = .034$). All these changes in strategy use were only observed for the two experimental groups; the control group did not show any changes in strategy use from pre-test to post-test. Also, some differences are found between the two experimental groups: The interview pre-test scores show relatively fewer students in the DI group to use the strategies "automatized," "splitting," "neighbour," and "repeated addition" ($p < .05$).

Table 3 Means and standard deviations for total of different strategies used (strategy repertoire)

	Paper-and-pencil test		Oral test	
	pre-test	post-test	pre-test	post-test
GI	2.90 (1.55)	3.47 (1.45)	4.03 (2.00)	4.00 (1.76)
DI	2.84 (1.35)	3.60 (1.27)	3.00 (1.98)	3.17 (1.94)
C	3.03 (1.39)	3.34 (1.26)	3.94 (1.85)	3.97 (1.69)

Table 4 Students (%) using the strategies at paper-and-pencil test (pp) and oral interview (o)

Strategy	GI pre-test		GI post-test		DI pre-test		DI post-test		C pre-test		C post-test	
	pp	o	pp	o	pp	o	pp	o	pp	o	pp	o
automatized	55	71	73	88	48	47	79	68	60	67	59	79
reversing	13	53	16	47	6	55	15	55	4	57	13	52
splitting +	55	52	82	55	51	39	82	47	59	61	72	66
splitting -	5	50	8	53	5	28	9	25	3	40	3	24
doubling	23	28	25	23	20	20	26	25	41	34	32	33
neighbour	10	50	14	53	14	29	16	29	12	49	14	52
mult. table	18	38	30	25	25	32	32	24	18	32	34	30
rep. add.	38	67	85	55	94	41	91	24	93	52	97	46
drawing	13	6	6	1	8	7	9	1	10	4	7	3
dividing	0	0	9	1	0	0	0	0	0	0	0	0

The same difference is still visible at post-test but has not increased. The post-test shows more of the students in the GI group to use division strategies and fewer to use addition strategies when compared to the students in the DI group.

A comparison between the two methods of testing shows that the strategy of "reversal" is more frequently observed on the oral than on the written test, $t(264) = 10.112$, $p < .001$. The same holds for the strategies of "splitting based on subtraction" ($t(264) = 10.662$, $p < .001$) and "neighbour" ($t(264) = 8.332$, $p < .001$). The strategy of "repeated addition" is displayed more often on the written test than on the oral test ($t(264) = 14.390$, $p < .001$). Conversely, "saying the table" is used more often on the oral test at pre-test than on the written test at pre-test ($t(264) = 2.629$, $p = .009$), but the difference disappears at post-test.

Because many different strategies were used, both alone and in combination with other strategies, it seems useful to study the *adequacy* of the students' strategy use. A distinction can be made between the use of retrieval strategies (automatized problems) and the use of back-up strategies (calculation of answers). Within the back-up strategies, a further distinction can be made between the use of adequate strategies (with only one intermediate step), semi-adequate strategies (with two intermediate steps), not very adequate strategies (with more than two intermediate steps), and counting strategies (repeated addition, the use of drawings or other materials). The use of the different categories of strategy adequacy is shown in Table 5.

Table 5 Relative frequency of strategies (in %) for paper-and-pencil test (pp) and oral interview (o)

Strategy	GI pre-test		GI post-test		DI pre-test		DI post-test		C pre-test		C post-test	
	pp	o	pp	o	pp	o	pp	o	pp	o	pp	o
no answer	30	25	21	11	39	32	23	16	35	23	25	10
retrieval	12	19	18	31	9	10	16	23	7	15	13	25
adequate	9	23	18	26	8	17	20	26	9	29	13	28
semi-adequate	1	8	1	6	1	6	2	6	1	8	1	9
little adequate	4	3	2	3	3	3	4	2	5	4	3	4
counting	22	20	22	18	21	15	20	11	24	16	22	18
unknown	22	1	16	1	19	2	16	1	18	0	22	0
total	100	100	100	100	100	100	100	100	100	100	100	100

Significant differences in the adequacy of the strategies used by the different groups of students were found at post-test. The students from both of the experimental conditions were found to use adequate strategies more often than the students from the control condition on the written test at post-test, $F(2,262) = 5.131$, $p < .001$. In addition to this, the students in the GI group more frequently used retrieval strategies than those in the DI group on the oral test at post-test, $t(264) = 3.468$, $p = .016$. The students in the GI condition were also better able to write down their solution strategies at post-test than the students in the DI condition (category "unknown", $p < .001$).

From pre-test to post-test, significant changes in the adequacy of the strategies used by the students were found for both the oral and written tests, indicating that the students use more frequently the strategies retrieval and adequate at post-test ($p < .001$). The difference was significant for all of the conditions, and a general decrease in the number of problems with no answer was also observed across conditions ($p < .001$).

The mean efficacy scores (see Table 6) also changed significantly from pre-test to post-test for both the written test ($t(264) = 8.720$, $p < .001$) and the oral test ($t(264) = 5.599$, $p < .001$). This shows the students to generally use more adequate strategies at post-test with the exception of the control group on the oral test. In other words, certain differences in the students' use of strategies were found to depend on the type of instruction they received but no differences in the efficacy of the strategies they used.

Table 6 Means and standard deviations for strategy efficacy

	Paper-and-pencil test				Oral test			
	pre-test		post-test		pre-test		post-test	
GI	3.61	(1.05)	3.03*	(1.03)	2.82	(0.99)	2.42*	(0.89)
DI	3.77	(1.02)	3.00*	(1.00)	2.98	(1.04)	2.46*	(1.15)
C	3.71	(0.94)	3.26*	(0.91)	2.75	(0.83)	2.56	(0.92)

* Significant difference ($p < .05$) between pre- and post-test

In sum, the students' strategy use is found to change with the students in the two experimental conditions using a greater number of different strategies at post-test than at pre-test. The adequacy of the strategies used is also found to improve for the two experimental groups but not for the control group.

Conclusions and discussion

In this study, the process of learning multiplication was investigated. The effectiveness of two experimental programs was compared to that of a control program (i.e., standard math instruction). In the following, the research questions will be examined in light of the present findings. Thereafter, some general conclusions will be presented and discussed.

Before discussing the results, some remarks can be made based on the observations. From the lessons we observed, one particular form of instruction did not appear to be better than the other. What we did see, however, is that some of the students react better to guided instruction while others react better to direct instruction. For example, a young girl who tends to have a fear of failure will probably not spontaneously tell the group about a newly invented strategy for fear of being wrong. Such a student will probably benefit most from direct instruction and then during the early stages of instruction in particular. However, a boy with an autistic disorder who rigidly but adequately applied the strategy of "doubling" to every problem did not benefit much from direct instruction and the requirement that other strategies be applied. In other words, taking the characteristics of the individual child into account to select the most appropriate method of instruction appears to be critical.

Question 1: The effects of different methods of instruction on test scores

As already mentioned, the math test scores for the students in all three of the study conditions were found to improve on both the written and oral tests. The effect sizes nevertheless show the two experimental groups ($d > 0.60$) to improve more than the control group ($d < 0.60$) on both tests. On the written test, the DI group ($d = 0.89$) improved even more than the GI group ($d = 0.61$). However, these results should be interpreted with caution as significant between-group differences were not found on the pre-test neither at post-test. Caution is also demanded because the DI students had received less multiplication instruction at the start of the intervention, but still showed the same multiplication level as the students in both other conditions. This could reflect a higher learning capacity or learning speed of the DI students, which could explain the differences found in effect sizes. Moreover, the strategies used by the students to obtain their answers are just as important as the results.

Question 2: The effects of different methods of instruction on strategy use

With regard to the students' use of strategies, the following conclusions can be drawn. First, the experimental conditions were both found to enlarge the students' strategy repertoires (i.e., the number of different strategies used) while the control condition did not. While the students in the DI group used a smaller number of different strategies than the students in the GI group, no significant differences in the expansion of the students' strategy repertoires were observed. Both of the experimental groups enlarged their strategy repertoires and also showed a change towards a more effective use of strategies: less use of repeated addition and more use of automatized multiplication facts. With regard to the adequacy of the students' repertoire use, all of the students were found to use more adequate strategies at post-test relative to pre-test (i.e., more "retrieval" and "adequate" strategies and fewer "no answer"). Only the two experimental groups showed increased efficacy scores at post-test. In addition to these findings, some small differences were found between the two experimental groups; namely that the students in the GI group used adequate retrieval strategies more often than the students in the DI group and were better able to write their strategies down than the other students. A few of the students in the GI group even applied spontaneously division strategies to solve some problems. In other words, the two experimental groups showed more improved strategy use than the control group, and the GI group improved slightly more than the DI group.

General conclusions

The students who participated in the present study showed clear changes in their strategy use. The experimental (GI and DI) students in particular showed an increased strategy repertoire and a shift towards more effective strategy use. These changes were also found to occur for both the students attending regular education and special education. In other words, even students with learning problems are able to expand their strategy repertoires and become good problem solvers when provided with appropriate instruction.

Although the students in both experimental groups learned to use more adequate problem-solving strategies and to discuss the application and use of the different strategies, the exact learning process was found to differ for the two groups. In the GI condition, the students discovered or learned to discover new strategies on their own; they also showed considerable commitment to the discussion of the different solutions. In the DI condition, the students more or less adopted the solution procedures presented to them by the teacher. Given that both of the instructional methods proved effective for students with math learning problems, direct instruction is not necessarily needed, as shown in the findings of former research and recommended in other literature (Jones, Wilson, & Bhojwani, 1997; Van Luit, 1994; Woodward & Baxter, 1997). However, the present results are based on mean group scores. It is possible, and also seen in the execution of the programs, that there are individual differences.

Some of the students in the GI condition appeared to be in the right place and managed to discover new strategies and solutions while others clearly needed a more structured example as provided in the DI condition. The observations showed that some of the students in the GI condition could not handle the "freedom" they were given and appeared to be overwhelmed by the different possible solutions and discussions of strategy use. Conversely, some of the students in the DI condition appeared to feel restricted by the strategies presented by the teacher and showed a preference for selecting their own strategies. In other words, one form of instruction cannot be judged as better than the other; the choice of instructional method, rather, must be based on the individual learning style and individual learning needs of the student in question. It is therefore necessary to diagnose the specific learning capacities of students prior to the initiation of an intervention program. When students need structure or are afraid of making mistakes, it may be best to start with direct instruction. When students find it difficult to use strategies other than the ones they already master, and when they are capable of inventing or acquiring new strategies and also applying the strategies they know to new tasks, guided instruction may be most suitable. It is also, of course, necessary to take a particular student's history of instruction into consideration. When a student is not accustomed to guided instruction, for example, he will need more time to adjust than a student who is already accustomed to such instruction.

A closer look at the results also allows us to draw some more specific conclusions about the students' strategy use. Ten different strategies were distinguished, and some of the strategies were obviously used more frequently than others. The strategies "automatized," "splitting," and "counting" were used most frequently at both pre-test and post-test. Given that all ten strategies were found in the tests but the students used an average of only three or four different strategies, it appears that different students may use different sets of strategies. Indeed, the students in both the GI and DI groups showed clear personal preferences with regard to strategy use. This could be expected for the GI group because the students in this group were clearly encouraged to rely on their own personal preferences. The finding is more surprising for the DI group, which was taught to strictly follow the strategies demonstrated by the teacher. Apparently as these students learn to apply different strategies, they also learn to solve problems in their own way. Contrary to expectations based on former research (e.g., Klein, Beishuizen, & Treffers, 1998), thus, the mathematical problem solving of the students in the DI condition proves to be just as flexible as that of the students in the GI condition.

A final conclusion concerns the differences between the oral and written tests. The oral test was used to measure relatively easy problems while the written test was used to measure both relatively easy and more difficult problems. With regard to the students' strategy repertoires, an increase was found to occur for the written test from pre-test to post-test but not for the oral test. At both pre- and post-test, however, the students demonstrate a greater repertoire of strategies on the oral test than on the written test. The students' mean efficacy is also found to be higher on the oral test at both pre- and post-test than on the written test. Clear differences were present in the strategies used on the oral versus written tests: Whereas the strategies "reversal," "splitting" and "neighbour" were used relatively more often on the oral test, "repeated addition" was used relatively more often on the written test. The students' use of the strategy of "saying/writing down the multiplication table" increased over time for the written test and decreased for the oral test. The question thus arising is just how the differences in strategy use found for the different methods of testing can be explained. One explanation may lie in different degrees of test difficulty. The tests clearly differed in difficulty, and it is therefore possible that the students used different strategies for easier problems (i.e., on the oral test) than for more difficult problems (i.e., on the written test). Another explanation may lie in the mode of testing itself (i.e., oral versus written testing). It was easiest to determine which strategy (or strategies) the students used on the oral test because the test assistant could always question the students. On the written test, we had to depend on what the students wrote down and it was basically impossible to discover what the students did when they did not write their strategy (or strategies) down. Nevertheless, the students were given scratch paper for the written test and this provided clear and relatively reliable insight into the strategy (or strategies) used by the students. On the oral test, students may be predisposed to give the answers that they think the test assistant wants to hear. In other words, the two methods of testing have clear advantages and disadvantages that merit further investigation. In other research (Verschaffel, De Corte, Gielen, & Struyf, 1994), oral report has been shown to provide a good picture of strategy use. Future research should nevertheless be undertaken to provide greater information on the reliabilities of both methods of testing.

In sum, it can be concluded that students who receive guided instruction acquire math problem-solving strategies in a different manner than students who receive direct instruction but that the differences in their actual test results are minimal. In both instructional conditions, the performance of the students with math learning problems from both regular and special education was found to increase. Their strategy use was also found to change over time with most of the students showing a larger repertoire of strategies and more adequate strategy use at post-test. Given the few differences between the guided versus direct instruction results, the effectiveness of the two instructional methods can be judged as equal and it is therefore recommended that the method of instruction always be tailored to the specific needs of the student in question.

References

Carnine, D. (1997). Instructional design in mathematics for students with learning disabilities. *Journal of Learning Disabilities, 30,* 130-41.

Case, L.P., Harris, K.R., & Graham, S. (1992). Improving the mathematical problem-solving skills of students with learning disabilities: Self-regulated strategy development. *The Journal of Special Education, 26,* 1-19.

Cawley, J.F., & Miller, J.H. (1989). Cross-sectional comparisons of the mathematical performance of learning disabled children: Are we on the right track toward comprehensive programming? *Journal of Learning Disabilities, 22,* 250-255.

Geary, D.C. (1994). *Children's mathematical development. Research and practical applications.* Washington, DC: American Psychological Association.

Geary, D.C., Brown, S.C., & Samaranayake, V.A. (1991). Cognitive addition: A short longitudinal study of strategy choice and speed-of-processing differences in normal and mathematically disabled children. *Developmental Psychology, 27,* 787-797.

Goldman, S.R. (1989). Strategy instruction in mathematics. *Learning Disabilities Quarterly, 12,* 43-55.

Jitendra, A.K., & Hoff, K. (1996). The effects of schema-based instruction on the mathematical word-problem-solving performance of students with learning disabilities. *Journal of Learning Disabilities, 29,* 422-431.

Jones, E.D., Wilson, R, & Bhojwani, S. (1997). Mathematics instruction for secondary students with learning disabilities. *Journal of Learning Disabilities, 30,* 151-163.

Kraemer, J.M., Van der Schoot, F., & Engelen, R. (2000). *Periodieke peiling van het onderwijsniveau. Balans van het reken-wiskundeonderwijs op LOM- en MLK-scholen 2* [Periodic measurement of the educational level. A report of the mathematics education]. Arnhem, The Netherlands: Cito.

Kroesbergen, E.H. (2002). *Mathematics education for low-achieving students: Effects of different instructional principles on multiplication learning.* Doetinchem: Graviant.

Klein, T., Beishuizen, M., & Treffers, A. (1998). The empty numberline in Dutch second grades: *Realistic* versus *gradual* program design. *Journal for Research in Mathematics Education, 29,* 443-464

Mercer, C.D., & Miller, S.P. (1992). Teaching students with learning problems in math to acquire, understand, and apply basic math facts. *Remedial and Special Education, 13* (3), 19-35, 61.

Montague, M. (1992). The effects of cognitive and metacognitive strategy instruction on the mathematical problem solving of middle school students with learning disabilities. *Journal of Learning Disabilities, 25,* 230-248.

Pellegrino, J.W., & Goldman, S.R. (1987). Information processing and elementary mathematics. *Journal of Learning Disabilities, 20,* 23-32.

Rivera, D.P. (1997). Mathematics education and students with learning disabilities: Introduction to the special series. *Journal of Learning Disabilities, 30,* 2-19.

Schopman, E.A.M., & Van Luit, J.E.H. (1996). Learning and transfer of preparatory arithmetic strategies among young children with a developmental lag. *Journal of Cognitive Education, 5,* 117-131.

Van de Heuvel-Panhuizen, M. (1996). *Assessment and realistic mathematics education.* Utrecht, The Netherlands: CD-b Press.

Van Luit, J.E.H. (1994). The effectiveness of structural and realistic arithmetic curricula in children with special needs. *European Journal of Special Needs Education, 9,* 16-26.

Van Luit, J.E.H., Kaskens, J., & Van der Krol, R. (1993). *Speciaal rekenhulpprogramma vermenigvuldigen en verdelen* [Special remediating program multiplication and division]. Doetinchem, The Netherlands: Graviant.

Van Luit, J.E.H., & Naglieri, J.A. (1999). Effectiveness of the MASTER strategy training program for teaching special children multiplication and division. *Journal of Learning Disabilities, 32,* 98-107.

Verschaffel, L., De Corte, E., Gielen, I., & Struyf, E. (1994). Clever rearrangement strategies in children's mental arithmetic: A confrontation of eye-movement data and verbal protocols. In J.E.H. van Luit (Ed.), *Research on learning and instruction of mathe-matics in kindergarten and primary school* (pp. 153-180). Doetinchem, The Netherlands: Graviant.

Woodward, J., & Baxter, J. (1997). The effects of an innovative approach to mathematics on academically low-achieving students in inclusive settings. *Exceptional Children, 63,* 373-388.

10
STRATEGY USE AND MATH INSTRUCTION FOR STUDENTS WITH SPECIAL NEEDS

Bauke F. Milo and Aloysius J.J.M. Ruijssenaars

Theoretical framework and research questions

Strategy development and learning problems

Learning is a process that is mainly characterized by qualitative changes in the cognitive structure. For example, skills are executed faster and with fewer errors after repetition and exercise, new information may lead to more insight and knowledge networks are constantly being extended. Description of these changes is an important theme in cognitive (developmental) psychology. The associated main question is: *what* develops? To answer that question researchers in the past examined the changes in cognitive strategies involved in solving a wide range of tasks (for example: Resnick, 1976; Siegler, 1978). This research about strategy use and learning is not less relevant today. In his recent work Siegler (1996; Lemaire & Siegler, 1995; Siegler & Jenkins, 1989) emphasized situation-bound use of and interaction between more and less time-consuming strategies, respectively more and less automatized or direct available. These strategies develop, become more sophisticated and more adequate with respect to the task that has to be performed. An increasing quality is also reflected in increasing speed and accuracy.

It is possible to describe the quality of strategies – and the change in them – by means of four parameters: the repertoire of available strategies, the relative preference in use of the available strategies, the efficiency in use (speed and accuracy), and the way the strategy-choice is adapted to the situation. Individuals differ in the degree to which these aspects have developed, or in their ability to learn. Learning ability is commonly considered as a synonym for intelligence, although many authors point to the fact that this theoretical view does not always fit the way intelligence is operationalized in intelligence tests (see for a review: Hamers & Ruijssenaars, 1984; Hamers, Sijtsma & Ruijssenaars, 1993; Van der Aalsvoort, Resing & Ruijssenaars, 2002). Commonly used IQ tests are static and not representative of the dynamics of learning processes.

Results (right/wrong, speed) are taken into consideration instead of solution- and learning strategies.

In the educational learning process, a proportion of the children drop out. They have relatively great difficulties in gathering new knowledge, fail to reach the level of automatization, use their knowledge insufficient and continue to be dependent on instruction. In many cases, further individual assessment takes place, in which generally the IQ is measured. Such children may be referred to special education, on the basis of a low IQ-score. These students with mental retardation (MR students) are expected to continue to have difficulty in acquiring new knowledge and using it in different situations. Other students who also drop out have an average IQ. Although their problem solving capacities do not show any shortcomings, they have great difficulties in specific scholastic skills as word identification or automatization of mathematical facts. When the amount they have fallen behind becomes too great then these students with learning disabilities (LD students) are often referred to special education as well.

Since the Dutch inclusion movement (Weer Samen Naar School: Together To School Again) came into effect in 1998, MR and LD students are placed together in the same educational setting. Given that they are in so-called schools for special primary education, the distinction between them has legally disappeared. Of course, an important question – because no research has been conducted before the implementation of this policy – is whether the two types of students benefit to the same extent from instruction. In this research, attention is also paid to this important question.

Instruction and cognitive possibilities

As is shown by the LD students, intelligence is not always sufficient to permit a child to benefit from instruction. For learning, specific academic skills are needed more than adequate learning competencies. Besides learner characteristics, another source for variance in learning results is instruction quality (Vedder & Koster, 1983; Ruijssenaars, 1992). Two students with comparable capacities may benefit to varying degrees from distinct types of instruction.

If we consider cognitive development as a qualitative change in processing and solution strategies, instruction can be characterized by the way strategies are handled. Instruction can vary in the extent to which direction of the learning process takes place or in the degree of explicitness. In an educational concept that is based on direct instruction, strategies are offered to students in a structured, directing way, centered on an explicit analysis of the learning task. The opposite of this concept is a didactic, which is based on the learner's (implicit) task perception and task approach. In the first concept, the contribution of the teacher is central; in the second it is the student's individual contribution. An important question is about which type of instruction is best in which situation. The importance of this question is connected to the change that is taking place in Dutch schools for special primary education with respect to mathematics education. It is expected that these schools, following regular schools for primary education, will implement a method, based on constructive, student-centered view of learning (in the Netherlands known as *Realistic Mathematics Education*). This implementation also means that the traditional, direct instruction will be replaced by an interactive, student-centered approach. It is expected that students with limited cognitive capacities – such as MR students – will benefit from direct instruction, whereas students with greater learning potential – such as LD students – will be able to develop their own constructions and make the most of their individual contributions.

The foregoing outlines the issue of this chapter. Students may get frustrated in regular primary education in such a way that a referral for a school for special primary education is necessary. Some of these students have intellectual capacities that are not significantly different from normal (LD); others function on a lower intellectual level (MR). In approaching their mathematical problems, a choice can be made for direct instruction or guided instruction, in which the instruction is connected to the individual contributions of the students. If the different kinds of instruction lead to different results for the two types of students, then this should be taken into account in schools for special primary education.

Solution strategies for addition and subtraction up to 100

With regard to solution strategies for addition and subtraction up to 100 the main distinction between the jump- and split strategy is widely acknowledged (Beishuizen, 1997; Fuson, Wearne, Hiebert, Human, Olivier, Carpenter & Fennema, 1997; Klein, Beishuizen & Treffers, 1998). In the split strategy tens and units are handled separately, after which the results are taken together, whereas in the jump strategy one starts from the first whole number, after which the tens and units are added or subtracted by *jumping*. The problem 53 + 16 can be solved by (50 + 10 =) 60 + (3 + 6 =) 9 = 69 (split strategy) or by 53 + 10 (= 63) + 6 = 69 (jump strategy). Fuson et al. (1997) also mentioned a combination of these two main strategies as a third strategy. The problem 53 + 16 is then solved by 50 + 10 (= 60) + 3 (= 63) + 6 = 69.

The main idea of the research reported in this chapter is that stimulating a repertoire of solution strategies promotes insight in the efficiency of the strategies (Van Lieshout, 1997). Flexible strategy use can then, consistent with the definitions by Gray and Tall (1994) and Blöte, Klein and Beishuizen (2000), be defined as *adaptation of the solution strategy to the number characteristics of the problem, minimizing the chance of a false solution*. Although an adaptation can also take place within a strategy, in this definition adaptation is a change of strategy choice. The latter part of the definition, *minimizing the chance of a false solution*, is important in order to make a distinction from the *number* of used strategies. The number of used strategies (*variety*) gives no information about their efficiency. With respect to the efficiency of the two main strategies, the split strategy is known to be problematic for some of the students in subtraction problems with regrouping (Beishuizen, 1997). The problem 62 - 25 might be solved by (60 - 20 =) 40 + (2 - 5 =) 3 = 43. Changing a ten in ten units is not mastered and/or applied in that case. For the same problem, the jump strategy is less problematic, because counting back takes place from the first whole number by jumping in a way that is connected to the child's ability level (for example 62-10-10-2-3 or 62-20-5).

With respect to MR and LD students, Harskamp and Suhre (1995, 1996) concluded that a *realistic* approach leads to good results. In their research, which involved addition and subtraction up to 100, instruction was adapted to students' preference strategies, aimed at reinforcing these strategies. The students generally benefited more than a control group. Because the training involved several directing aspects, like the use of step-by-step strategy cards and directing hints given by the teacher, and the fact that the control group did not receive extra help, it is unclear to what extent the contributions made by the students were responsible for the progress. Woodward, Monroe and Baxter (2001) investigated whether different types of students (average ability students, at-risk students and students with learning disabilities) benefited from instruction in which the contributions of the students were central. The research was conducted in regular class situations, and classes in which a traditional method and didactics was used were compared to classes that used a modern, Standards-based (NCTM) method and instruction. At first sight, the students with learning disabilities seemed to benefit most from the modern didactics, but further analysis showed a clear split within this group: some of the students had benefited much, whereas an equal number of the students showed hardly any progress.

Research questions

We have mentioned that students with mathematical problems differ in intellectual capacities. Prior to the inclusion movement in the Netherlands, the distinction between MR and LD students was obvious. In this research we take the same position.

The choice made for optimal didactics can vary from starting from students' contributions and adapting instruction to their strategies, to direct instruction with respect to fixed strategies. This distinction is also central in this research. With respect to direct instruction two variants are being used, following the earlier mentioned two main solution strategies for addition and subtraction up to 100: the jump strategy and the split strategy.

The main question is about the effectiveness of the guided instruction (GI), in which students' contributions are central, and the two types of direct instruction (DI) for the two distinct groups of students (MR and LD students). Effectiveness then is related to strategy use, connected to accuracy in addition and subtraction up to 100. The specific research questions are:

1. To what extent does stimulating several solution strategies (GI) versus offering and allowing only one strategy (DI) result in different performance (*accuracy*) for special needs students? Do differences become apparent between MR and LD students?
2. To what extent does stimulating several solution strategies (GI) versus offering and allowing only one strategy (DI) result in a different *variety* in strategy use? Do differences become apparent between MR and LD students?
3. To what extent does stimulating several solution strategies result in *flexible* strategy use and do students, characterized with respect to flexibility, obtain different performance scores? Do differences become apparent between MR and LD students? This last question will be answered not only for the whole sample, but also for the GI students separately, as flexibility was an explicit goal for them.

Method

Subjects

The sample consists of 70 students from three schools for special primary education in Leiden, the Netherlands. Selection was based on mathematics ability: instruction with respect to addition and subtraction up to 20 had to be completed. No instruction had taken place with respect to addition and subtraction with regrouping. Addition and subtraction up to 100 was not mastered yet, so it seems reasonable to assume that a (taught) strategy preference had not developed. After deliberation with the teachers, students who were supposed to be unable to work as intended - as a result of behavioral problems, limited verbal capacities and/or reading level - were excluded. The mean age of all the students at the start of the program was 9;10 years ($SD = 11$ months). The mean IQ was 81.5 ($SD = 13.3$). The participants were 34 mildly mentally retarded students, whose mean age and mean IQ were respectively 10;2 years ($SD = 10$ months) and 72.0 ($SD = 9.6$), and 36 students with specific learning disabilities, whose mean age was 9;7 years ($SD = 10$ months) and mean IQ 90.4 ($SD = 9.6$). As gender was not considered in the selection, the over-representation of boys in schools for special primary education is also found in the sample: 44 boys and 26 girls took part in the research. For the students with specific learning disabilities this over-representation (20-16) is less clear than for the mildly mentally retarded students (24-10).

Materials

Worksheets

Two points were of main concern for the worksheets: they had to stimulate interaction between the students through clear and motivating contexts, and they had to be suited for special needs students. After some try-outs and conversations with participating teachers, objections were raised to the existing methods. Standard methods contained few interaction-provoking contexts, while the page layout of modern methods was too distracting. A great diversity of contexts and a heavy demand on reading ability were considered so time-consuming that we decided to use a limited amount of standard contexts. As a consequence, the worksheets for the group lessons and class situation were therefore not identical to existing methods, but based on them. For each lesson 5 worksheets were available: 1 with formula problems and 4 with context problems. On the worksheets for the start of the program in the DI condition the model involved (number line for the DI-jump and number position scheme for DI-split) was printed on the worksheets. In the GI condition, both models were shown, so the students could choose which model to use. Later in the program, the models were omitted, but on each page some empty space was left to draw the model when desired.

The worksheets were adjusted to the ability level of the children: to start with, the problems were related to addition and subtraction without regrouping. At about the eighth lesson regrouping was introduced, after which work was done towards the targeted ability level, addition and subtraction up to 100 with regrouping. The last 10 lessons (and the individual lessons in the classroom in the same period) involved the whole domain of addition and subtraction up to 100.

Instruments

Before the main program started, a performance test was administered as pretest. The same test was administered as posttest, together with a transfer test.

The addition and subtraction test was constructed by selecting 40 addition and subtraction problems from the databank of the National Institute for Educational Measurement (CITO). The selected problems were context and formula problems and covered the whole range of addition and subtraction up to 100. The test was divided in two parts: 20 items had to be calculated mentally, the solution steps for the other 20 could be written down on the answer sheet. The test was administered group wise and the items were read aloud by the researcher. There was no time limit.

The flexibility test for addition and subtraction up to 100 (Milo & Ruijssenaars, 1999) consists of 20 items. Half of the items relate to context problems; the other half consists of the same type of problems in formula. The test was administered individually without a time limit. The interviewer wrote down the solution steps on the answer sheet in such a way, that it was obvious which strategy the student had used. The test was intended to determine the used strategies and a possible adaptation of the strategy with respect to the number characteristics of the problem. The types of problems were chosen with respect to the number characteristics: they cover the whole range of addition and subtraction up to 100. The formula and context problems both contain 5 addition problems and 5 subtraction problems, of which 3 subtraction problems with regrouping (for example: 53-16 and *You drive at a speed of 63 km/h. Then you slow down by 17 km/h. At what speed are you driving then?*). The chosen contexts were the same as in the program.

Procedures

General

Before the start of the program, the trainers were given training. In the training, theory and practical examples with respect to instruction were discussed. The instruction was related to mathematical issues, interaction and behavioral norms. The training ended with a discussion of a videotaped, try-out lesson. All trainers were senior students in

Education (specialized in Learning Problems). Six of the seven students were experienced teachers and/or remedial teachers.

After the training the groups were assigned to the trainers. We attempted to assign groups of different conditions, different schools and/or different types of student (MR/LD) to each trainer. During the program, several discussions took place with all trainers to guarantee maximum agreement between them. In these meetings, videotaped lessons were used to start discussion.

After finishing the pretest (see Table 1), the students were instructed for a half year period in a way that placed students' contributions central (*guided instruction*) or in a way in which the instruction was directing and a solution strategy was central (*direct instruction*). In the first condition, both the jump strategy and the split strategy were introduced in the introduction program, and both were sustained during the whole main program. The teacher made no directing remarks with respect to strategy use: the students were free to choose their own strategy. For both strategies a supporting model was introduced: the number line for the jump strategy and the number position scheme for the split strategy. The main idea was that by comparing the strategies the students would acquire insight in the efficiency of the strategies and be able to use them in a flexible way (Van Lieshout, 1997). In the GI condition either the jump strategy, supported by the number line, or the split strategy, supported by the number position scheme, was introduced. Only the introduced strategy was allowed during the program. The main idea was that by using only this strategy, students would master the strategy.

The LD and MR students were trained in separate groups of 3-5 students. Students from the same class were trained in the same group. They were trained two times a week during math lesson. For the other lessons in the classroom worksheets were available. These worksheets could be filled out individually or, whenever possible, in cooperation with a student who was in the same instruction group. The students did not receive instruction from the class teacher for addition and subtraction up to 100. For different math domains, the students joined the class instruction. After the training period, the same tests, as in the pretest, were administered as posttest, together with some specific tests (including the flexibility test).

Table 1 Research design: number of students in each condition (total N = 70) and time schedule

Condition	Number of students
Guided instruction	13 MR students
	13 LD students
Directing jump-instruction	11 MR students
	11 LD students
Directing split-instruction	10 MR students
	12 LD students
	Time schedule
Pretest	January: performance test
Treatment-program	Jan.- July: introduction and 25 lessons
Posttest	July: performance- and flexibility test

The program consisted of two parts: an introduction program and a main program. The introduction program (between 4 and 6 lessons) was meant to demonstrate the strategy/strategies and supporting model(s), and also to introduce group work. Because for the GI students more strategies and models had to be presented, their introduction program consisted of a few more lessons. It also appeared necessary to pay attention to group work to a different extent for the groups. For this reason behavioral agreements were made ('social norms', see Gravemeijer, 1996; Lo & Wheatley, 1994; Yackel & Cobb, 1996), of which the students could be reminded during the main program. The lessons in the introduction and main program lasted (about) 45 minutes, depending on the normal length of the lessons in the school. The actual mathematics lessons were in the main program - 25 in total - of which some could not take place for practical reasons. In each condition the lesson started with an interactive phase, based on a specific context. In the GI condition, the students could contribute their solution strategy to the discussion, after which the contributions could be compared. In both DI conditions some students demonstrated the (only sustained) strategy, and the teacher and/or other students discussed the accuracy of the strategy use.

Procedure for characterizing flexibility

Strategy use is considered flexible whenever a solution strategy is adapted to the number characteristics of a problem in such a way that the chance of a false solution decreases. If students use a less error-prone strategy for subtraction with regrouping than the strategy they use for the other problems, they are considered to be flexible.

To characterize the students for flexibility, we used a number of decision rules. The (few) problems for which no strategy use could be determined were not included. Whenever a student used one solution strategy for at least 75% of the problems, that student was characterized as *jumper* or *splitter*. A consequence of this decision rule was that students who consistently used one solution strategy (for example the jump strategy) could not be characterized as flexible. Students who used more than one solution strategy, but not in a way that the chance of a false solution decreased, were characterized as *unfocussed* ('trial-and-error'). The students that used the jump- or combination strategy for at least 5 of 6 subtraction problems with regrouping, while for the other problems they showed no clear preference or mainly used the split strategy, were characterized as *flexible*.

Results

Because very few students actually made use of the opportunity to write down solution steps on the performance test, the distinction between the two parts of the test vanished. To examine whether the test could be analyzed as one, correlations were computed for the pretest and the posttest. As these correlations were considerable ($r = .71$ on the pretest; $r = .73$ on the posttest), it was decided to use the sum of the two scores as variable. The test is then considered as a performance test.

The first question we need to answer was whether condition had an effect on the results on the performance test by means of a covariance analysis (with pretest-score on the performance test as covariate). Consequently the flexibility characterizations were compared to each other with respect to their score on the performance test. This analysis is executed for all subjects as well as for the students in the GI condition, as these students were expected to become flexible strategy users through adapting the instruction to their contributions. The results were each time analyzed for the sample as a whole at first, after which the two types of students were considered as two distinct groups. In all analyses a correction has been made for the influence of gender and age by using them as covariates.

The effect of condition on performance

For the sample as a whole, a significant effect of condition on score on the performance test appeared ($F(2,63) = 4.80$, $p < .05$). Direct jump instruction resulted in higher scores than direct split instruction ($F(1,38) = 4,60$, $p < .05$), but also higher than guided instruction

($F(1,43) = 8.09$, $p < .01$). The mean scores on the pretest and posttest are presented in Table 2. The effects were not significant for the LD and the MR students as separate groups, but the same trend was visible.

Table 2 Score on performance test (max. = 40) (pre = pretest; post = posttest)

Condition			Total			MR			LD	
		N	M	SD	N	M	SD	N	M	SD
Guided instruction	pre	26	14.12	7.01	13	12.31	6.26	13	15.92	7.49
	post	26	21.35	8.80	13	20.38	9.12	13	22.31	8.72
Directing-jump instruction	pre	22	12.68	7.58	11	11.64	7.89	11	13.73	7.48
	post	22	25.50	6.91	11	25.45	5.72	11	25.55	8.23
Directing-split instruction	pre	22	12.41	6.55	10	9.90	4.56	12	14.50	7.38
	post	21	21.10	7.48	9	20.78	2.68	12	21.33	9.82

Characterizing flexibility

Characterizing flexibility resulted in the distribution of students in the different conditions as presented in Table 3. All students but 2 were directly and clearly characterized. The two exceptions were the result of ambiguous scoring by the teacher. Their results were not included in the further analysis.

Each individual characterization was presented to the trainers to check whether these characterizations were recognizable to them. This appeared to be the case: students that always used one solution strategy in the training were characterized that way (*jumping* or *splitting*) and the students that used different strategies during training also proved to be characterized as *flexible* or *unfocussed*.

Table 3 Type of flexibility: number of students in each condition (total (MR - LD))

Type of flexibility Condition	Flexible	Jumping	Splitting	Unfocussed
Guided instruction	5 (2 - 3)	5 (2 - 3)	13 (7 - 6)	2 (1 - 1)
Directing-jump instruction	4 (0 - 4)	17 (10 - 7)		
Directing-split instruction	1 (0 - 1)		21 (10 - 11)	
Total	10 (2 - 8)	22 (12 - 10)	34 (17 - 17)	2 (1 - 1)

The great number of splitting students in the GI condition is striking. Only 5 students were characterized as flexible. The distribution of LD and MR students appeared to be the same: few students were flexible, some mainly used the jump strategy, most students were characterized as splitting and an individual subject used different strategies in an unfocussed way.

As was expected, no splitting students appeared in the DI jump condition and no jumping students in the DI split condition. In these conditions no unfocussed students were identified, but there were still some flexible students: four students in the DI jump condition and one student in the DI split condition. All were LD students. The MR students all used the strategy that was central in the training.

Performance and flexibility characterization

For the analysis with respect to the flexibility characterization, the two unfocussed and mutually incomparable students were excluded.

Table 4 Score on performance test by type of flexibility (max. = 40) - all students (pre = pretest; post = posttest)

Type of flexibility			Total			MR			LD	
		N	M	SD	N	M	SD	N	M	SD
Flexible	pre	10	15.60	7.21	2	13.00	4.24	8	16.25	7.87
	post	10	27.50	7.26	2	34.00	2.83	8	25.87	7.18
Jumping	pre	22	13.36	6.88	12	11.75	7.40	10	15.30	6.00
	post	22	25.32	6.13	12	24.17	5.41	10	26.70	6.93
Splitting	pre	34	11.65	6.05	17	12.76	6.70	17	12.76	6.70
	post	33	19.18	7.53	16	19.63	5.60	17	18.76	9.15

Covariance-analysis for the sample as a whole showed significant differences between the students, characterized by flexibility ($F(2, 56) = 8.75$, $p < .01$). The flexible and jumping students acquired higher performance scores than the splitting students (respectively: $F(1,38) = 6.89$, $p < .05$, and $F(1,50) = 10.73$, $p < .01$). There was no difference between the flexible and the jumping students.

For the MR students, the high scores of the flexible students are remarkable, given that their performance on the pretest did not differ from the others. For the LD students, the flexible and the jumping students attained relatively high scores. In Table 4 the mean pretest and posttest scores are presented for the flexibility characterizations.

When we focused on the GI condition - as these students were familiar with different strategies and stimulated to use them in a flexible way - it appeared that the students using flexible and the jumping strategies attained higher scores than the splitting students. The difference proved significant only for the flexible students ($F(1,13) =$

5.80, $p < .05$). In Table 5 the mean scores of the GI students, characterized by flexibility, on the pretest and posttest are presented. Nothing can be concluded about the flexible MR students as a result of their small number, but their high score on the posttest is intriguing. For the LD students we can conclude that the flexible and jumping students perform better than the splitting students.

Table 5 Score on performance test by type of flexibility (max. = 40) - guided students (pre = pretest; post = posttest)

Type of flexibility		Total			MR			LD		
		N	M	SD	N	M	SD	N	M	SD
Flexible	pre	5	17.40	5.77	2	13.00	4.24	3	20.33	5.03
	post	5	29.40	5.90	2	34.00	2.83	3	26.33	5.51
Jumping	pre	5	18.40	4.39	2	19.00	7.07	3	18.00	3.61
	post	5	25.60	5.68	2	21.50	6.36	3	28.33	4.04
Splitting	pre	13	10.77	5.12	7	11.43	6.48	6	10.00	3.35
	post	13	16.85	7.32	7	18.14	8.01	6	15.33	6.83

Conclusions and discussion

Although this research project has not been designed to be a test of Siegler's ideas, it may be interesting to examine to what extent an interpretation of the results is possible with respect to the four parameters that are used to describe the development of strategies (Lemaire & Siegler, 1995). We will discuss the first, second and fourth parameter (respectively: *the repertoire of available strategies*, *the relative preference in use of the available strategies*, and *the way the strategy choice is adapted to the situation*) and will relate the results of the first and fourth parameter to the third. This third parameter, *the efficiency in use of the strategies* will be discussed with respect to accuracy, as no suitable speed scores are available.

The first parameter, *the repertoire of available strategies*, is a central aspect of the research project. Emphasizing a repertoire of strategies (GI) in contrast to offering and allowing only a single strategy (DI) is an important, clear distinction between the conditions. In each GI group several strategies were centrally discussed. A main question of the research was whether having more strategies at one's disposal would lead to better results on the performance test. This appeared not to be the case. Stimulation of, discussion about and exercise of several strategies did *not* result in better performance scores. Direct jump instruction appeared to yield higher mean scores on the performance test compared to guided instruction. As the scores of the direct jump instruction students were also higher than the scores of the direct split instruction students, not only the number of strategies, but also the kind of strategy is of great importance. The strength of the jump strategy (supported by the number line) compared to the split strategy is well known (Beishuizen, 1997; Beishuizen, Van Putten & Van Mulken, 1997; Fuson et al., 1997; Klein, Beishuizen & Treffers, 1998). It offers the possibility of adapting the solution steps to the individual ability level. Moreover, visualization by means of the number line - which relieves working memory - provides insight into the solution procedure. After a while, the number line may serve as a *mental model* (Beishuizen, 1993).

We investigated the second parameter, *the relative preference in use of the available strategies*, by considering the number of solution strategies in the variety of problems of the flexibility test. Most directed students (directed jump students *and* directed split students) appeared to mainly use the strategy taught. Some of them also used the strategy that was not taught, even as this was not allowed during the training. It was striking that these were all LD students. Only 7 of the 25 GI students appeared to use several solution strategies. The other 18 all used a single strategy, even though they had several strategies at their disposal. Stimulating a repertoire of solution strategies results in actual use of these strategies only for a few students with special needs. As Harskamp and Suhre (1995, 1996) showed, these students often have a (taught or self-chosen) favorite strategy, which they do not abandon easily.

The fourth parameter, *the way the strategy choice is adapted to the situation*, has been examined through the characterization of flexibility. It is striking that a few LD students turned out to be flexible strategy users, while they were allowed to use one single strategy in the training. No directed MR students showed flexible strategy use. They all used the strategy taught. Of the guided students, who were stimulated to use a repertoire of solution strategies, 18 students did *not* use several strategies. Moreover, 2 of the 7 students using several strategies, did it in such an inconsistent, unfocussed way, that the chance of a false solution did *not* decrease. For the sample as a whole, flexible and jumping students appeared to attain equal scores, but splitting students attained lower scores. The difference in performance seems possible to derive from the type of strategy used.

Although the scores of the MR and LD students did *not* differ on the performance test, some important distinctions became apparent. Firstly, only 3 of the 32 MR students used more than one solution strategy (of whom 1 unfocussed), while 9 of the 36 LD students did (of whom 1 unfocussed as well). The fact that no directed MR student used a non-taught strategy, while 5 LD students do, suggests that instruction creates different effects for the two types of students. It is worth mentioning the fact that jumping LD students acquired the same performance score as the flexible students, which is higher than the score of the splitting students, while for the MR students no difference was seen between the jumping and splitting students, and only 2 students became (high-achieving!) flexible problem solvers. This last conclusion is consistent with the conclusions of Woodward et al. (2001). They concluded that adapting instruction to students' contributions leads to dichotomous results for students with learning disabilities: some students show strong improvement after instruction, while just as many students show hardly any improvement at all.

The research we have reported has some restrictions. The most important is the fact that the students have been trained in small groups, so generalization to instruction in whole class situations is not possible. We should also mention that after consulting the teachers some students were excluded from the selection if there was a suspicion that the working procedure would not be successful as a result of problems relating to behavior, reading ability or verbal capacities. Nevertheless, it is important to ask whether interaction as intended is possible in a group of 15-20 students with special needs. The influences of specific learner characteristics on the group process as well as the benefit of the guided instruction for students with complex problems are unclear. Nevertheless, some important conclusions can be drawn from the results.

Firstly, the research sheds light on the effects of students' contributions, one of the central aspects of realistic mathematics education. Students with special needs benefit most from structured, direct instruction compared to adaptation to and stimulation of a variety of strategies. Use of the jump strategy seems to result in the greatest proficiency. The fact that these students benefit more from direct instruction than guided instruction is very important with respect to the current implementation of realistic methods in schools for special primary education. Results of the last Dutch national assessment program in 1997 showed that in regular primary education, 74% of the schools used a realistic method (Janssen, Van der Schoot, Hemker & Verhelst, 1999), while this percentage was respectively 56% and 9% for LD and MR students (who were still educated separately at that time) (Kraemer, Van der Schoot & Engelen, 2000). Special needs students with mathematical problems have often become stranded in regular primary education before. Therefore, it is not yet obvious how guided instruction can be transferred to schools for special primary education. The ratio of number flexible (5) and non-flexible (20) students raises questions about the need to force adaptation to students' contributions. The effects on insightful, flexible solution behaviour seem limited and do *not* result in higher achievement scores. Swanson, Hoskyn and Lee (2000) and Butler, Miller, Lee and Pierce (2001) also emphasized the importance of a certain amount of direction of the learning process. They showed by means of a meta-analysis that students with learning disabilities obtain their best results through didactics in which elements of direct instruction are obvious. Explicit instruction, frequent feedback, ample drill-and-practice (Butler et al., 2001), sequencing, segmentation and strategy cueing (Swanson et al., 2000) proved to be instruction components that strongly related to positive effects.

Secondly, this study shows an important age difference between the LD and MR students that have acquired certain mathematics abilities. This reflects the fact that MR students despite their greater educational experience do *not* gain higher achievement levels. This does not mean that joint education - a policy aim of the inclusion movement - is impossible, but it does not argue in favor of natural integration of the two groups for mathematics education. The most recent Dutch national assessment program in schools for special primary education (Kraemer et al., 2000) showed that MR and LD students reach different ability levels at the end of primary education. For LD students the conclusion was that half of the 12 year olds do not master addition up to 100, but 13 year olds master addition and subtraction to 100 fairly well. With respect to MR students the conclusion was that at least 25 percent of the 12 year olds do not master addition and subtraction up to 20, and 13 year olds do not reach higher achievement levels.

References

Beishuizen, M. (1993). De lege getallenlijn als (sober) mentaal model [The empty number line as a (sober) mental model]. *Tijdschrift voor Nascholing en Onderzoek van het Reken-wiskundeonderwijs, 11*(3), 16-19.

Beishuizen, M. (1997). Development of mathematical strategies and procedures up to 100. In M. Beishuizen, K.P.E. Gravemeijer & E.C.D.M. van Lieshout (Eds.), *The role of contexts and models in the development of mathematical strategies and procedures* (pp.127-162). Utrecht: Freudenthal Instituut.

Beishuizen, M., Van Putten, C.M., & Van Mulken, F. (1997). Mental arithmetic and strategy use with indirect number problems up to one hundred. *Learning and Instruction, 7*, 87-106.

Blöte, A.W., Klein, A.S., & Beishuizen, M. (2000). Mental computation and conceptual understanding. *Learning and Instruction, 10*, 221-247.

Butler, F.M., Miller, S.P., Lee, K., & Pierce, T. (2001). Teaching mathematics to students with mild-to-moderate mental retardation: a review of literature. *Mental Retardation, 39*, 20-31.

Fuson, K.C., Wearne, D., Hiebert, J.C., Murray, H.G., Human, P.G., Olivier, A.I., Carpenter, T.P., & Fennema, E. (1997). Children's conceptual structures for multidigit numbers and methods of multidigit addition and subtraction. *Journal for Research in Mathematics Education, 28,* 130-162.

Gravemeijer, K.P.E. (1996). Het belang van social norms en socio-math norms voor realistisch reken-wiskundeonderwijs [The importance of social norms and socio-math norms for realistic mathematics education]. *Tijdschrift voor Nascholing en Onderzoek van het Reken-wiskundeonderwijs, 14*(2), 17-23.

Gray, E.M., & Tall, D.O. (1994). Duality, ambiguity, and flexibility: a "proceptual" view of simple arithmetic. *Journal for Research in Mathematics Education, 25,* 166-140.

Hamers, J.H.M., & Ruijssenaars, A.J.J.M. (1984). *Leergeschiktheid en leertests. Een leertestonderzoek bij eersteklassers in het gewoon lager onderwijs* [Learning ability and learning tests. A learning test study in third grade children.]. Harlingen: Flevodruk (Published in 1986 by Swets & Zeitlinger, Lisse).

Hamers, J.H.M., Sijtsma, K., & Ruijssenaars, A.J.J.M. (1993). *Learning potential assess-ment. Theoretical, methodological and practical issues.* Lisse: Swets & Zeitlinger.

Harskamp, E.G., & Suhre, C.J.M. (1995). *Hoofdrekenen in het speciaal onderwijs* [Mental arithmetic in special education]. Groningen: GION.

Harskamp, E.G., & Suhre, C.J.M. (1996). Hoofdrekenen tot honderd op maat [Adapted mental arithmetic up to one hundred]. *Tijdschrift voor Orthopedagogiek, 35,* 115-130.

Janssen, J., Van der Schoot, F., Hemker, B, & Verhelst, N. (1999). *Balans van het reken-wiskundeonderwijs aan het einde van de basisschool 3. Uitkomsten van de derde peiling in 1997* [An account of mathematics in primary education. Results of the third Dutch national assessment program at the end of primary school 3]. Arnhem: Centraal Instituut voor Toetsontwikkeling.

Klein, A.S., Beishuizen, M., & Treffers, A. (1998). The empty number line in Dutch second grades: realistic versus gradual program design. *Journal for Research in Mathematics Education, 24,* 443-464.

Kraemer, J.-M., Van der Schoot, F., & Engelen, R. (2000). *Balans van het reken-wiskundeonderwijs op LOM- en MLK-scholen 2. Uitkomsten van de tweede peiling in 1997* [An account of mathematics in the education of children with specific learning disabilities and mildly mentally retarded children 2. Results of the second Dutch national assessment program]. Arnhem: Centraal Instituut voor Toetsontwikkeling.

Lemaire, P., & Siegler, R.S. (1995). Four aspects of strategic change: contributions to children's learning of multiplication. *Journal of Experimental Psychology, 124,* 83-97.

Lo, J., & Wheatley, G.H. (1994). Learning opportunities and negotiating social norms in mathematics class discussion. *Educational Studies in Mathematics, 27,* 145-164.

Milo, B.F., & Ruijssenaars, A.J.J.M. (1999). *Flexibiliteittoets optellen en aftrekken tot 100* [Flexibility test for addition and subtraction up to 100]. (Unpublished test). Leiden: Leiden University.

Resnick, L.B. (1976). *The nature of intelligence.* Hillsdale, NJ: Lawrence Erlbaum.

Ruijssenaars, A.J.J.M. (1992). *Rekenproblemen. Theorie, diagnostiek, behandeling* [Mathematical problems. Theory, diagnostics, treatment]. Rotterdam: Lemniscaat.

Siegler, R.S. (1978). *Children's thinking: What develops?* Hillsdale, NJ: Lawrence Erlbaum.
Siegler, R.S. (1996). *Emerging minds. The process of change in children's thinking.* New York: Oxford University Press.
Siegler, R.S., & Jenkins, E.A. (1989). *How children discover new strategies.* Hillsdale, NJ: Lawrence Erlbaum.
Swanson, H.L., Hoskyn, M., & Lee, C. (2000). *Interventions for students with learning disabilities. A meta-analysis of treatment outcomes.* New York / London: the Guilford Press.
Van der Aalsvoort, G.M., Resing, W.C.M., & Ruijssenaars, A.J.J.M. (2002). *Learning potential assessment and cognitive training: actual research and perspectives in theory building and methodology.* Oxford: Elsevier Science Ltd.
Van Lieshout, E.C.D.M. (1997). *Optimalisering van onderwijsleerprocessen bij de verwerving van rekenkennis* [Optimalisation of teaching and learning processes with the acquisition of mathematic knowledge]. Subsidie-aanvraag NWO, afdeling SGW.
Vedder, P., & Koster, K. (1983). *Rekenonderwijs in de fout* [Mathematics education mistaken]. Apeldoorn: Van Walraven.
Woodward, J., Monroe, K., & Baxter, J. (2001). Enhancing student achievement on performance assessments in mathematics. *Learning Disabilities Quarterly, 24* (Winter), 33-46.
Yackel, E., & Cobb, P. (1996). Sociomathematical norms, argumentation, and autonomy in mathematics. *Journal for Research in Mathematics Education, 27,* 458-477.

Aknowlegdements: The research described in this chapter was financially supported by the Foundation for Society- and Behavioral Studies (MaGW), which is subsidized by the Dutch Organization for Scientific Research (NWO), nr. 575-36-002

www.ingramcontent.com/pod-product-compliance
Ingram Content Group UK Ltd.
Pitfield, Milton Keynes, MK11 3LW, UK
UKHW021834140426
5217IPUK00021B/1453